WITHDRAWN

OCT 2 1 2015

THE BATTLE OF ALBERTA

MARK SPECTOR

WITH A FOREWORD BY THEOREN FLEURY

THE
BATTLE
OF ALBERTA

THE HISTORIC RIVALRY BETWEEN THE
EDMONTON OILERS & THE CALGARY FLAMES

McCLELLAND & STEWART

Copyright © 2015 by Mark Spector

All rights reserved. The use of any part of this publication reproduced, transmitted in any form or by any means, electronic, mechanical, photocopying, recording, or otherwise, or stored in a retrieval system, without the prior written consent of the publisher – or, in case of photocopying or other reprographic copying, a licence from the Canadian Copyright Licensing Agency – is an infringement of the copyright law.

Library and Archives Canada Cataloguing in Publication
is available upon request

Published simultaneously in the United States of America by McClelland & Stewart, a division of Random House of Canada Limited, a Penguin Random House Company

Library of Congress Control Number is available upon request

All photos in the inserts are courtesy Pro Am Sports.

ISBN: 978-0-771-07806-4

ebook ISBN: 978-0-771-07807-1

Typeset in Electra by M&S, Toronto

Printed and bound in the United States of America

McClelland & Stewart,
a division of Random House of Canada Limited,
a Penguin Random House Company

www.penguinrandomhouse.ca

1 2 3 4 5   19 18 17 16 15

Penguin
Random
House

WHITCHURCH-STOUFFVILLE PUBLIC LIBRARY

This book is dedicated to my dear wife, Shelka, who encouraged me to take this project on and then doted on me while I wrote, and wrote; to my children, Rudy and Haley, whose father loves them endlessly; to my father, Milt, who gave me my love of sports, and my mother, Ruthe, who taught me that good writing matters and provided me with the guidebooks that helped me to find the right words for this project; and to Nike, my little Schnoodle writing companion, whose expiry date sadly came before the final edit.

CONTENTS

Foreword by Theoren Fleury   ix

1   **IRON SHARPENS IRON:** The Oilers and the Flames Evolve   1

2   **MATCHING THE OILERS BLUEPRINT:**
U.S. College Talent Boosts the Flames Roster   21

3   **DISSECTING THE OILERS DYNASTY:** Glen Sather and the Art of Experience   36

4   **CLIMBING THE MOUNTAIN:** Bob Johnson Fuels the Flames' Rise   58

5   **LEADING BY INCLUSION:** Oiler Mark Messier's Subtle Direction   75

6   **OF MICS AND MEN:** Reporting from the Battle Press Box   94

7   **BEING NEIL SHEEHY:** The Battle's Most Hated Villain   108

8   **UPSIDE-DOWN LAND:** The Flames Capture the 1986 Battle   121

9   **THE RIGHT PLAY THE WRONG WAY:** Oiler Steve Smith's Unforgettable Goal   141

10   **STRIPES AND STARS:** Reffing the Battle of Alberta   156

11   **CONTAINING THE GREAT ONE:** Like Trying to Hug Fog   172

12   **THE MOUNTAIN CLIMBED—FINALLY:**
The Flames' Lanny McDonald Hoists the 1989 Stanley Cup   191

13   **STU GRIMSON VERSUS DAVE BROWN I AND II:**
The Night the Battle Went Too Far   210

14   **TWO HUNDRED FEET AWAY, MILES APART:**
Flame Réjean Lemelin versus Oiler Grant Fuhr   234

15   **THE LAST GREAT BATTLE:** Theo Fleury's Anger Pours Gas on the Battle's Fire   250

Conclusion   267
Acknowledgements   271
Index   272

FOREWORD

People talk about destiny, or karma. That certain people were "born into" their role or their job; how, let's say, a player like Mark Messier was a "born leader."

Well, I don't know whether I was born to play in the Battle of Alberta or not. But there hasn't been a brand of hockey played before or since that suited my game and my attitude toward life better than Calgary versus Edmonton. (Although the "friendly" competition between cities existed long before professional hockey entered the scene, the Battle of Alberta got really intense in the Oilers versus Flames rivalry in the 1980s—and especially bitter in the second half of the 1980s.)

I grew up in Russell, Manitoba, and spent my teenaged years in Saskatchewan, busing across the prairies while playing for the Moose Jaw Warriors in the mid-1980s. I didn't know it then but learning to survive as a five-foot-six, one-hundred-and-fifty-pound seventeen-year-old in the Western Hockey League was an apprenticeship of sorts for where I was going to find myself as a pro a few years later. It was survival for me as one of the smallest guys in a league full of players like Dave Manson, Ken Baumgartner, Shane Churla, and Todd Ewen.

I remember one time in my first season getting hit by Manson in Prince Albert. Nearly broke me in half, he hit me so hard. It was my first "Come to Jesus" moment in hockey because I knew that that couldn't keep happening. On the bus ride home that night I thought about how a guy my size was going to survive in hockey the way it was played in the 1980s. I figured out pretty quickly that not getting plastered by huge defencemen was a place to start, but in order for that to stop happening, I had to make them not want to run me every time I had the puck.

In short, I had to become a dangerous little prick. A guy who'd shove his stick down your throat without blinking an eye. Who'd cut your eye out or wasn't afraid to get even with a full baseball swing. A guy who didn't give a shit if the hit was clean but only cared about getting even. More than even, actually. Those skills would serve me well later on, as it turned out.

We got most of the Calgary–Edmonton games on TV in Saskatchewan, and I watched as many as a junior kid could, considering we played seventy-two games a season ourselves, plus playoffs. The playoff series, I just remember how intense they were. How much they mattered to everyone—the players, the TV announcers, the fans, and, of course, the players.

The Flames drafted me in 1987, but I didn't fully understand the hatred between the two teams until I arrived in Calgary in 1989. Then I realized how totally important the rivalry was.

Shortly after I got called up, we played the Oilers in back-to-back games. The first game, I scored my first two NHL goals on Grant Fuhr, on *Hockey Night in Canada*. The next night we went to Edmonton, and Kevin Lowe tried to take my head off. That's when I became fully submersed into the Battle of Alberta. I'd gone around him the game in Calgary. He was probably a little bit pissed off.

I knew then that my worth to the Flames would be measured, to a large extent, by how I handled myself against Edmonton. I knew that the Oilers would try to intimidate me.

It's no different than what every junior opponent did. I was small, and I was supposed to go away when they inflicted a little pain on me.

But surviving and thriving in the Battle of Alberta was imperative for me. So I had to make those guys think twice (or three times) before they took a run at me. That's what made the Battle of Alberta so much fun.

Those games were circled on the calendar. Playing the Washington Capitals on a Tuesday night in Calgary wasn't going to have the same juice that a Saturday night in either Edmonton or Calgary was going to have. Jeff Beukeboom suckered me once, then bragged about it in the papers the next day. I thought that was pretty low at the time, but to be honest, I likely had it coming. I must have slashed him as hard as I could fifty times before he caught me with that punch.

Looking back through the hatred, the fear, the competitiveness, we made each other better. All of us. Finding those opponents to play against that make you elevate your game or else be left in the dust. Both organizations in the 1980s and early 1990s were model franchises.

If you were born in the 1980s or later, you might doubt that some of the things found in these pages really happened. Well, they did happen, and it's amazing we all lived to tell these tales. I can only speak for myself, but the attitude I took into every installment of the Battle of Alberta was like Mel Gibson's in *Braveheart*. Remember that scene where they ask Mel's character, William Wallace, what he was doing? He says, "I'm going to pick a fight."

That's what the Battle of Alberta was like every night. It's one of my favourite movie scenes of all time because that was me: "What are you doing?" "Well, I'm going to see if I can pick a fight with someone tonight."

Somebody once asked me if I would want my own son to experience what I experienced in those games. Of course I would. That was when men were men. You better grow some balls or you're not going to be very successful playing in those games. And those are the kind of games you want to play in, as a professional hockey player, a professional athlete. The higher the intensity, the more you want to be part of it. Those are the games that make you grow, make you better. You find out what you're really fuckin' made of in those games.

When people look back on the history of the game, there is a place that Calgary versus Edmonton holds. I'm not sure there is another rivalry on the same level. People who lived out East, I'm not sure they realize the intensity of the Battle of Alberta. How important it was to the people who lived in Calgary and Edmonton during those years.

It was some of the greatest hockey that has ever been played at a club level. You think about the greatest series, the greatest games every played, you're always referencing Canada–Russia or Canada–U.S. But from an NHL perspective, there wasn't a rivalry quite like it.

To walk into the trainers room after a Battle of Alberta game was like walking into a M*A*S*H* unit. And that series in 1991 — it doesn't get any better than that. That was the only Calgary–Edmonton series in which the team that won the series didn't go on to the Stanley Cup final.

Edmonton couldn't. Minnesota mopped them up in the next series — not because they were so much better than the Oilers but because the Oilers had nothing left. And we likely wouldn't have either. We literally kicked the piss out of each other. And it's ironic that it went to overtime, where Esa Tikkanen scored the winner. That game could have gone on forever and neither team would have backed down.

I have the fondest memories of all the battles within the big Battle. Glen Sather was such a smart hockey man. Jeff Beukeboom and Steve Smith beatin' the crap out of me every chance they got, and me getting them back with a two-hander every chance I got. Tikkanen, yappin' at you in whatever language he was speaking. I never figured out what he was saying.

There are so many incredible characters on both sides. Guys like Colin Patterson, Rick Wamsley, who never really got the attention but were so key to the Battle of Alberta. The Oilers had those guys too: Dave Lumley, Dave Hunter. I was standing right there when Dave Brown caved in Stu Grimson's face that day. *Holeee*.

I went on to play with Mark Messier, Wayne Gretzky; Steve Smith I played with in Calgary. I played for Sather in New York. They all turned out to be great guys that I learned to have a tonne of respect for. So there was a respect for one another, I guess.

But during the Battle, more importantly, there was a total dislike for one another. They didn't like me in Edmonton, and that was fine. We didn't like them either. In fact, we hated them. I'm not sure that anything close to that hatred exists in the National Hockey League anymore. But, boy, how I hated those bastards back then.

This book should have been written a long time ago. Enjoy.

Theoren Fleury
March 31, 2015
Calgary, Alberta

1

IRON SHARPENS IRON

The Oilers and the Flames Evolve
"It was real then. There were going to be fights."

Wayne Gretzky is sitting on the Edmonton Oilers' bench, watching one of his teammates duke it out with one of the Calgary Flames.

This time it is Kevin McClelland, and the Oilers are losing big-time to the Flames. The last time it was Dave Semenko in a lopsided Edmonton win. The next time? Dave Brown in a tied game. In the Battle of Alberta, the scoreboard changed but the routine stayed mostly the same.

As Steve Smith said, "When you look back and you think about the Battle of Alberta, every time you went into that building, you knew you were going to shed some blood. And hopefully you were going to take some with you."

Gretzky didn't have to take, or give, any blood. When you average about three points a game, you get a pass on the whole blood-spilling thing. But on this night, Gretzky had a front-row seat to a fight that, for some reason, he remembers ahead of so many others he'd seen over the years.

"We were losing 7–2, or 8–2. There was about four minutes left in the game, and Kevin McClelland and Tim Hunter drop their gloves right in front of our bench. They're both tough guys, and they were going at it pretty good," Gretzky said, now twenty-five years after the fact. "Hunter hit McClelland so hard that his nose shattered. It was almost on the other side of his face. The whole bench just kind of went, 'Oh my God . . .'"

Among all the castes on a hockey team, fighters are perhaps the most complex breed. Their worth as teammates is measured far less on the result of each bout, assuming they can win their share. It's more about them being there to put up a fight when a fight is needed, like when you are down by five or six goals.

Whichever team got a lopsided lead in the Battle of Alberta, their tough guys would do exactly what McClelland was doing on this night. Was it kind of dumb? Yes, sometimes—by today's standards—it got kind of dumb. But this was the 1980s National Hockey League (NHL), a far different place than today's NHL.

It was a time when the Edmonton Oilers and the Calgary Flames combined for 780 goals in a season (those same two teams might hit 420 today). It was less about defensive systems and Department of Player Safety videos and more about scoring goals and throwing down, when two of the NHL's best teams were also two of the league's toughest teams.

In this bout, however, McClelland was getting a bad case of east–west nose from Hunter. He took a big shot, the Oilers bench cringed, and then he did something Gretzky will never forget.

"Without missing a beat, McClelland turns to our bench and says, 'It didn't hurt! I didn't feel a thing!'" Gretzky says. "I remember Tim Hunter looking at him, like, 'Are you serious?'

"It was almost like a piece out of a movie, and it said to us, 'You guys can do whatever you want to us. We're not going to back down. We're going to keep coming.' We all rose about six inches off the bench. He just made us all that much bigger. I remember after that game, all of us saying, 'That's it. We're not going to lose to this team.'"

You cannot capture the Battle of Alberta with one story—or even one series. But the McClelland–Hunter incident encompassed as many elements of the epic Oilers versus the Flames crusade of the 1980s as you could ask for.

It included the greatest player the game has even seen, yet it involved a level of fury that made you want to avert your eyes; a dash of slapstick comedy, as McClelland somehow timed his delivery to the very moment his nostril reached his own ear; and a pinch of wrestling-like thuggery. Like the time Mike Bullard hopped off that stretcher underneath the stands or the night a roundly beaten-up Doug Risebrough used his skates to slice Marty McSorley's jersey to bits while sitting in the penalty box.

We Albertans, we didn't have a clue about how good we had it in the 1980s. We laughed at teams like the Toronto Maple Leafs and Detroit Red Wings that would limp through "Death Valley," a two-game Alberta trip that was pointless in every sense of the word. Back in the day, Albertan hockey fans rode a pretty high horse, which has now turned into a stick pony as both the Flames and the Oilers reside nearer to the bottom of the NHL standings, immersed in rebuilds today, in hopes of one day being as mighty as they were during the 1980s.

Think of it like this: an eighteen-year-old Flames fan in 2014 had not seen his team win a playoff round since he was seven years old. The same Oilers fan has not even seen a playoff *game* since age nine. There has been one Stanley Cup appearance for their team in each of those fans' lives: 2006 in Edmonton and 2004 in Calgary. Both ended in identical, heart-wrenching Game 7 losses, followed by a steady decline to that synonym of organizational failure: the Rebuild.

Now, let's go back to 1983, when an eighteen-year-old kid growing up in Edmonton—which is exactly what I was—had watched his club get swept by the four-time-champion New York Islanders in the Stanley Cup. It was, history records, the last time in nearly a decade that hockey's power base would exist outside of Alberta.

Spring 1984 would see the Flames and Oilers clash in a stunning seven-game series. The Oilers would overcome the Islanders for the first of five Edmonton Stanley Cups in seven years, and from years eighteen to twenty-five in the life of this fabulously spoiled young Alberta kid, no other team would represent the Clarence Campbell Conference (renamed the Western Conference in 1993) in the Stanley Cup than the Oilers or the Flames.

The mission in Calgary, it became painfully clear, was to catch up to Edmonton. The problem was, the Flames did such a fine job of it that the competition just kept making Edmonton better and better. The goalposts never stopped moving. As such, the hockey just got better and better.

"Ali needed Frazier. That top opponent that pushes, and challenges, and makes you better," Mark Messier said of the Flames. "If you're an Albertan, you're having a pretty good time."

Hockey people would say that the Battle of Alberta began when the Calgary Flames moved north from Atlanta for the 1980–81 season, one year after the Edmonton Oilers had merged into the NHL as one of four survivors from the World Hockey Association (WHA). But no visceral, loathsome rivalry just fires up when two teams arrive in two geographically linked towns. A proper rivalry has to simmer through political decisions, to amateur sports, to fights over services and education. In Alberta, the competition began long before Highway 2—the north–south ribbon of highway between the two cities—was even paved.

In the 1800s, the two settlements fought over which one would get the first Canadian Pacific Railway terminal. Calgary won that round but was sour when Edmonton was named the provincial capital and then designated as the location for the University of Alberta in the early 1900s.

In an early-1980s Angus Reid poll, Calgary finished far ahead of Edmonton as a city Canadians said they would move to, provided they would not lose their standard of living. That prompted Edmonton alderman Ron Hayter, coincidentally a bigwig in the local Boxing and Wrestling Commission, to quip: "Every day spent in Edmonton is as good as a week in Calgary."

"Edmonton is not the end of the world," countered former Calgary mayor Ralph Klein. "It's just easier to see it from there."

Edmonton hosted the Commonwealth Games in 1978? Calgary got the Winter Olympics a decade later. The Calgary Cannons won a couple of divisional pennants in Triple A baseball's Pacific Coast League? The Edmonton Trappers won the league title four times, thank you very much. In the Canadian Football League (CFL), the degree of hate in the Labour Day Classic has always transcended wherever the clubs are in the standings, and it was Warren Moon's Edmonton Eskimos that set the table for hockey's battle so perfectly when the Esks won five consecutive Grey Cups between 1978 and 1982, often stepping on the Calgary Stampeders' dreams along the way.

As the oil business has evolved, Calgary has become the white-collar Dallas while Edmonton is the Houston that services the oil patch. Calgary's airport gets more and better international flights. Edmonton has a better arts scene. You name a forum and

I'll show you a place where one city is trying to one-up the other.

By the time the two NHL teams had been established in Alberta, however, so was the pecking order of the two sports towns. Edmonton called itself the City of Champions, which took some nerve considering its hockey team was in its infancy. But they had a better football club, a better football stadium, and a better and newer hockey rink. And they had Wayne Gretzky, the great difference-maker, whom some Edmontonians believed might one day be known as the best player the sport of hockey has ever seen.

Behind the Oilers bench resided Glen (Slats) Sather, a smug young savant with a scar on his lip that gave him a perma-smirk. He was cocky, and so was his team. "Sather had a right to be. They won," said Flames centre Joel Otto. "You have to be confident to be good, but it rubbed me the wrong way. A lot of our guys knew they had a smugness to them, in our minds."

Sather surrounded Gretzky with reams of toughness, perhaps even more skill, and patterned the Oilers' game after the Swede-heavy Winnipeg Jets of the WHA.

"Edmonton played hockey the way you're supposed to play hockey," said Calgary Flame Mike Bullard. "It was just 'Let 'em loose, Bruce.'"

"I don't think we realized it at the time," said Mark Messier, who entered the battle as an unknown kid from St. Albert and left it as one of hockey's legendary leaders. "A lot of us came here when we were eighteen years old. We were just trying to hang on to the rope, to stay in the league. We were scared to death, and the best way to stay out of trouble against the big, bad Flyers—and a lot of the other teams—was to skate as fast as you could. So skating, the free flow, really became a staple of our game."

Some old-time hockey players were still in the mix, including Ken Houston and Eric Vail, left over from Calgary's days as the Atlanta Flames; and Al Hamilton and Dave Dryden (Ken's brother), hanging on from Edmonton's time in the renegade WHA. None of those names would last for long on two teams that changed the way the game was played (the Oilers) and altered the way an NHL general manager built his team (the Flames).

"I remember playing on a line with Ron Chipperfield and Bill (Cowboy) Flett, God rest his soul," Messier said. "It was the middle of the game, and somehow I ended up inside our zone on his side of the ice. He looked at me and he says, 'Get the hell outta here!' He was from the old school, up-and-down-the-wing kind of hockey, while we were trying to play this innovative, European, more weaving style.

"As time went on, we realized that the style of play we were introducing, it forced the league to change because of us. If they were going to compete against us, they were going to have to skate, and up their talent level as well."

The first team to realize that was Calgary, and make no mistake—the Flames were in the chase position for the first several years. Eventually Flames general manager Cliff Fletcher would piece together a lineup that could give Edmonton a game on a nightly basis. Of course, it was easier to catch up in toughness and attitude before actually collecting enough Joe Mullens, Doug Gilmours, and Joe Nieuwendyks to challenge Edmonton's collective skill set.

So Calgary fought with and intimidated Edmonton as best it could while trying to build a team that could actually play with or, on occasion, outscore Edmonton.

"I remember before a game," said Flames winger Jim Peplinski, "Bob Johnson says to us, 'Well, boys, it's going to be a war tonight. So I want you to look at the guy beside you and know who you're going to be in that foxhole with.'"

The toughest Flame was Tim Hunter, who could handle himself any night in any rink against any opponent. He was a big, mean, Calgary-born winger who'd put together a couple of 300-penalty-minute seasons in the Western Hockey League.

The Flames' best player in those days was Kent Nilsson, one of those Swedish Jets with marvellous skills. Skills, shall we say, that were spoken of more often than his heart and will.

"So I look to my one side," continued Peplinski, "and it's Timmy Hunter. I think, 'Okay.' Then I look to the other side, and it's Kent Nilsson. And he's shaking his head."

"Well, one out of two isn't bad . . ."

They still tell the story about Nilsson having a hat trick and two assists in the first period one night. Johnson could see his star was jumping. "You could really rack up some points tonight, Kent," he said. "Keep 'er goin'. There's still forty minutes left! You might set a record!"

Nilsson, however, was never known as an avid perspirer. He had three times the talent of 90 percent of the NHL in those days, but the Flames already had this one in hand, and Nilsson, nicknamed The Magic Man, told Johnson: "Bob, five points is enough. If I get more, they'll expect that from me every night."

Edmonton, of course, was the polar opposite. Sometimes it looked like the Oilers played their hardest when they were crushing some unfortunate Norris Division team and the points were easier to get. When goalies like Don Beaupre, Allan Bester, poor Murray Bannerman, or Gretzky's childhood buddy Greg Stefan set up in the Northlands Coliseum crease, their success was measured not in goals allowed but whether they lasted two periods before getting the hook.

It could have been Gretzky's example, as he was noted for never taking his foot off the gas, even in a blowout. Or perhaps it was their coach and general manager, whose career as a journeyman winger taught Sather never to give a sucker an even break.

"They had something very unique," said Peplinski. "That was Slats's ability to cause Dave Hunter to be better than you'd think he should be. To cause Pat Hughes to be what he was. To cause Dave Lumley to perform the way he did. To give Semenko the confidence to play on a line with Wayne Gretzky and not just be a tough guy but score once in a while. Kevin McClelland, Marty McSorley . . . Somebody gave those guys some confidence, believed in them.

"If it was 6–1, it was going to be 7–1 if you didn't keep playing," Peplinski said. "They just came in waves. We had a stretch where we couldn't get through the start of a game where they wouldn't score in the first thirty-five seconds."

If there wasn't a goal scored in the opening thirty-five seconds of the Battle, then there might be a five-on-five brawl. Nobody could promise, when you bought a ticket for Edmonton–Calgary, whether the game would have an R rating or merely PG. The guarantee was, however, that you would be entertained.

Craig MacTavish played 1,093 NHL games, so the dates and seasons blend together somewhat when he reaches back into that helmetless memory bank for some data on another train wreck of a night in the Battle of Alberta. Much water has flowed under a bridge that was constructed in 1980 when the Atlanta Flames couldn't make it in the South anymore and the original "Man Who Sold Wayne Gretzky," Nelson Skalbania, led a group that purchased the Flames and moved the club to Calgary.

It began in the old Stampede Corral in 1980, where the boards were so high they made grown men look like pee wee players, and 300 kilometres north, inside the Northlands Coliseum. That building had various names over the many seasons, but that same edgy tension always existed when the two best teams in the NHL met during the mid- to late-1980s.

"We'd been beaten in Calgary, and it was a back-to-back game," began MacTavish. "We knew we had to answer the bell here in Edmonton. I started the game; Kevin [Lowe] started the game. Well, after the first shift, Kevin and I are both back in the locker room taking our gear off.

"He looks at me and he says, 'Boy, were we ever on the same wavelength.'"

That wavelength was often of a violent nature in the Battle, whether it involved Marty McSorley skewering Mike Bullard, Dave Brown busting up Stu Grimson's face, Carey Wilson losing his spleen, or Jamie Macoun busting a cheekbone on a blindside punch from Mark Messier. Somehow the Oilers gave better than they received when it came to injurious acts that ended up in a hospital visit.

"My sense would be that we were much more the recipients than the instigators," said Peplinski. "We were a team that were much happier to play a hard game up and down. The Oilers seemed to be much more about wolf pack. They bordered on the personality that Slats had as a player—an irritant or an agitator.

"When I think back to The Rat [Ken Linseman], when I think back to Lumley, to Kevin McClelland, even Wayne. I don't think we were near as yappy as they were either. Then again, maybe that's just me remembering it the way I would have liked it to be."

It was Paul Bunyan rules most times when these teams met. And God forbid there was a three- or four-goal spread as the clock ticked down.

"They were big, strong, physical. They were dirty, just like us," said Oilers defenceman Jeff Beukeboom. "They did everything in their power to win, as did we. We adjusted to them, and they adjusted to us. It was like the nuclear war of hockey: you were constantly trying to arm yourself in a way to beat them. They did it too, vice versa."

"You would never turn your back on anybody," said Lowe. "As a defenceman, if the play went up the ice, if Tim Hunter was behind me, or beside me, I'd never take my eye off him. He'd chop you on the back of the legs or on the wrist. In front of the net in scrums, you never took your eye off anyone or the guy would pop you. Your guard was always up."

Once the game was decided, the winning team tended not to keep taking cheap shots. You were already thinking about next time out, and there was no point in fuelling that fire. "The shoe could be on the other foot next time," Lowe said.

How about this Kodak moment, from long-time Oilers equipment man Lyle (Sparky) Kulchisky, taken from a typically rough night in the old Corral: "Middle of the second period, brawl breaks out, and into the dressing room comes Dave Semenko and Don Jackson," he said. "Same ice bucket—Sammy had his right hand in there, and D.J. had his left. They sat there next to each other and watched the rest of the game on TV."

It was a style of hockey that time has forgotten. Or is trying to forget.

"You always knew going into it that there was going to be blood shed, and it was going to be some of your own. That was a certainty," Steve Smith said. "It was real then. There were going to be fights. You were going to be part of fights, and you were expected to be part of fights and physical hockey. If you were going to win, you were going to take some real severe hits to make plays. You knew that.

"And if you weren't going to be physically beat, you could be mentally beat by the end. You knew it was a sixty-minute game, if not longer, every single game. With no easy times at any point in time during one of those series."

As the NHL game has grown more civil, the smallest indiscretion has people calling for a suspension. If the NHL's Department of Player Safety had existed in the 1980s, they might have built a separate wing in the New York office for the Battle of Alberta. Luckily, it was a time before the league was technically able to capture every transgression. By the time that VHS cassette had been Fed Ex'ed to NHL president John Ziegler's New York office, well, usually everyone had already moved on.

The result was that few across the hockey world actually witnessed all of Messier's Gordie Howe–like elbows. And that classic playoff spear — McSorley versus Bullard, April 23, 1988 — garnered not a game's suspension yet goes down as a classic moment in the Battle.

"Gary Roberts went in the corner and absolutely tattooed McSorley," remembers Bullard, a short-term tenant in the Battle who would be dealt away in a package that brought Doug Gilmour to Calgary. "It was a huge bodycheck. He really hurt him, and just as McSorley is coming by our bench [Flames head coach Terry] Crisp calls my name. I hop over the boards, and, well, there's nothing like being in the wrong place at the wrong time, eh?"

McSorley arrived in ill humour, dazed and furious, on his way to the Edmonton bench. He was like an enraged bull, and there was Bullard, wearing a bright red jersey.

"As soon as he saw a Calgary player, he was going to pitchfork them. It just happened to be me," Bullard said. "Marty and I are good friends, we'd played together in Pittsburgh. But in the Battle, there were no such things as friends. Marty and me? We hated each other.

"It was about Calgary and Edmonton. It wasn't about hockey anymore. It was about which city was a better place to live. Who drives the nicer cars. Which restaurants were better. Which rink had better fans. I think we became secondary as players on the ice," he said. "So they take me off on the stretcher, into the room, and I say to [Flames trainer Jim] Bearcat Murray, 'We need a win here. I'm okay. Go tell Crispy.' He goes out to the bench, Bearcat, and right where the players can hear, he says to Crispy: 'Bully says he's okay. He can play. Do you want him?' And Crispy yells back, 'Hell, no. He hasn't done a goddamned thing yet anyway. Leave him in the room.'

"I knew Crispy wasn't gonna keep me. I'm just telling you from the horse's mouth. The real story is the bugger didn't want me to come back."

Ex-players are excited to tell their Battle stories some twenty-five or thirty years later, but while the Battle was still burning hot, the truth and the quotes did not always intersect. Like the next morning at practice, when the journalists arrived, looking to mine McSorley for an explanation of his Zorro routine.

"Everyone is waiting for McSorley to come to his stall in the room. There's a big group of us around his cubicle," recalls Al Maki, a columnist for the *Calgary Herald* at that time. "He walks into the room, sees us, and you can see him think, 'Uh, oh.' Slats motions him over, and they step into the corner, and they're talking. They're getting their stories straight.

"So McSorley walks to his locker, he stands in, and the first question comes: 'What happened?' He says, 'I don't know. I have no recollection of what happened.' He just blew it all off. Pleaded amnesia."

Of course, the Flames remembered what had happened. The victims, it seemed, always had a clearer recollection of crimes committed than did the perpetrators. Assistant coach Doug Risebrough handled the press briefing that day, working himself up into quite a lather: "'That's the most vicious thing I've seen in hockey!'" Maki recalls him saying. "'An abomination!'"

On one hand, the game is clearly a better place now that players have stopped spearing each other in the jewels. On the other hand . . .

"That's the thing we're missing in the game today. Emotion," said former Flames goalie Mike Vernon. "Those games had so much emotion, and those things were all real. Emotions were high, and there was a price that had to be paid. Like the time Dave Brown fought Stu Grimson. Grimmer sat in the penalty box for ten minutes with a broken face.

"You want to see real? That's real."

The Battle of Alberta, however, was filled with these strange dichotomies. On one hand, as the 1980s unfolded, Edmonton and Calgary became the two best teams in the West every year—and in the entire NHL most times as well. But at the same time, each team made sure they were the toughest, buttressing their immense skill with plenty of players who could and would do the dirty work of the day.

For two teams that scored nearly twice as many goals as a good team does today, fighting and physical play was always held in high esteem. If you won the game, but my team won the fights? Well, I hadn't completely lost, had I?

"There had to be a lot of pressure on those guys [who fought a lot]," said Lowe. "Knowing that they're carrying not only the team but the fans, almost the whole city for that matter. [Winning fights] was almost like a badge of honour. Bragging rights the next day."

Behind the bench, Flames coach (Badger) Bob Johnson was a professorial type out of the U.S. college ranks who'd never played an NHL game, brandishing a notebook and a pen like McSorley wielded his Koho. Meanwhile, Sather was this street-smart journeyman who wore slick suits and operated with a swagger that came to define the Oilers organization. To the naked eye, they were nothing like each other. Both, however, possessed immense motivational skills, even if they came at the task from opposite ends of the earth, it seemed.

Even ownership was contradictory: the Flames were run by a conglomerate of well-heeled, respected Calgary businessmen who would only step behind a microphone when they were announcing money donated to put a wing on a hospital for children. Whereas in Edmonton, Peter Pocklington was brash and entrepreneurial, with a portfolio that went up and down like the hood of a car. He didn't always pay his bills, but if a hockey writer wanted a quote from Peter, you just phoned his home number, and after a few minutes of chatting with his wife, Eva, she'd hand him the phone.

Another strange branching of this plant was the level of hucksterism that pervaded the Battle, perhaps a homage to the days when WHA co-founder Bill Hunter operated his junior Oil Kings out of Edmonton, and his partner in crime, Scotty Munro, was hawking tickets for the Calgary Centennials down south. Truly, the roots of the Battle began in senior hockey, where the Edmonton Flyers and Calgary Stampeders went at it with straight sticks and horsehair goal pads, and filtered through the junior ranks to the Oilers and Calgary Cowboys of the WHA.

"You grow up in Edmonton, it starts out as a kid," said Kulchisky. "You get to provincials, you often had to go to Calgary to win the province. The Labour Day Classic, you had to beat Calgary. When I grew up, it was the Calgary Centennials versus the Edmonton Oil Kings. Scotty Munro versus Bill Hunter. You just had a dislike for Calgary, whether football, hockey, volleyball, basketball . . . Calgary was the enemy."

"It was bred into us here," said Otto. "Cliff, Coatesy, [assistant to President Al Coates] Al MacNeil, they were all good hockey men and they had a job to do. That was to get on par with

Edmonton. It was instilled that this was the enemy up north. And that's the way it was. I took it to heart. I was playing for the crest, and they were the enemy."

Behind the scenes, Bearcat and his Flames equipment man, Bobby Stewart, cooperated famously with Kulchisky, head Oilers equipment man Barrie Stafford, and medical trainer Ken Lowe, who was Kevin's older brother. Whichever team was on the road, if the other guy needed a helmet repaired or an extra pair of laces, they were welcome inside each other's equipment rooms. They were the Switzerland in the greater picture, and awfully busy some nights when the fists started flying.

"I had to go out on the ice one time for Kevin," remembered Bearcat. "He'd been bodychecked behind the net and hit his head on the glass. Kenny was busy and had gone to the dressing room. So I said, 'Kevin, it's Bearcat. You hit your head. Kenny's busy, but everything's going to be fine. Just relax. By this time, Kenny was there.

"So, we're coming off the ice now and I say to Kevin, 'You've got to start smartening up because you're married now. You've got a wife now. Somebody to look after you, and somebody to look after. And it's about time you showed her some respect and starting wearing something on your head to protect yourself other than that goofy [Jofa] helmet. I give it to him all the way off the ice.

"Kenny had been trying and trying to get him to change helmets too, and he wouldn't do it. But you know what? When he recovered from that, and he came back, he was wearing a proper helmet. I went up and shook his hand and he says, 'Bear, you were right.'"

Kulchisky agrees—but only to a point.

"We'd do anything for them and vice versa. But once the game started, it was a different world. You'd look down that bench and you'd think, 'Go eff yourself, Bearcat,'" he said. "Win the game or go down swinging. From my view behind the bench, listening to the coaches between periods, and listening to the players. That's what I got out if it."

It was in Calgary in January 2003 when Craig MacTavish, by then the Oilers head coach, reached over the glass and grabbed Flames mascot Harvey the Hound by the tongue after the six-foot-six plush dog taunted him repeatedly. Oh, how Neil Sheehy would have liked to do the same to Esa Tikkanen a decade before. "I was surprised by how easy it came out," MacTavish said afterwards. "It was one of those tear-away tongues."

Some of the strangest confrontations occurred not on the ice but in the stands behind the teams' benches. Remember, it wasn't until the mid-1990s that the NHL mandated teams have extra-high glass behind the benches, so interaction between fans and the coaching staff were known to boil over.

In Calgary, Oilers head coach Glen Sather had a long-running feud with a Flames season ticket holder who rankled Sather for years in the Stampede Corral and Saddledome. When you see the 1988 highlight of Gretzky streaking down the left wing and blasting a slapper high to Mike Vernon's glove side in overtime of a playoff game, the clip always includes Sather fist-pumping at someone behind the Oilers bench in Calgary. That's the guy, and Slats couldn't wait to shove it up the rear end of some shmoe who'd paid his way in. The high ground, it must be said, was seldom travelled in the Battle.

Off the ice, that is. On the ice, as the two teams matured, most nights they cut through the rest of the Campbell Conference like butter. In those eight Stanley Cup seasons, when the Flames or the Oilers emerged from the Smythe Division to play against the survivor of the Norris, the Alberta teams went a combined 32–10 in the conference final. The Chicago Blackhawks, a pretty fine team in the 1980s, had four cracks at getting to a Stanley Cup. In those four conference finals, the Blackhawks won but five lonely games.

It is said that one of the reasons the Oilers went from being a collection of good players to a championship team of the highest order was because of the Flames and the level of play required just to get out of the Smythe. Bob Johnson always had a "seven-point plan" on how to "get to the top of the mountain," but once again, Johnson's strategy often came with a gimmick.

Prior to the Oilers–Flames playoff matchup in spring 1986, Johnson dressed two college goalies in Oilers uniforms and ran them out on the ice for the Flames shooters to fire away at. Of course, this infuriated Sather, who thought the entire exercise to be bush league. But it distracted the Oilers that day, so in some small way, Badger had succeeded.

In his heart of hearts, Johnson knew that the Oilers had him outmanned in most positions. But he always believed there was a way to coach his team up to that level, and damned if he did not accomplish that in 1986, when the Flames' courageous pursuit of the two-time Cup champions resulted in a Game 7 victory for Calgary in Edmonton with "the Steve Smith goal," an own goal that is burned into the memory of every Flames and Oilers fan born after about 1980.

It was a goal for the ages, a Game 7 winner banked in by the Oilers defenceman off of the back of goalie Grant Fuhr's leg and credited to Calgary's Perry Berezan—an Edmonton native, no less. What rankled the Flames was that here they'd knocked off the champs in a seven-game series and the only goal anyone remembers was the one they didn't even score themselves.

"Everyone talks about the Steve Smith goal," grouses Lanny McDonald. "Well, they forget it was a seven-game series. We had to find a way to win three other games. If that happened in Game

3 or 4, no one would be talking about it. They'd be talking about what an unbelievable series it was. And it was."

From that moment on, once Calgary had checked in with its first series win over Edmonton, the complexion of the Battle would never be the same. Equal footing had been attained, and with that came a higher level of respect from Edmonton.

"All the most important, most memorable team meetings we ever had were in that dressing room in Calgary," MacTavish said. "We were the best two teams in the NHL of that day, and we would meet very early in the playoffs. It was good because the players weren't worn down from the rigours of three previous series, and they were absolute wars.

"A pleasure to be a part of, in hindsight."

Said Peplinski: "I continue to be shocked and amazed that there were not more serious injuries from those games. There was a never a game that wasn't vicious . . . and violent."

Was the hockey better? Well, if you grew up watching 5–4 hockey games with two or three fights, as I did, you are likely going to say there was more entertainment in a night of the Battle than when those same teams play a fightless, 3–2 game today—at four times the ticket price.

As for the players on the ice, they would probably rather get paid like today's NHL player, and not fearing for your life wouldn't be such a bad thing. But as Craig MacTavish said, sometimes when the old fight-or-flight response gets activated, the rush can feel pretty good once you're back in that dressing room, a cold beer in hand.

"For me, it was where we really challenged each other—in a lot of aspects of the game, but mostly the toughness part of it," he said. "Everybody had to get outside of their comfort zone for what they were willing to do from a toughness standpoint, and there is a lot of satisfaction when that happens. When everybody does it on your team, and you win.

"I mean, those games were highly satisfying. They were big games. We were the two best teams back in that era. You didn't have to look too long into the tea leaves to see what was ahead. It was going to be a tough, hard game.

"And those playoff series? Everybody in the league was watching them. It was just a battle of attrition."

Years later, in 2003, the Oilers, toiling in obscurity and playing inside a building renamed the Skyreach Centre, were scraping along the bottom of the NHL standings and fixing to welcome an only slightly better Flames team that night. The pendulum had swung on the Battle of Alberta, and the chances of ESPN dropping its American coverage to televise the Battle—as the network had done in the 1986 playoffs—was a distant memory.

Oilers president Patrick LaForge was asked if his club had anything special planned for that night's tilt, the first meeting between the Calgary Flames and Edmonton Oilers since MacTavish had poached Harvey the Hound's tongue.

"No," replied LaForge. Then he thought for a moment.

"Other than to beat the shit out of the Flames."

2

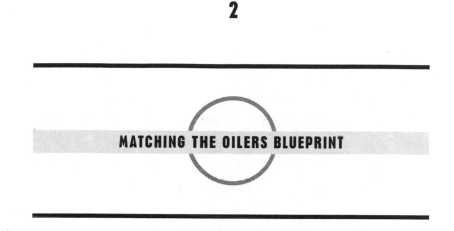

MATCHING THE OILERS BLUEPRINT

U.S. College Talent Boosts the Flames Roster

"Really? I didn't have a clue . . ."

Jamie Macoun would play more than a thousand NHL games eventually. But on January 22, 1983, he was as naive as a college kid could be, surrounded by NHL executives in the front seat of a rented car heading for an airport hotel in St. Louis.

Macoun, a defenceman, was facing his first four-on-one as a Calgary Flame. "Cliff Fletcher is in the front seat, and Al Coates, Al MacNeil, and Badger Bob Johnson are in the back seat," Macoun recalls. "I met the team down in St. Louis. I'm sitting there negotiating my own contract, right out of college."

Still a student at Ohio State University, where he'd had a total knee reconstruction the year before, Macoun had no idea what lay ahead. But he was already the consummate Calgary Flame before he'd even shaken general manager Cliff Fletcher's hand that day in Missouri.

You see, while Edmonton chief scout Barry Fraser had hit five or six early home runs, drafting five Hall of Fame players plus defensive rock Kevin Lowe in his first three NHL drafts, Fletcher was catching up with his own bird dog, a U.S. college scout by the name of Jack Ferreira.

If the Oilers were two or three years ahead of Calgary in the Battle of Alberta, and they surely were with players like Wayne Gretzky, Mark Messier, Grant Fuhr, Jari Kurri, and Paul Coffey, then it didn't make much sense for Fletcher to think he would ever catch up to Edmonton using the NHL draft. Any eighteen-year-old he could draft would always be at least two years behind the crop that Fraser had drafted, and as each season passed, two years turned into three, and into four, and so on.

Meanwhile, Ferreira, who would go on to become an NHL general manager himself, was in the midst of a forty-year career in the game. He had found quite a lode in these older, twenty- and twenty-one-year-olds coming out of the U.S. college ranks, and it made a ton of sense, snapping up players like Joel Otto out of Bemidji State; Colin Patterson from Clarkson; Eddy Beers, a Merritt, B.C., kid on scholarship at the University of Denver; and Gino Cavallini, a Toronto boy who went south to Bowling Green State University. Especially considering that Fletcher had gone out and hired a head coach named "Badger" Bob Johnson, a National Collegiate Athletic Association (NCAA) legend who was fresh out of the University of Wisconsin.

(The Flames had so much success with college guys, they would even sign a defenceman named Charlie Bourgeois out of the Université de Moncton. He came with a tragic back story, retold a little further below.)

On this day it was Macoun's turn to make the jump from college to pro. There was, however, a little matter of a contract to be hammered out. But Macoun was college-educated, so he didn't require an agent, right?

Well . . .

"Being in college, you didn't see a lot of the NHL down in Columbus, Ohio," he remembers. "I'm thinking, 'The Calgary Flames. Okay.' I know a couple of names, and I'm checking out the standings. But to be honest, it was pretty new to me. They're telling me, 'Well, Timmy Hunter is in the minors for us, and this guy's here, and that guy's there.' But really? I didn't have a clue."

Macoun always had the gift of the gab, and though he likely could have used an agent to negotiate his contract, he surely didn't need one for self-promotion.

"We'd brought him in," said Al Coates. "He'd watched the game, and now we're talking to him. He's telling everybody what kind of a player he is. He's saying, 'I can really skate, I'm a great first-pass player. I hit like a truck, I see the ice really well . . .' Finally, Badger says to him, 'Well, do you have any weaknesses at all?' And Jamie stops, thinks for a minute, and says, 'Well, every once in a while, on a two-on-one I run at the wrong guy. Other than that, I'm a pretty good player.'"

Finally, the management team asked the twenty-one-year-old Macoun what it would take to get his name on a contract. Again, Macoun was at a loss for any real negotiating strategy.

"My only thought was, 'I'm in college right now, and I'm getting paid to go to college.' If I could somehow guarantee that my college would get paid for if these guys decided they didn't want me in a year, then I'm happy," he surmised. "So I say, 'Are you going to pay for my school?' And they say, 'Absolutely. And we're going to pay you to go to school.'

"We used to get $300 a month at school for food. They were going to pay me $2,000 a month. I'm going, 'This is unbelievable!' They were paying me if things didn't work out and I went back to school, and they paid me when I went back to school in the summertime. Talk about a no-lose situation. I'm thinking, 'If I can get a chance to play one or two games . . . Or maybe I'll get lucky and play twenty or thirty games. And, I've still got my schooling!'"

But wait, they said to Macoun. How much did he think he should earn if he was actually playing for the Flames full time? Well, that thought had never even entered the steel trap that was Macoun's mind. Playing in the NHL? Was this a real possibility?

"I remember saying to myself, 'Bankers are getting this much, I should get as much as a banker.' They say, 'Sure, this year that's great. But what about next year?' I go, 'You mean, everything changes . . . ?'"

The Flames management could have taken advantage of these kids, locking them into deals they would have regretted the moment they arrived at their first NHL camp and found out what everyone else was making. But Fletcher and MacNeil were fair-minded people, entering into what they hoped would be a long-term relationship. As it turns out, with many of these guys it was long-term, so you can imagine the error it would have been to have started that relationship on nefarious footing.

"I look back now, I was treated incredibly fair," Macoun said, long after his 1,128-game career was done. "Cliff Fletcher, Al MacNeil, Al Coates, they are all great family people. Like Badger Bob, there was a genuine concern about what you were all about. Compare that to how Sather would have dealt with Jamie Macoun when I was coming out of college. Different schools, let's put it that way."

Thirty years later, and still lobbing shots at one another.

While Edmonton was owned by the high-profile Peter Pocklington, who was always accessible to the media though less so to collection agencies, the Flames ownership group was financially comfortable, highly respected in the community, and, as a rule, quiet as a mouse. The Flames had Badger Bob, the university professor with the wrinkly tie he would, every so often, use to wipe his nose on. Edmonton had Glen Sather behind its bench, wearing a smirk and a suit from Sam Abouhassan, Edmonton's clothier to the stars. Wipe your nose on Slats's tie and you'd need a lot more than a strip of silk to stop the bleeding that would ensue.

And when it came to building their rosters, they were similarly dissimilar. Johnson, whose roots were in the U.S. college game, was not only receptive to having college grads in his dressing room, it was probably a necessary route for his boss Fletcher to pursue. Had you stocked the room only with Canadian junior players in the early 1980s, then put an NCAA-trained coach in charge of them, you'd likely have had a mutiny.

Frankly, Calgary would have been crazy to believe that they could amass as much raw skill as the Oilers possessed. The solution for the Flames would come from masterful coaching and the devising of systems that when executed with precision— could stymie Edmonton's free-flow, freelance offence. And as any coach will tell you, that level of execution requires a unanimous buy-in from your roster. Twenty men would need to be 100 percent committed to Johnson's teachings if Calgary was going to pull this off, so the fact the dressing room was being salted with players whose backgrounds were identical to Badger Bob's was part of the design.

From the players' side, each and every one of them had been overlooked by the NHL into his early twenties. So guys like Colin Patterson, a Rexdale, Ontario, kid who had found his way down to Clarkson University in Potsdam, New York, viewed the Flames as one last chance at playing pro hockey.

"None of us were drafted," Patterson said. "We got a chance to play, where otherwise we probably wouldn't have. And Badger Bob was the coach at the time, so we all blended in."

From a roster-integration standpoint, there are mileposts throughout hockey history that are frequently acknowledged as game-changing trends. The moment the NHL finally abolished the Montreal Canadiens' territorial rights to the best young French-Canadian players was one milepost. The rise and fall of the WHA was another. The Winnipeg Jets gathering Ulf Nilsson, Anders Hedberg, and several other Swedish players together to produce a WHA team that would, most believe, have beaten many NHL clubs on a regular basis was yet another. When the Stastny brothers arrived from Czechoslovakia. When the Red Army began to disseminate, and Russian players began to appear in NHL uniforms.

The Calgary Flames' success with undrafted U.S. college players was something, however, that few saw coming. Today, of course, it seems like there is a Danny DeKeyser or a Torey Krug coming out of the NCAA every spring and walking right into a feeding frenzy of NHL general managers. But in 1982 there was no frenzy. Just an airport hotel in St. Louis and a rental car full of hockey men.

"At that time, there was a stigma about U.S. college hockey players, that the only hockey players there were played in the Canadian major junior hockey leagues," recounts Fletcher. "Bringing Bob Johnson to Calgary was the easiest decision because at that time if you suggested that Calgary was a little redneck-y as sports fans go, you wouldn't be far off. But we needed someone to make our players better and I thought if anybody could do it, he could."

Necessity, as always, became the mother of invention. Fletcher needed to play catch-up with Edmonton. "I was just looking for an edge. Being innovative. When I was working in St. Louis we were at the start of what turned out to be the origin of scouting combines. We got involved early in computerized scouting. I was just a guy looking for an edge over my opponents . . . and we were just looking at it as a possibility of acquiring players who'd make us better quicker—without having a lot of competition to get them. The scouts did a great job. Three [undrafted NCAA players] played on our Stanley Cup team, and three more were traded for a Hall of Famer [Joe Mullen]."

While Edmonton had drafted their crop of Hall of Famers, Fletcher was in the process of trading for a group of his own. Over the years he acquired Lanny McDonald and Doug Gilmour and traded three of those college kids (Beers, Bourgeois, and Cavallini) to St. Louis for Mullen, the Hell's Kitchen, New York, native who would reward the Flames with a fifty-one-goal season in their Cup year of 1988–89. Then the Flames would draft Joe Nieuwendyk, Al MacInnis, and Brett Hull, all of whom have been awarded plaques inside the Hockey Hall of Fame in Toronto.

"You land a fifty-goal guy out of players who had been acquired—not through the draft system—but through the college ranks? It gave you assets to deal with," Coates said. "All of a sudden there was some depth within the organization, and almost without exception they were character people. Still not as good as the Oilers but getting closer every year."

Slowly, Calgary checked off the boxes: Neil Sheehy would become Gretzky's personal discomfort zone. On every night of the Battle, No. 99 would wear the Flames defenceman "like a hair shirt," as Hall of Fame *Edmonton Journal* writer Jim Matheson used to say. Paul Reinhart, a power-play quarterback, was Calgary's answer to Paul Coffey in Edmonton. Hakan Loob was Calgary's Jari Kurri, Tim Hunter rivalled Dave Semenko, and so on.

But perhaps the most difficult matchup fell to Joel Otto. He was a six-foot-four centreman, strong in the faceoff circle, and with decent foot speed. So that paired Otto up with Mark Messier. The two couldn't have come from more divergent backgrounds.

"Badger was way ahead of his time with line matching, and I was out whenever we could [against Messier]," Otto said. "My role was to be strong, and as best I could, nullify him. It gave me a focus, a responsibility. For him, he probably had that guy every game [on the other side]."

Messier had grown up in a Northern Alberta hockey family, his father trekking through the minor leagues before coming home to wage the Battle of Alberta as a senior player with the Edmonton Monarchs in 1969–70. Messier himself had left home to turn pro at age seventeen, quenched like molten steel in a World Hockey Association culture that was both tough and unfair in equal portions. He learned to fight at fifteen, and as a sixteen-year-old racked up 194 penalty minutes as an ironically named St. Albert Saint in the Alberta Junior Hockey League.

Otto, meanwhile, was nine months younger than Messier and miles behind when it came to the style of hockey that the Battle would require. With seventy-five points in just thirty-one games during the 1983–84 season, Otto had led his Bemidji State Beavers to a national Division II title in his final year of college. By that time, however, Messier had played in two Stanley Cup finals, winning the Conn Smythe in 1984 as Edmonton ended the New York Islanders dynasty.

Within a season, Otto was busting helmets—going Cooper to Winnwell—with Messier, a lot to ask of a college kid making his first couple of tours through the NHL. Otto was physically up to the task right away. But the mental part? It would have to come over time.

"He was unpredictable," Otto said of Messier. "I approached him like I was going into the cage with a lion. You had to be careful. He brought something that not many guys did, and that's a lot of everything. There aren't many more complete players than he was, and he's not one to back down.

"Hey, Edmonton games were nervous. It was an important part of our era . . . and it kept me focused because I had to know his unpredictability. And he had the entire package."

In hindsight, going head to head with Messier was, in a perverse way, the safest place to be in the Battle. It kept Messier in front of Otto at all times, and the Flames centre could be excused for never letting Messier out of his sight—which was always the safest vantage point when Calgary met Edmonton.

"I know he gave it to Nats [Ric Nattress] with an elbow one time. Couner [Macoun] once, just about killed him," Otto listed off. "And I'm missin' a couple others. Caught Perry [Berezan] with his head down once . . ."

It became a fascinating clash of twosomes in the Battle: Messier and his sidekick, Glenn Anderson, against Otto and his permanent right-winger, Jim Peplinski. "Pep and I were together for most of the five years we played [in Calgary] together," Otto said. "And I owe Pep all my penalty minutes 'cause he'd start the stuff, I'd wade in. You'd get ten minutes back in those days."

Otto has been quoted many times on Messier, saying, "I owe him my career, basically." That may be a tad charitable, as it is hard to believe there weren't twenty other teams that would have loved to acquire a six-foot-four centreman with all of Otto's attributes for their lineup. But, like many of these college grads who gravitated to Cliff Fletcher's team in Calgary, Otto still holds a special reverence—almost an indebtedness—to the Battle.

"Well, it got me in the league, personally. I've said that to many people," Otto said. "Calgary trying to find a blueprint that would match Edmonton. That's what it was all about. It gave me the opportunity to play, and I was lucky enough to be in the right place and make the most of it."

"For us," echoed Patterson, "without them, we would not have formed our team the way we did. For me personally, had it not been for them, I don't know if Calgary would have signed me."

Getting conscripted into the Battle of Alberta in the early 1980s was one thing. Finding the games on television or radio outside the province of Alberta was quite another. In the 1990s, when Glen Sather was no longer behind the Oilers bench, sometimes he would be out of the market when the Oilers were playing. Unable to find it on television, he would call home and instruct one of his family members to place the receiver near the radio so he could listen to the radio play called by Rod Phillips.

A decade before that, remember, there was no Internet and no Centre Ice package on digital TV. Even when the Battle burned the brightest, it was difficult to tune in from anywhere outside what was then a 403 area code that enveloped the entire province of Alberta.

"It wasn't like the CBC was carrying Edmonton or Calgary games every weekend," Patterson recalled. "There was no double-header on Saturday night. Unless you were going to stay up 'til midnight and get a satellite dish that could give you illegal access to the game, you weren't seeing it.

"My parents lived in Toronto, and they'd try to listen to our games on the radio. My dad was an electrical engineer, so he had all these hookups. They'd pick up some station from another station, from another station, but they could never get the game. So you'd phone them after it was over and tell them the score. Or if you couldn't call [there were no cellphones in the mid-1980s], they'd pick up the paper the next *afternoon* to get the score.

"So many of Gretzky's feats weren't even seen nationally. Can you imagine?" said Patterson. "People outside the province, I don't think they understood how good the hockey was. You'd have to ask [CBC producer] John Shannon, but I'm pretty sure that '86 series cost him his job with CBC. 'We're not leaving this broadcast. We're not going to show The *Pig and Whistle*, or whatever the hell was on at the time. That's how you knew, people didn't know about the Battle."

The Battle left a tattoo on the hearts, however, of those who were on its front lines. Even years later, with careers now winding down and both teams far removed from any Stanley Cup chatter, there was a certain feeling that lasted — in the pit of your stomach, a tension that still had a grip.

"I can remember being in the locker room before an Edmonton game," Otto said. "This is my eighth, ninth year in the league. It was just another game in the regular season, and I turned to Pep and said, 'I'm nervous.'

"I was never nervous before any game, but I was nervous because of what's at stake. The rivalry. The way the game's going to be played. There was going to be fights, there was going to be physicality. It was going to be that type of game."

It's almost uncanny the way the matchups formed, as if they were keeping up with the Joneses. Even as insignificant as it may seem, there were two stay-at-home defencemen registered in the Battle who came from the Canadian university ranks. One resided on each team's blue line.

Edmonton had a big, red-haired graduate of the University of Alberta's Faculty of Medicine named Dr. Randy Gregg, whose skating style was best described by Oilers play-by-play man Rod Phillips, who would greet a Gregg puck rush with, "Here comes Randy Gregg, snow-shoeing up through centre-ice . . ." I played baseball with Gregg on a men's team called the Edmonton Tigers. He was a sharp-fielding third baseman with a fine arm who, as a hitter, could launch the ball a mile. He was, like most NHLers, simply an excellent all-around athlete.

Of course, Calgary would have an answer for Gregg, and that came in the form of Charlie Bourgeois, a similarly safety-conscious defenceman out of the Université de Moncton. Gregg had been the premier defenceman in what was then the Canadian Inter-university Athletic Union—they have since named an award after him, given to the top academic hockey player—before joining the Canadian Olympic team in 1979. Two years later Bourgeois would be named an All-Canadian defenceman and take his Université de Moncton Aigles Bleus to the national tournament.

It was at another of these tournaments, in spring 2005, when I ran across Bourgeois again, now the U of M's head coach, as he brought his Aigles Bleus to Edmonton for a University Cup championship tournament. Bourgeois's team practised at Clare Drake Arena on the University of Alberta campus, not 100 metres away from the U of A Pavilion that only two weeks previous had held one of the largest funerals in RCMP history, as the four Mounties killed in the Mayerthorpe massacre were laid to rest.

Officers Anthony Gordon, Lionide Johnston, Brock Myrol, and Peter Schiemann were executing a property seizure on a farm near Mayerthorpe, a rural community in North Central Alberta, when they were ambushed by James Roszko in what was the worst multiple-officer killing in modern Canadian history.

"My dad was a good cop. A real good cop," Bourgeois told me that day. "I remember, he'd run into a drunk, and some nights he'd bring him to our house instead of taking him to [the station]. Just a good cop. Very fair, but tough.

"He was just a good man. He wanted to help people."

Charlie Bourgeois's story begins in the 1960s when a young cop named Aurele Bourgeois moved his family from Toronto to Moncton. "There was less danger," recalls Charlie as the reason for the move. For those who serve the public the way the RCMP do, the concept of "less danger" may be attainable. A workday without any danger, however, is not something they sign up for.

And so it was that two members—Cpl. Aurele Bourgeois and Const. Michael O'Leary—were dispatched with $15,000 in ransom money in December 1974, instructed to free fourteen-year-old Raymond Stein from a pair of local thugs. One of the kidnappers was the notorious James Hutchison, who, like Roszko, had a litany of violent offences on his record when he shot his way into Canadian history books.

"It was a kidnapping—the son of a wealthy restaurateur in Moncton—which had never happened in the city," Bourgeois recalled. "My dad and his partner, Constable O'Leary, were responsible for delivering the ransom. That's where there were several errors. There was no backup, and they were caught by surprise. They boy was let go safely, and my understanding is [the kidnappers] were able to get the gun off one of the police officers and forced the other police officer to put down his weapon. Since then, the law has changed. A police officer is never to put down his weapon."

Bourgeois was fourteen, going on fifteen years old when this tragedy played out. He was playing minor hockey in Moncton. His dad came to as many games as his shift schedule would allow. Even when he was working, you might have seen a patrol car parked outside the local hockey rink for twenty minutes or so, when young Charlie's team was on the ice.

"There were several days when we didn't know what was happening. Dad didn't come home," Bourgeois remembers. "Those three days of not knowing, those were trying times. Back home, nothing like that had ever happened. The police force just wasn't prepared. There was a series of . . . mistakes. There was no backup. My dad and his partner couldn't have access to the shotguns. Looking back now, they just didn't take all the pre-cautions. It was a small community."

Bourgeois and O'Leary's last contact was made when they radioed their dispatcher to say they were in pursuit of a Cadillac that contained the kidnappers. Something went wrong, however, and before long the two officers were on their hands and knees in the woods north of Moncton, digging their own graves. Both were killed execution-style, with their own revolvers. Hutchison and his accomplice, Ricky Ambrose, purchased shovels at a local hardware store a few hours later and buried the bodies. The graves were found two days later by an elderly trapper.

Aurele Bourgeois was just forty-three years old, with a wife and four kids. The Bourgeoises did not attend court proceedings or demand an inquiry.

"As a family . . . we just kind of wanted to push it away. Our mom sheltered us from it, and kept us away," Bourgeois said. "My dad. My hockey coach. Building the outdoor rink in the back, he'd be out there hours in the night, flooding a big outdoor rink. Wouldn't miss any games, even if he was on duty. You'd see up in the corner of the building, a guy dressed in his uniform, sneaking in. He never played the game, but he had a great pas-sion for it. He just loved the game of hockey. He's probably why I'm still involved in this game at forty-five years old."

But even that was a close call for a while. Bourgeois nearly quit the game after his father died. "I was fourteen. In high school," he said. "It was tough, at first. It was devastating. I just stopped playing."

It is hard to know if Bourgeois found the Battle of Alberta or if it found him. But he was cut out for the work: a big, burly defence-man with a chip on his shoulder who wasn't about to take any crap from anybody.

"The first NHL game I saw live was the first NHL game I

played in: at the old Stampede Corral against St. Louis. Fought Brian Sutter," he said. "My first game at the Forum, the twelfth game of my NHL career, I had my family and friends there and I scored that night. My first NHL goal.

"It's as clear as if it happened yesterday: Mel Bridgman making the pass back to me; just a shot from the point; Richard Sévigny, a shot over his shoulder; Willi Plett picking the puck up and giving it to me . . ."

It was the first of only sixteen career goals for Bourgeois in a stay-at-home, 290-game career. "The odds of my mom and my family being in the rink where I'm going to score a goal? My *first* NHL goal? And growing up as a Montreal Canadiens fan? My dad and I watched the Canadiens every Saturday night. That was his team. So, for that all to happen, you wonder if somebody upstairs wasn't looking out for you."

Ricky Ambrose, now sixty-three, was paroled in July 2000. He changed his surname to Bergeron and was living in Edmonton when his parole was revoked. He is, by all reports, still in the system. James Lawrence Hutchison died in the Kingston Penitentiary in 2011 at age eighty-three. Both had been sentenced to hang as cop killers, but their sentences were commuted to life without parole for twenty-five years when capital punishment was abolished in Canada.

Charlie Bourgeois has settled in Atlantic Canada, where he is heavily involved in youth hockey programs. He is a good man who has been through a lot.

3

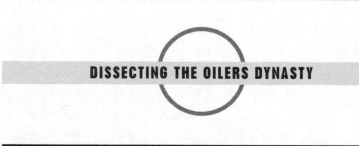

DISSECTING THE OILERS DYNASTY

Glen Sather and the Art of Experience

"Your parents aren't here.
Your agents will run from you.
You come to me and I'll be able to help."

Wayne Gretzky scanned the lineup of former Oilers greats and focused on his old boss, Glen Sather, at the end of the line. They were sitting on a stage reminiscing about that first Cup, won three decades ago. Messier, Coffey, Fuhr, Anderson, Lowe . . . A pretty good band, to be sure, but even the finest orchestra needs a damned good conductor.

"I once told Glen," Gretzky said, "for a six-goal scorer, he had tremendous hockey sense."

When it came to those Oilers teams, Sather was the mother-board. He ran everything, and everything ran through him. Yet, because of Sather's keen awareness of when and when not to get involved, you could never call Sather a micromanager.

He trusted people, and if they performed and were honest, he remains loyal to them to this day.

For any leader, knowing when to step in is no more or less important than knowing when to stay out of something. Whether that concerned a player's learning curve or the all-import drafting process that built this Oilers dynasty, Sather possessed this innate ability to make the right call.

"Here's what the media's misconception of [the draft] always is," said the Oilers grizzled former chief scout, Barry Fraser. "They think the managers go out and see all these [junior] guys play? They've never seen 'em play at all, most of them."

This was where Sather had the good sense to hire smart people and let them do their jobs. It's true—he had very little to do with those drafts. But when he struck his nose in, Sather's touch was perfect. Like the time some kid named Mark Messier was next on Edmonton's draft list.

"He wanted to take Messier in the third round, and I wanted to wait one more round," Fraser remembers. "I mean, he'd only scored one goal the year before [in Cincinnati of the WHA], and it was one that hit him in the ass and went in, as I remember."

"I said, 'No, we're taking Messier now,'" Sather recalls. "I'd seen Mark when he was a kid playing in St. Albert. He was just a kid, but he had tremendous instincts."

Between the two, after twenty-three NHL drafts together, that was the only memorable conflict they could come up with. If you knew the smug, cocky Sather in the mid-1980s, you might find it hard to believe that one of his strongest qualities as a leader was knowing when to get the hell out of the way and trust his people.

"I found that out very early in the whole process," Sather said. "Barry would see 230 games a year, and all of his scouts would see over 175. I went to see Grant Fuhr [play junior] in Victoria, and he was awful. I saw him at the Memorial Cup at Windsor? He was awful. And I remember talking to Barry about it, and him saying, 'This guy is going to be a great goaltender. We're drafting him.'

"I went to see Paul Coffey when he was playing junior hockey. Barry was telling me about this guy, and how he was going to be a great player," said Sather, who didn't exactly fall in love with Coffey's game that day. "But I didn't argue with him because I could see that he could skate and shoot the puck."

Once Fraser drafted the players, they were turned over to Sather to mould into NHL players—and to turn into men. And not necessarily in that order. Sather leaned hardest on the guys he knew would and could deliver his message. The players he trusted the most? They got the most heat.

"He was harder on us than our parents were," Gretzky said. "The very first phone call you ever made if something bad happened, or something wasn't right, if you called Glen he was going to take care of it. So he really became a father to all of us, especially those of us who were here at eighteen, nineteen, twenty."

On the other end of the scale was Fuhr. His finances were a wreck, and his level of maturity simply wasn't sufficient to handle all that came along with NHL stardom. Yelling wasn't going to help, and Sather likely fathered Fuhr more than any other player.

"I might be responsible for a lot of those grey hairs on his head now," laughed Fuhr. "Financially, as an eighteen-year-old kid, just because all of a sudden you have money doesn't mean you know what to do with it. So, he helped me buy my first house here in the city. Basically, he helped me along until I figured it out, if I ever figured it out.

"He gave us a lot of rope, so that we could learn on our own. But he also knew when to yank on the rope to reel us back in," Fuhr said. "So he let us grow, thinking it was our idea."

Covering Sather's teams for more than a decade, one consistency I observed was his affinity for doing exactly what you thought was not necessary. Just when you figured you were coming down to the rink to cover a bag skate, he would run a teaching practice. And when things were good, and Sather perceived his team might be getting a little fat and sassy? He'd skate the hell out of them.

Inside the dressing room, the guys who produced the most also got the most heat when things were slipping.

"Most of the meetings that Glen had were one-way meetings, you know? You kind of took it," Gretzky remembers with a wry smile. "As coaches have to do, he called out guys. But Glen's forte was, he never picked on guys he didn't think were front-line guys. He was the hardest, always, on myself, Kurri, Messier, and Coffey. He believed that, if he could get through to us, get us to play the system he wanted, then everybody else would conform to it."

It worked the same way with the journalists who covered the team. He'd test you, and if you responded with a strong backbone, you had his respect. If you shied away, you were irrelevant. He had little time for the weak, whether on the ice or off.

I can attest, as a young reporter for the *Edmonton Journal*, his modus operandi was always the same. Where some coaches would pull you aside and berate your story, or a line of questioning in private, Sather wanted it well known that he was taking you to task. In my first couple of years on the beat, he would challenge me in the midst of a scrum of my colleagues.

It would happen during his interview session, in his dressing room, with many of his players within earshot. On his turf, by his rules—that was always Glen's M.O.

At first I wouldn't see it coming, and thought I tried not to let on, here was the great Glen Sather questioning something you'd written in front of everybody. I was rattled—exactly as Sather wanted you to be. But you had to stand up to him. You couldn't cower or apologize because in the big picture it was a test. He wanted to know what kind of adversary he was facing, and you had to show him that you were going to chase the next story as hard as you'd chased the last one.

Once, in the mid-1990s, I had a story about a young Oilers player who had fathered a child out of wedlock. That fact alone wasn't so newsworthy, but the legal process that ensued was crushing the player mentally. He was missing practices to attend the legal appointments, and his game had fallen off a cliff.

I confronted the player, got all the quotes, and although we couldn't run the story that day, it would certainly be vetted by the *Journal* lawyers and run the next day. I went to bed late and was startled to hear my home phone ring at 6:45 a.m. It was Sather.

"You'll never cover another game in our rink," he threatened. "Your career will be done if you run that story."

I was still half asleep while he was sharp and pushing the conversation. He had created an advantage for himself, a skill at which Sather was masterful. I told him the story was running, that I had it nailed with all the player's quotes, and if he wanted to talk to me about it I would add in his perspective.

"I'm not going to talk to you about that!" he shouted. The thought of actually helping me with the story had never crossed his mind. I was scared as hell, truthfully, but the story ran and there wasn't a single repercussion.

Sather's bark was worse than his bite, which I would later learn was a pattern with those whom he liked or at least respected. I'd passed his test enough times, I guess.

⭐

It doesn't take a genius to figure out that a general manager can't win games in the NHL. No one in a suit has the ultimate control over a game. So a GM's job description is to put the right people in all the right places—the amateur scouts, the pro scouts, the head coach, the assistant coaches, the training staff—to deliver his plan. But when the WHA closed its doors in 1979—with the Edmonton Oilers, Quebec Nordiques, Winnipeg Jets, and Hartford Whalers merging into a now twenty-one-team NHL for the 1979–80 season—to say Sather had even the skeleton of a team that would become a dynasty would be stretching it.

What he had was Wayne Gretzky, the odd Blair MacDonald and Brett Callighen, a Stan Weir here, a Dave Dryden there . . . and not much else. The NHL fathers, bitter that the WHA had driven up player costs (the Canadian NHL teams were also sour that *Hockey Night in Canada* revenue would now have to be split among three more Canadian clubs), made sure that the four merging WHA teams were stripped bare. They allowed each team to keep just two skaters and two goalies. Every remaining player who had been drafted by an NHL team reverted to becoming that team's property again.

"They took Bengt Gustafsson. Screwed us on that one," spat Sather, still sour some thirty-five years later about losing to the Washington Capitals what had been a savvy, late-season acquisition in the WHA's final campaign by Sather. But the Oilers were able to keep Wayne Gretzky, and history shows, he was the only player from that last WHA team that really mattered, right?

Wrong. The Oilers brought Sather into the NHL as well, and without him the words "Edmonton Oilers" and "Stanley Cup" might never have been found in the same sentence. For one, Sather had instructed owner Peter Pocklington to acquire Gretzky in the first place, and he did so on November 2, 1978, from Nelson Skalbania, whose Indianapolis Racers were said to be losing an unheard-of $40,000 per day in their WHA operation. It gave Sather a centrepiece around which to construct a hockey club, and surprisingly, there was relatively little push back by the NHL teams about allowing Gretzky to remain with Edmonton.

"They knew that we had to have a good player. And a lot of the guys in the NHL were not convinced that Wayne was going to be a good player. I don't think a lot of them looked that hard [at the WHA]," Sather said. "There were lots of other pieces we had to surround Wayne with, and those pieces changed all the time. It was a matter of developing them, taking your time, encouraging them, building them. Getting them to do the right things. Getting them to be disciplined on the ice, but letting them grow into mature young men."

Sather had been perhaps the last of hockey's player/coaches when he replaced head coach Armand (Bep) Guidolin behind the Oilers bench midway through the Oilers 1976–77 WHA season. It was Guidolin's idea, the kind of thing they did in the days of the WHA. The move was made partly because Guidolin was aware the team had stopped responding to him—and that Sather was the smartest hockey man in his employ—and partly because ownership didn't feel like adding another contract to the payroll.

Sather, as it turns out, had been running many of the Oilers practices anyhow. He was clearly the next in command, by then a savvy, thirty-two-year-old left-winger who would find a way to score the overtime winner in his first game as player/coach. It was in Sather's DNA to always be looking ahead, setting up his next move in life. And as Sather surmised the similarly aged players on the Oilers roster—Bill (Cowboy) Flett, Norm Ullman, goalie Dave Dryden—he saw men whose hockey careers were drawing to a close.

The WHA was an iffy proposition on the best of days, and Sather wasn't going to be caught without a chair when the music stopped on that rickety old circuit. So he took the job as head coach.

"The thing about the WHA is, it offered opportunities," said Dryden in Ed Willes's excellent book, *The Rebel League: The Short and Unruly Life of the World Hockey Association.* "My brother [Ken] played with Slats in Montreal, and he said, 'He's got a lot of confidence and he's smart,' and that was pretty accurate. He was a horse trader and he was good at picking up information by asking the right questions and talking to the right people. Once he got behind the bench, I really liked the way he handled things. He didn't over-coach. He was clear and direct. Then, when we got Wayne, he made sure [Gretzky] was surrounded with the right guys who'd teach him the right things."

The career that would land Sather in the Hockey Hall of Fame began the day he replaced Guidolin behind that Oilers bench, with eighteen games remaining in another middling Oilers WHA season. The kid with the brush cut out of High River, Alberta, had eked out 658 games for six NHL organizations, plus another 81 games in that final WHA season in Edmonton. By the time the 1976–77 campaign had ended—despite scoring nineteen goals, thirty-four assists, and fifty-three points, all career highs—Sather knew his future was behind the bench. He hung up his skates after that season, and it was at that moment that Glen Sather the plugger—nicknamed "Slats" because of all the time he'd spent on the end of a bench—began the transformation into Glen Sather the Hall of Fame builder.

"How does anybody become what you become? You become a lot of things by chance, by luck, or by planning for the future," Sather, now seventy-one years old, said when we spoke. He was sitting in the Rexall Place press box, in the visiting team's booth. The cigar he chomped for all those years was absent, but the hint of smugness, the "here's how it works" demeanour, was as strong as it ever was, even if some of the details from those old games have blurred a tad.

"The first few years I played pro, I ran hockey schools in Red Deer, in Banff, in Kimberley. Ran three of them at one time. I was organized. I planned. I liked the kids. I liked teaching. And I knew how to get the best out of them."

We are all a product of our surroundings, and nowhere is that more true than in sports. You might have one or two wives in your life and think you know about relationships. But a guy like Sather—loyally married to Ann for forty-six years—played for a dozen or more coaches along the way. Some of them were Hall of Famers themselves, and each taught Sather a little something different.

"You think of Harry Sinden, Emile Francis, Scotty Bowman, Red Kelly . . . I learned something from all of those guys. I learned things to avoid. I learned things that I liked, and I knew what the players liked. I had a chance to analyze the game from [the bench] because I was playing ten minutes a game. I wasn't playing eighteen minutes a game."

In 1979 the Oilers were coming off a loss to Winnipeg in the Avco Cup, the WHA's corporate, less historic version of the Stanley Cup. That loss was meaningless as soon as the final horn sounded, as everyone knew the next game would be with the big boys in the NHL. That first NHL game, on October 10, 1979, inside the old Chicago Stadium, was a milestone, to be sure. But the most important thing that Glen Sather—now the Oilers' general manager and president as well as head coach—did in that first year? Well, it didn't even happen in a hockey rink.

It occurred August 9, 1979, at the Queen Elizabeth Hotel in Montreal—exactly nine years to the day before Sather would be forced to sell Gretzky to the Los Angeles Kings. It was here that Sather's trust policy really began to pay dividends.

It was the Oilers' first NHL draft after joining the league as a WHA survivor alongside the Winnipeg Jets, Quebec Nordiques, and Hartford Whalers. Sather and Fraser chose Kevin Lowe with their first pick, twenty-first overall. They traded their second-round pick to Minnesota to secure North Stars property Dave Semenko, whom the Oilers had lost off their roster under the terms of the WHA merger.

(The trade went like this: Edmonton's forty-second-overall pick [which Minnesota used to select Neal Broten], plus Edmonton's sixty-third-overall to Minnesota, for Semenko and Minnesota's forty-eighth-overall pick. The Oilers re-acquired the heavyweight they'd lost in joining the NHL, and their plan worked perfectly when Messier was still available six choices later at forty-eight.)

Fraser drafted Lowe thinking he would be the glue guy, that high-in-character, stay-at-home defenceman whose pain threshold was out of sight. He was right. Lowe emerged as a shut-down defender whom Sather could play against the best in the NHL. A guy who wore a letter yet conducted himself every night as if he were still trying to make the team.

"He didn't make many mistakes, a sound guy," said Fraser when asked what he saw as he scouted Lowe in junior paying for the Quebec Remparts. "He was an English captain of a Quebec Major Junior team, which was rare. His competitiveness . . . ? They didn't call him 'Vicious' for nothing. He had a temper for sure, and I liked that."

Lowe was known in his younger years as "Vish." It was derived from Sid Vicious, a singer and bass player for the punk band The Sex Pistols, and its origins described perfectly what Sather liked in a player. Lowe wouldn't travel across the zone to injure anyone. In fact, he was highly respected as a stand-up player by his peers. But if you thought you might run Lowe, he would not hesitate to hold his stick in such a way that bodychecking Lowe meant going through his stick to get to him. Call it the ol' Sher-Wood sandwich. Lose a few teeth? Well, maybe you should have tried to hit someone else, eh?

That a player with Lowe's characteristics would be the first-ever draft pick seems like a sound investment in the future. In the here and now, boardrooms full of hockey men would debate the merits of which position should be attacked first. Do they build from the goal out? Do they start with a big, right-handed centreman? How about a quarterback for the power play?

In those days, however, the consultation was minimal.

"We didn't have a whole lot of discussions about anything like that," Fraser said. "Glen was coach, general manager, and president of the team. He didn't have a whole lot of time for this stuff. I was pretty much left on my own. He never entered into any of it."

In a time long before analytics, Fraser's gut was operating at a level far above what any math whiz could attain. We didn't know it in 1979, but Fraser could hardly miss. His draft picks would form the basis of a team that is in the conversation for the best team in NHL history, and when he saw Anderson practise, he just knew that this was a kid you wanted on your side.

"His speed, his recklessness . . . I mean, here's a guy who was going to play on the Canadian Olympic team at eighteen years old. That's outstanding enough as it is," Fraser said. A year later they held the draft in an NHL arena for the first time, moving down the street to the old Montreal Forum. That year, Fraser only drafted two Hall of Famers—Paul Coffey and Jari Kurri.

"Coff played for the Kitchener Rangers, and I lived in Kitchener," Fraser said. "I got to know him, I saw him a lot, and his coach [Bob Ertel] was a friend of mine. There was a lot of speculation about how good a defenceman he was going to be, but there was no doubt in my mind that if he couldn't be a defenceman, he surely could be a winger.

"He was just so smooth, so effortless. He could go like hell. Went through the whole team in junior just like he did in the NHL."

Kurri was a sighting from a trip the Oilers had made into Finland to play some exhibition games when they were still in the WHA. Then, in the seventh round, Fraser took a flyer on a kid out of Penticton, B.C., a little goalie named Andy Moog who would turn out just fine, playing eighteen NHL seasons and over 700 games. Just in case though, Fraser used his first pick the following year to select Grant Fuhr at number eight overall in 1981.

"Glen said, 'Well, you know we have a pretty good goalie [in Moog]?' And I said, 'Well, now we've got two,'" Fraser remembers. "That was about the extent of the conversation we had. He never bothered me in that respect at all."

Trust.

Of course, nobody knew back then that Fraser had, in his first three NHL drafts, collected the guts of one of the all-time great teams. Not even Sather. All he knew was, he was going with a young, young core, and he had to surround them with the right types of veterans. Fraser had provided some mighty good groceries, but Sather needed to find the right recipe to spice the dish the right way.

Meanwhile, he couldn't take his eye off the stove. So he laid down some rules, and rule number one was that if you got into any trouble, call Sather.

"That's the rule we had," Sather said. "I told 'em, 'There isn't anyone who is going to help you. Your parents aren't here. Your agents will run from you. You come to me and I'll be able to help.' I just knew that I had enough friends around town that if they had a problem, I could help solve it for them."

During Sather's time in Edmonton, the Oilers used Floyd Whitney, the father to 1,300-game NHLer Ray Whitney, exclusively as their practice goalie. More importantly for Sather's purposes, however, Floyd was a senior member of the Edmonton Police Service (EPS). That made him an avenue of warning or intelligence on things like bars or restaurants that the EPS suspected of being inhabited by the wrong types of people, or an inroad into any possible troubles with the law that an Oilers player or employee might stumble into. Floyd was part of Sather's network, his way of warding off problems before they happened.

There was also a fixture in the coach's office, a man named (Bullet) Bob Freeman, who was listed on the Oilers ledgers as a scout. But really he was more like Sather's "fixer."

Bullet was one of the true characters of the game in the 1980s. And he had some scouting chops, having dug Semenko out of the Brandon Wheat Kings in the mid-1970s. A man of few words, Bullet quietly listened to everything that was going on, and never missed a practice or game. He was just . . . around all the time. No one was completely positive what it was that Bullet did once he'd come off the scouting trail.

"I remember one time," said the *Edmonton Journal*'s Jim Matheson, whose father, Jack, was a renowned sports writer in Winnipeg, "my dad had written something about a boxing card in Winnipeg, that it had been a waste of time or something. Not a very good event. And he got a call from the promoter, who wasn't a real savoury guy. He told my dad, 'You shouldn't have written that. You're going to regret it.'

"Well, I mentioned this to Bob, who had roots in Winnipeg. He said, 'I'll look into that for you.' About a week later, Bob stopped me and said, 'Tell your dad it's taken care of. That promoter won't be a problem again.'"

In a small city like Edmonton, those were the kinds of valuable connections that Sather knew would come in handy. It was just another piece in the puzzle of parenting the young Oilers until they could figure things out for themselves.

"That's part of the job. You have to watch out for them, and at the same time you have to let them grow. Allow them to become young men. They have to make mistakes. They have to learn to be responsible," Sather said. "Mark [Messier], he was a young stallion. Two things I did with Mark: one, I found out that he had a motorcycle. I told him to get rid of the motorcycle. He got rid of the motorcycle. The time before that, he was late for a plane, I sent him to Houston for four games. Look what he is today? All those guys, they all had some warts on them, but they all grew into tremendous players."

Grant Fuhr was as erratic off the ice as anyone. He admitted to cocaine use and was suspended by the NHL. Was he the only one? Sather had done his level best to keep Fuhr's revelation under wraps, but even his efforts failed. Despite media reports, no other Oilers player was ever officially linked to drug use.

"We were all eighteen, nineteen, twenty years old," Fuhr said. "We needed a little parenting, for sure. Slats probably had one of the harder jobs. One, we were having success, and along with success comes a lot of options. Options to probably, how would you say . . . not stay out of trouble?"

Even the media were subject to Sather's lessons. I recall leaving a rink in Denver after a morning skate one lunch hour as Sather was stepping into a cab—to the hotel, I assumed. "Hop in," he said to me, and I did. Once we were en route, he mentioned, "We just have to make one stop."

He was heading for a gun shop, as it turns out. Sather was quite an outdoorsman, and on this day, he'd drag a young writer along while he handled several long guns and talked ammunition with the local storekeep at the Denver gun shop. The assumption, of course, was that he might buy them all. He surely could afford to, though I never knew if Sather bought any of them that day.

"Ever shoot one of these?" he asked me. I had not. "Well, hold it against your shoulder like this, and lean your cheek in here . . ."

The most dangerous weapon I had ever held was a Marriott pen after a 10–2 loss by the team I was covering, but here I was in a Denver gun shop, getting a lesson on how to shoot a very expensive rifle. It mattered not that I did not hunt, and to this day I have never had the urge to shoot a rifle of that heavy gauge. When you were with Sather, he would show you a thing or two. That was his way.

"He had a lot of passion for life away from hockey," said former Oilers centreman Craig MacTavish. "That did a lot in terms of building the camaraderie among the group. We'd go on hunting trips. We'd go snowmobiling. You'd never do that today, but he was an outdoorsman and a real active guy. A big kid."

Sather held all the cards in the Oilers organization: head coach, general manager, president. He was the centre of power, and there was not a single person, from the lowliest "Radio Johnny" to the president of major sponsor Molson Breweries, who didn't know exactly who was in charge.

Behind the bench, Sather owned a steady hand and a smart hockey mind. His general manager duties would take him away at times from both practices and the odd game, and while Sather was one of the best at motivation, pushing the right buttons, and getting the most out of his players, he needed a right-hand man who could match wits with the Bob Johnsons of the world when it came to Xs and Os.

John Muckler would be that man, joining the Oilers as an assistant coach in 1981. He was promoted to co-coach in 1985 and would become the Oilers' head coach when Sather went upstairs for good in 1989. Muckler, trusted implicitly by Sather, would guide Edmonton to its final Stanley Cup in 1990.

"It was a perfect mix of a coaching staff," MacTavish recalls. "Glen was the manager, and he was fully in charge. Muck was the tactician. Very capable. He had a head-coaching persona, so when Glen was away doing managerial stuff, Muck took over, and there was no drop off in authority. Everyone had a very high regard for Muck.

"It was back in an era where it was a much more dictatorial relationship than what coaching and managing is today, where it's more of a cooperative collaboration between manager, coach, and player than it ever was then. Back in those days, Glen told you what to do and you did it. Today, you tell them what to do, and why to do it. Then you try to convince them that it's their idea so they'll execute it better."

When the young Oilers were at the rink, Sather's word was gospel. Nobody disrespected Sather inside the Northlands Coliseum — not in front of his face or behind his back. Honestly, there wasn't a popcorn salesman or floor sweeper who would have spoken ill of Sather in the mid-1980s around Northlands. He was unilaterally respected and feared by anyone within arm's reach of the Oilers organization. He was The Boss — period.

But as they say, heavy is the head that wears the crown. Sather had this wonderful crop of high-pedigree players, yet he drove to the rink every morning trying to figure out what lesson it was that they would need most that day.

"It's is one thing to have talent. It's another to allow yourself to be developed into the kind of players they all became," Sather says. "They have to have the attitude and desire to get there. There were a lot of things we did to make sure that they did develop.

"One of the things I always said was, we practised hard. But you never sat on the ice, you never kneeled on the ice, and if you were hurt, you got off the ice. We were in the ['88 Cup final] against Boston, in triple overtime. I looked down from the press box and all the Bruins guys were sitting on the boards, sitting on the ice . . . There wasn't one Oiler sitting down. That's one piece of the training that they learned. They weren't going to give up. They weren't going to show the other team that they're soft. They're ready to win."

Of course, the lessons that were borne out in those later Cup victories were learned the hard way, often against Calgary. Sather—like Fuhr, Messier, Calgary native Mike Vernon, and equipment man Sparky Kulchisky—had all grown up with the Battle of Alberta. It was in their DNA that their team was supposed to kick the crap out of the provincial rival any chance it got. So many of Sather's lessons that would apply in Cup finals against the New York Islanders, Boston, or Philadelphia were Battle-tested against Calgary.

"They were both ferocious teams, and they really hated each other. At the same time they respected each other—but they wanted to win," Sather said of the rivalry. "I remember the night that [Calgary's Jamie] Macoun cheap-shotted Messier. Mark was back just two games from a separated shoulder, and he knocks Macoun out with one punch. That was it. You get even. You kill the penalty off, that's it. It's over."

Well, except for that ten-game suspension Messier received for sucker-punching Macoun. Though clearly, Sather didn't see it that way.

As we spoke, Sather looked down at the Rexall ice after a tame affair in which Sather's Rangers had won 2–0. There had been three minor penalties assessed in the game—all for hooking. The stats crew counted twenty-three hits for Edmonton, seventeen for the Rangers, but like so many games, asked to recall any of those "hits" post-game, a fan would have been hard-pressed to recollect more than two or three decent bodychecks thrown all evening.

"Look at the game tonight," Sather said afterwards, disdain in his voice despite having reaped the two points. "Nobody wants to hit anybody and that's the way the rules are today. Move the puck, skate, dump it in, dump it out, and wait for a break. It's all it is."

The removal of the red line has played a big part, he said, because under the old system the puck had to be carried through the neutral zone. That meant that a Calgary player would stand up an Edmonton player before that red line far more often than he would today, and that physical confrontation led to all kinds of different shenanigans. Today, on so many occasions, a defence-man rifles a pass along the boards that is simply deflected at high speed by a winger and it serves as a dump-in. No one had the puck long enough to get rocked, so nobody got upset. The game may have more skill today, and it definitely has more speed. But it cannot be argued that today's NHL does not also lack the emo-tion it did during the days of the Battle.

Today, you'd rather have a great "first-pass" defenceman on your team than a guy who punishes opposing forwards in his own end. Corsi numbers have exposed the stay-at-home defence-man as a guy who plays in his own end so much because he lacks the puck skills to get the puck out.

Clearly, replacing the Paul Baxters and Don Jacksons for today's Justin Schultzes or T.J. Brodies has sped up the game. That is indisputable. But it also robs from the physical brand of hockey that used to add a great deal of value to the entertain-ment dollar.

Attend a game in the Battle and you might leave the rink talking about the fantastic goal Doug Gilmour or Kent Nilsson scored for Calgary. You might marvel at Paul Coffey's skating ability or something Gretzky did that you'd never seen before. But on the rare night that the defenders won the day, that meant big hits, certainly a couple of fights, maybe a cheap shot or two, and an overall heightened energy level. Blood would be spilled, and who knew what might happen after that?

Basically, if the Hakan Loobs and Jari Kurris didn't entertain on a given night, the Dave Semenkos and Tim Hunters did. So often today, when a game lacks offence like that Rangers–Oilers game did, there is no facet to replace that entertainment value for fans. Unless, for your $150 ticket, you are happy with a load of blocked shots and some "smart dumps," you go home like everybody did that night in Edmonton, with little to tell the boys at work about the next morning.

"There's not as much playing between the two blue lines," Sather said. "Now the puck is passed from the goal line to the far blue line, they tip it in, the other guy gets it, they chip it back out. In the game you saw in the 1980s, you had to control the puck. And you had to move it to the right people."

Of course, Sather's strong suit was finding those right people and surrounding himself with them. He had a great nose for talent and an uncanny ability to judge character.

"Sather knew they were better, and they were," said Calgary journalist George Johnson. "And there's nothing that ticks you off more than the truth. Like Muhammad Ali said, 'It ain't bragging if you can back it up.' And they could back it up.'"

The headlines will always revolve around the greatest players, but hockey isn't basketball. In a rivalry as heated as the Battle, sometimes the fifteenth, sixteenth, or seventeenth man on the roster became the difference-maker. That's where Sather's instincts took over. Once Fraser had furnished him with his top eight or nine players, a group that was superior to the top eight or nine of any team in the NHL, Sather—who had spent a career on the bottom half of an NHL roster—knew the right people to place in support roles.

"They had great players, yes," said long-time Flames winger Colin Patterson. "But it was their supporting cast. Guys who would come through when you least expected it. Dave Lumley. Dave Hunter. Pat Price. Esa Tikkanen was a great player. Sather was so good at resurrecting guys' careers and bringing players in that maybe other players didn't want anymore. MacTavish. Keith Acton had a great career there. [Ken] Linseman. The list goes on and on. Kent Nilsson came back and played with the Oilers [after his career with Calgary had closed]."

It was equal parts star power and role player that made Sather's team so consistently formidable. Like the night—February 3, 1984—when I arrived at Northlands for the sixth installment of the Battle, a nineteen-year-old and his late, great father, Milt, settling into a nice pair of seats about thirteen rows up in the corner. Then came the announcement that, though seldom heard, was every fan's worst nightmare: "Not in the Oilers lineup tonight, number 99, Wayne Gretzky."

There weren't many nights in the 1980s when a guy didn't get his money's worth at the Northlands Coliseum, but on the rare occasion that neither team had any jump, Plan B was always there. You could simply watch Gretzky, from the time he hopped the boards to the moment he went back in the gate. Watch seven or eight Gretzky shifts in a row and I defy you not to come away with something to try on the outdoor rink the next Saturday afternoon.

On this night, however, there would be no Gretzky. Instead, a journeyman winger named Pat Hughes—who had come in a trade with Pittsburgh a few years previous for a defenceman named Pat Price—would score five goals in a 10–5 win over Calgary. A five-goal performance at Northlands. And not only was Gretzky not scoring the goals, he wasn't even setting them up!

Hughes averaged twenty-five goals a year and won two Cups in Edmonton but resided far down the list when it comes to the average hockey fan's recall of those Oilers teams. He would move on to Buffalo for the 1985–86 season, the kind of small tweak Sather always made to keep his lineup fresh.

"Glen always changed a spare part," marvelled Al Coates, the director of public relations for Calgary. "Whether it was a sixth or seventh defenceman, or a fourth-line centreman or winger, just to bring in someone different. That came from the Eskimos. The Edmonton Eskimos won five Grey Cups in a row, and they changed a couple of pieces on an annual basis. Just to get someone new in there who was fresh and hungry."

Sather had built a lineup that, on the top half, was untouchable. A bunch of young stallions growing into their roles as elite NHL players, dominating the Canada Cup rosters, and winning Stanley Cups. Gretzky became the quiet leader by example. Messier's more overt style was louder and more physically intimidating but every bit as easy to follow once the puck dropped. There was enough toughness, plenty on defence, and between Fuhr and Moog, goaltending that other general managers would kill for.

The only thing that could hurt the Oilers now was chemistry, or commitment to the cause. Sather had studied this closely on his lengthy tour through various NHL dressing rooms as a player. He'd played for coaches who got too involved, and he'd seen what happens when the coach wasn't involved enough.

"You can leave them alone," he said of his players, "but you've got to be really careful you don't leave them alone so much that they think they run the team. You've still got to be the boss. There is only one leader, and you can't have it any other way. The players who are your leaders still have to respect you enough to follow your direction. You can't turn it over to them and say, 'Run the team.' You're looking for chaos."

In the end, Sather worked that balance almost to perfection. There were some slip-ups along the way—no doubt far more than were ever made public thanks to Freeman, Whitney, and the rest of Sather's network—but by and large, Sather was spared of having to make too many difficult decisions.

Asked for one, he replied, "I didn't want to trade Semenko, but I had to trade him." Sather wouldn't say why, remaining ever loyal to a player who had always shown great loyalty to him. It is well known, however, that Semenko's lifestyle had spun out of control in Edmonton. For Semenko's own good, and the good of the team, Sather had chosen to trade Semenko to Hartford. Another well-known secret was that Sather had gone to great lengths to help Semenko through his troubled years, ultimately helping him to get healthy again. Sather hired Semenko back as a pro scout, and to the day of this writing Semenko works for the Oilers as a pro scout, a happy, healthy former Oiler still working in the game.

"Any other decisions that were forced upon you?" I asked Sather.

"Gretzky's situation was out of my hands. But it still wasn't a trade," he said, looking sour at the memory of having to be the general manager who dealt away Wayne Gretzky. "Even trading Mark—someday I may tell all these stories that everyone wants to know. But I'm not ready to do all that."

And with that, the interview was over. Sather trusts that you enjoyed it.

4

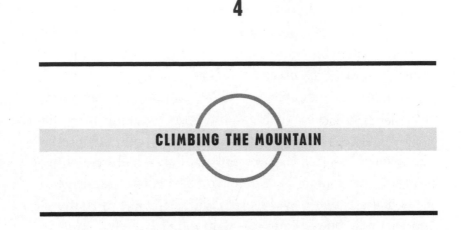

CLIMBING THE MOUNTAIN

Bob Johnson Fuels the Flames' Rise
"Beat the drums, boys! Beat the drums!"

Bob Johnson had dropped into the Battle of Alberta from the University of Wisconsin, as if out of the future. "It's a great day for hockey!" was his mantra, and all you had to do if you wanted to hear his trademark slogan was to greet him with a "How ya doin' today, Bob?"

He was serial happy—no, perpetually pumped—about the game. He'd come from the Wisconsin Badgers in 1966, made seven trips to the NCAA tournament (winning three), and left as a legend, bringing the whole U.S. college experience with him to Calgary. He was a Korean War vet, a former head coach of the U.S. Olympic team, and, when it came to the game he loved, a human pep rally.

"There were a lot of old-guard guys on that team, like Lanny, and John Tonelli, who kind of looked at Bob and thought, 'What is all this college bull?'" observed Calgary scribe Al Maki. "I remember one time, we were talking with Lanny, Steve Simmons, and I. And Steve put it to him: 'What is it? Why is there this unspoken dislike or distaste for this guy?

"'Is he too high school?' Lanny says, 'Naw.' Steve says, 'Does he mix his lines around too much?' Lanny goes, 'No, that's not it.'

"So finally I say, 'What is it, Lanny? What's the problem?' And Lanny thinks for a while, then he says, 'He's too positive!'"

To describe Badger Bob's attitude as merely sunny is to say that Sofia Vergara isn't bad-looking. The guy was not only eternally optimistic, but it also took him only minutes to figure out that, as the head coach of the Flames, job 1-A was to get everyone else feeling the same way. Especially when it came to playing the Oilers, who, when Johnson arrived in the summer of 1982, enjoyed likely the biggest advantage on the Flames in the history of the Battle.

Any coach walking into that assignment was going to have to have a psychology degree to go with his practice planner. As such, Badger Bob Johnson was general manager Cliff Fletcher's perfect hire.

"You have to understand people, and what makes them tick. That was Bob's M.O.," said McDonald, who had 674 NHL games under his belt before Johnson had even signed his first pro deal in Calgary. "Whether it was an hour before practice, or in the evening when you ran across him in the hotel lobby on the road, he was always [McDonald evokes the squeaky voice of his Bob Johnson impression], 'Hey, I've been thinking about this . . . Do you think this'll work. . . ?'

"You'd say, 'Well, let's talk about it, Bob. . .' Career coaches. When they love what they do, what's wrong with that?"

Al Coates, assistant to the president in Calgary, recalls being approached by two veteran Flames. One of them said, "Coatesy, we have a big favour to ask of you." And the other one says, nodding toward the coach's office, "Whatever he's on, can we have some of it?"

"They couldn't get over it. Every day was non-stop enthusiasm," Coates said. "It was something that veteran NHL players just weren't used to because that wasn't normal coaching. Bob was just a total deviation from that norm. And really a breath of fresh air. And his wife, Martha, was exactly the same way. He was just someone you wanted to be around all the time.

"Drive you nuts once in a while? Sure. But still, his enthusiasm for winning, and to get better and better on a daily basis. . . ." It was off the charts.

In the early-1980s NHL, coaching staffs held as many meetings in the bar the night before the game as they did at the rink the next morning during a road trip. As for players, they had their fun as well. It was a time before physical fitness, when players showed up at camp to get in shape, and the teams obliged them by scheduling eleven or twelve preseason games. There was no riding bikes after a game in those days, and in a time before charter flights, a morning commercial flight meant a post-game beer or two for the boys.

Why do you think the two traditions of a morning skate and an afternoon nap were developed for grown men in their twenties and thirties? The skate was to get them out of bed and sweat out the booze. And the nap was, well, what do *you* do on a Sunday afternoon after a Saturday night on the town?

The year before Johnson arrived, the Flames dressing room inside the old Stampede Corral was still inhabited by veteran Atlanta holdovers like Ken Houston, Willi Plett, Don Lever, and Eric Vail. Between the young, fast team up the road in Edmonton and general manager Cliff Fletcher's intent on handing the project over to his new John Wooden prototype, the Flames' front office knew it had to begin to turn the roster over even before, and after, Johnson was hired.

"There was some movement of players going out who, well, they just weren't going to get it, for Bob," said Coates. "But it was hard for guys because practices were different. He had this playbook, and he believed in building from one day to the next. There would be something he was trying to build in a week's time. So you'd start on Day 1, do something else on Day 2, and hopefully you were there at the end of the week. And the next week, it was something else. It was a year-round thing with him. It never ended."

Players didn't always like to think that much in those days. It was the same backlash that video pioneer Roger Neilson had faced—and not unlike the analytics scene today—in that changing a player's routine was met with opposition by a percentage of the roster.

Ironically, they had tried the same thing in Edmonton a decade before, in the early years of the old WHA. There, Clare Drake, the legendary coach from the University of Alberta, had been hired to coach the 1975–76 Oilers.

Now, Drake was Johnson before Johnson was Johnson and, like Badger, had already forgotten more about the game than many NHL coaches in those days would ever know. Today, such prominent NHL coaches as Mike Babcock, Ken Hitchcock, Barry Trotz, and Willie Desjardins proudly claim to be from "The Clare Drake School" of coaching, a collective of hockey knowledge that has been passed down by Drake to ensuing generations of Canadian coaches. In the mid-1970s WHA, however, the stigma surrounding these "college guys" was even stronger.

If the coach hadn't played pro, and he did things a little differently, then there was always going to a big enough faction in any professional dressing room that would push back. It only takes a few hard-headed players to render a coach's system useless if they are not willing to execute it—or, more so, pay attention long enough to learn how to execute it. That attitude neutered Drake, whose absence from the Hockey Hall of Fame today is truly an act of blaspheme, in my opinion. He posted an 18–28–2 record and was fired in Edmonton after forty-eight WHA games.

So, Johnson was Alberta's second coming of Drake, in many ways, whom Fletcher was in awe of as soon as he watched Badger run a practice.

"He was one of the big guys in U.S. college hockey. I just watched him run a couple of practices and I thought, 'I've never seen anyone run practices like this guy,'" Fletcher said. "It was tremendous how he documented what he did, every drill, every practice, in his notebooks. How he prepared his team. I'm sure there were better bench coaches than him once the game started, but in preparing teams and improving players on the team, he's the best I've come across in my years in the game."

It was the perfect union of the right coach for an ongoing organizational build. Fletcher, with U.S. scout Jack Ferreira, had decided that the best way to reload the Flames was by raiding the NCAA of undrafted graduates who would show up at twenty-one or twenty-two years of age and be far more ready to play than the traditional eighteen-year-old NHL draft pick. Each of those incoming young players—guys like Joel Otto, Jamie Macoun, Colin Patterson, Neil Sheehy, Gary Suter, Eddy Beers, and Gino Cavallini—walked in the door knowing exactly who Bob Johnson was, revering him in many cases. And as each showed up, with help from Ferreira, the Flames had a better chance of unearthing the *next* graduating NCAA player who could join their "program."

"Coming out of Wisconsin, he knew players and he knew people," Coates said. "You'd walk into his office and he'd have newspaper after newspaper on his desk. College this, college that . . . He'd be looking at some alumni messaging—anything where he might find one snippet of information, where we might find a player attached to the end of that line. Somebody who we could go chase down.

"There wasn't a day that went by, and I am serious about this, where Bob Johnson wouldn't say to you, 'What are you doing today to make the Flames better? What are we going to do today to get to the top of that mountain?'"

Climbing the mountain: those three words would become synonymous with the Calgary Flames' quest to catch, then knock off, their northern foes in Edmonton. Johnson hadn't been in town for five minutes when he started talking about "climbing that mountain," and the mountain was, figuratively, the team up the road that was about to have five or six of the best players in the world.

The analogy was positively accurate, as the Oilers and Wayne Gretzky loomed like Mount Everest. Meanwhile, the Flames— with a bunch of college kids, a college coach, an old goalie out of the *Slap Shot* movie named Reggie Lemelin, and a few legit NHLers like Kent Nilsson, Doug Risebrough, Mel Bridgman, and Lanny McDonald—were truly in need of a Sherpa and a compass to find their way out of the Smythe Division.

In his first season behind the Flames bench, Johnson's teams went 2–4–2 against Edmonton, matching the Oilers with thirty-seven goals apiece. Not bad, right? It's something to build on.

Well, in season number 2 for Badger Bob, Edmonton won seven of eight games. The teams tied the other one.

"I still remember playing one game in Edmonton, we're down about 4–0, and it's early," said assistant coach Bob Murdoch. "Bob Johnson walks by the guys and down to me, and he says, 'Bob, we might lose by 20!'"

The Oilers won every game in Calgary that season, outscoring the Flames two to one, and at that point the mountain couldn't have looked any larger from a Calgary perspective.

It's not that the Oilers had won more than the Flames at that point. It was, in fact, worse than that. They had lost, and lost some heartbreaking series to some very good teams. Edmonton had already gone through that process of learning in defeat and were poised now to use that experience to reach the Stanley Cup finals in Johnson's second and third years in Calgary.

So imagine being the Flames. The team up the highway has a guy who averaged over 200 points per season for the period from 1981–86, and behind him were three more 100-point players. To put that in perspective, the entire National Hockey League has not had four 100-point players in the same season since the 2009–10 campaign.

Johnson's team, to the eye of any realistic thinking person, couldn't have been in a more wrong place at a more improper time. His players would go out and play against the Oilers, and they would get crushed. Then Johnson would gather them up the next day and you know what he'd do?

"He'd see you in the morning and he'd ask you, 'What did you have for breakfast?' 'How many pushups did you do?' 'Are you ready to play tonight?'" said defenceman Jamie Macoun. "He gave the impression, and it was a truthful one, that he really cared. He cared about you as a person, and he cared about you as a hockey player. That was a more unique attitude in the NHL."

The fact that Johnson actually hauled his team to the top of that mountain in 1986 was, as most folks would say, his greatest accomplishment as the Flames' coach. But spend some time around the game and watch a few coaches come and go. For me, the most amazing thing that Badger Bob accomplished was, he got the same buy-in from professional players that he used to get from those kids back at Wisconsin.

He convinced those men that he had a plan, he believed in that plan, and he was willing to live that plan. And they should too. I mean, really live it. Wear it, eat it, sleep with it. Dream about it.

"The guy used to live and breathe hockey. Twenty-four hours a day he was into hockey," said Murdoch. "We'd go on the road, and his workout would be that we'd go and have a sauna. You'd sit there, and you'd be going over plays in the sauna. Then you'd go for dinner, and the salt-and-pepper shakers, and the water glasses, they became our rotation on our penalty kill. It was twenty-four hours a day.

"Most players enjoyed playing for him," Murdoch said. "Some guys didn't like him, but the key guys bought into him. And you need the key guys."

That took innovation. For generations, coaches have written on the whiteboard (or chalkboard) on the dressing room wall while their players sit in their stalls, eyes darting from the floor to the ongoing lesson. Johnson had already figured out that he would do his coaching in a more convenient spot.

He would have a hockey rink taped out on the dressing room floor, and then he could move the pucks around with a hockey stick—right there in front of the players. Then he garnered some buy-in by charging different players with the responsibility of making the hockey tape rink on that dressing room carpet, a duty in which some players took much pride.

"He had pucks for our team, with numbers on the pucks," said Patterson. "Then he had blue pucks. They were the Oilers. So we would have someone tape the hockey rink on the floor. If you did a good job, you were doing it again [in the next town]. If you did a bad job, you weren't doing it again."

Well, wait a second there. If you did a bad job and the Flames won, you might just get the roll of white tape again in the next town. Because one thing that defined Johnson was his superstitions. He had his own brand of hockey voodoo for everything and was steadfast to his superstitious routines until they ceased to provide Ws. Then he'd change them.

"The most superstitious man I've ever been around," said Peter Maher, the play-by-play voice of the Flames, who learned of this Johnson trait while taping the daily coach's show for his game broadcast.

We've all heard of the coach who wouldn't change his tie during a winning streak or a player who bought the same coffee at the same time at the same coffee shop on the way to the rink during good times—then switched routines when he found himself in a scoring slump. Well, Johnson's thing—or one of his things—was to re-enact the *Coach's Show with Maher.*

"We'd do it in the morning, before or after the morning skate," Maher recalled. "Whenever the team was on a winning streak, the interview had to be conducted where it was the last game. One time, he went up and sat on the Zamboni, and I had to climb up to do the interview with him. Because we'd won the last game, with the Zamboni."

When the Flames were losing, Johnson felt like he needed to explore the realms of the Saddledome to find that obscure, never-before-used spot that could change his team's luck. Once he found it, Maher knew he was stuck with the routine at least until the Flames posted an L.

"The boiler room was the most successful one in the Saddledome, overall. There would be a streak, then we'd lose a few, and it would be, 'Let's go back to the boiler room.' Then there would be another few games.

"Then there was one time, we had to go sit in the row number of the win the team was looking for. They were looking for win number thirty? We had to sit in the thirtieth row."

Seriously?

"Seriously," said Maher. "But the worst of all was in Vancouver. The winning streak was in the penalty box.

"I've just been in the league a few years, but Bob had all these things that had to be done. So we're doing it the night of the game—must have been back-to-back games. No skate. And Bob says, 'Okay, we've got to get to the penalty box.' We're in the old building in Vancouver (the Pacific Coliseum), and the only way to get there was to walk across the ice. Well, we get there, and the door is locked. So Johnson gets up on the top of the boards, and the glass was lower then, fortunately, and he climbs over the glass, goes down, and opens the door. We do the coach's show.

"I go up into the booth afterwards, to do the game, and [Vancouver play-by-play man] Jim Robson comes over and says, 'Why was Johnson climbing over the glass to get to the penalty box?' I say, 'You really don't want to know . . .'"

It didn't take long for Johnson to become accepted in Calgary, a citizenry that—because of the oil business—was receptive to having Americans living among them. As in any town, Flames fans wanted to buy into the new program, and Johnson was as convincing as they came in those lean years before the team's performance could do the talking for him. At the same time, he and his wife, Martha, became honorary Calgarians. They would return to the States shortly after his tenure in Calgary came to a close, but while Johnson loved among Calgarians, damn it, he would be one of them.

"He would come walking into the rink and say, 'What a great town! Everybody recognizes you! And they'll come up and talk about the game last night, and talk hockey! What a great hockey town!'" Murdoch laughs. "Well, he's wearing

Calgary Flames–coloured running shoes. Calgary Flames socks. He's got a Calgary Flames sweatsuit. He's wearing a Calgary Flames hat. He'd be walking down the street and be surprised when somebody recognized him. Well, he practically had a neon sign that read: 'I'm Bob Johnson, coach of the Calgary Flames.'"

Johnson had been galvanized in that college football atmosphere, and when the scribes would gather on the day before a visit by Edmonton—or a visit to Edmonton—Johnson would always stop for a little pep talk just to make sure they had what they needed to properly stoke the fires of the Battle. Some believed him to be a little too camera-hungry, and if that was true, you could chalk it up to a man who had been the face of a program at Wisconsin for most of two decades and simply took that role up to Calgary.

"A lot of the veterans thought that Bob liked to be the show," confided Maher. "He had practices that were probably too long. Some of the players thought, 'He's just there because he wants to get the publicity.' There was a lot of that, or some of that. But it didn't bother [Johnson]."

And it didn't bother the fans or media, who grew hungrier for the Battle with every step forward that the Flames took.

"If you went to cover a Battle of Alberta game in those days, you knew that every check was going to be finished," said Calgary columnist George Johnson. "That everything would be contested at this seismic level that you'd never get if the Hartford Whalers were in town. You'd look forward to them. We all would.

"Whenever the Oilers were coming in, Badger would walk into the [media scrum] and say, 'Beat the drums! Beat the drums, boys!' He wanted the hype because everyone was at this playoff pitch for Game 44 of the season."

Johnson had his notebooks at hand at all times, giving him that professorial air that he loved. In those notebooks were line combinations likely going back to his first gig at Colorado College in 1963 and various other thoughts that would pass through the winding road that was Badger's mind.

There's no doubting the fact that he was very smart, but not many accused Badger of fully thinking out all of his hare-brained schemes. He was the king of holding team meetings in the highest rows of the Saddledome and getting Murdoch and some scrubs to re-enact the Oilers' breakout while he yelled for them to stop and start from Row 58.

It seems innovative until you realize that Neilson had already introduced both video and radio headsets to the NHL a few years previous. But that was Badger. He always had a plan—it was just a matter of how fully cooked the plan was. Some schemes, like keeping a left winger back to turn the puck into the middle, would morph into a defensive scheme used by likely two-thirds of the league in the mid-1990s.

Another—like Johnson's mythical Seven Point Plan—existed in two worlds. It was both a tangible and an intangible, a tenet of every Flames player's experience in Calgary, yet a manual on "How to Beat Edmonton" that none of them can recite from start to finish.

"Bob would never throw all of the Seven Point Plan at you at once," Murdoch said. "It would be over the course of the series. I think it started out as a four-point plan and turned into a seven-point plan."

"I also heard it variously described as a five-point plan. To me, it was a myth," added Hockey Hall of Fame hockey writer Eric Duhatschek, who's been around Calgary as long or longer than anyone. "I think it was a one-point plan: if the game went longer than three hours, the Flames had a chance. If the game went shorter than three hours, they didn't. It was, 'Try to win the games between the whistles, rather than during the play.'"

Johnson's plan was both mythical and masterful, falling perfectly into the college drum-beating that this old schoolman lived for. And it was brilliant really: everyone talked about the Seven Point Plan, yet no one could ever divulge it because it had never been laid out specifically in front of everyone, all at once, to be memorized. If Badger were here today, he would likely swear by its existence. But the simple fact that it was perceived to exist was enough to accomplish the goal of planting the intrigue.

The Oilers never had a Seven Point Plan. Why did Calgary? What was in this closely guarded plan, and why wasn't anyone ever allowed to see it, point by point? It was the Bat Cave of hockey strategies—everyone assumed it was somewhere, but nobody really knew where to look.

The Seven Point Plan was likely a list of strategies that Johnson found effective, built over time rather than conceived all at once and thrust upon his team, like some game plan from the Hockey Gods.

"Having a left winger back, to turn Coffey in [toward the defencemen]," began Murdoch. "Their tendencies on a power play. Being able to neutralize certain players . . . It wasn't anything magical, but it was something we gave our guys so they could look at it and say, 'Yeah, goddamnit. We can win this game.'"

"In many ways it was Bob Johnson's brain versus Edmonton's talents," said then CBC producer John Shannon. "I don't think there ever was a Seven Point Plan."

"He believed it, and I think we believed we could beat Edmonton," Patterson said. "But we didn't necessarily know how to. He gave us the tools to compete as well as you could."

There is no question that Johnson was an accomplished coach and one of the premier tacticians of his day. Then he was smart enough to take that plate of solid meat-and-potatoes coaching skill, gravy it up thick with hype and magic beans, and then sprinkle a little Stu Hart "Stampede Wrestling" huckster-ism on top.

Johnson might have had seven points, five points, three points . . . who really knew?

"I remember one time reading the paper going into a series," said Wayne Gretzky. "They had asked Bob Johnson what he was going to do. He said, 'I've got Plan A. If that doesn't work, we've got Plan B. And if that doesn't work, I've got Plan C.' That's the hockey man he was—a really smart, astute student of the game. He designed a system that made it really difficult for us to play the style we wanted to play."

Was there really a Plan C? As long as Gretzky believed there was, that's all that truly mattered.

Of course, the dichotomy between Bob Johnson and Glen Sather was as stark as you could imagine. One was college-bred, the other educated on hockey's streets. It was book-smart versus wily. Guts versus brains, and it made for a fantastic coaching matchup.

"He was a very good tactician. Always trying to find a way to throw us off our game," said Sather. Prior to the 1986 series against Edmonton, Johnson dressed a pair of junior goalies in Oilers jerseys and had his players shoot on them at practice the day before Game 1. They were former University of Calgary Dino Al Hryniuk and ex-Calgary Canuck Jamie Bowman. Johnson told the media it was no different than when a football coach uses a scout team, dressing players in the same uniform numbers of Sunday's opponent. But his true theory was that his players would get used to seeing rubber fly by that Oilers jersey, and they would have a psychological edge come game time.

"I've never seen that tactic before," Sather said at the time. "It must be something you learn in college in the U.S. Of course, he's an American. I guess he thinks differently than I do. Me, I'm

Canadian-born, in Alberta . . . in High River. I probably think more logically than he does.

"When he quit the Flames, I sent a note to him. I told him I was sad to see him leave," said Sather. "He had all those notebooks, but why not? He did things one way and I did things another. He was a complete coach. He took advantage, technically and psychologically."

Johnson's Flames would climb Mount Oiler in 1986, knocking off Edmonton and finding their way into the Stanley Cup final against Montreal. The Flames had spent the majority of their oxygen getting out of the Smythe Division in that memorable seven-game series, however, and mistakenly allowed an inferior St. Louis Blues team to take them to seven games once more in the Campbell Conference Final. It crippled their Stanley Cup hopes.

Johnson's Flames won Game 1 of the Stanley Cup final in Montreal, but they couldn't summit, losing the next four games to a rookie goalie named Patrick Roy and his Canadiens. It was as close as Johnson would come in Calgary, and the loss stayed with him.

The next season, 1986–87, Edmonton, Calgary, and Winnipeg would finish as the three top teams in the Campbell Conference, and place first, third, and sixth respectively in the NHL. Edmonton drew Los Angeles in Round 1 of the playoffs and scored thirty-five times in a five-game series win. Calgary got the Jets, in what would be Johnson's finale behind the Calgary bench.

Winnipeg won that opening round series in six games, capping it with a resounding 6–1 trouncing of the Flames. It seems the Jets had their own mountain they were climbing, and while Johnson and the Flames were focused on Edmonton, the Jets were beating a goat path right past Calgary in that series.

In the meantime, USA Hockey had been courting Johnson,

and that summer he and Martha decided to return to the States and live in beautiful Colorado Springs, and Johnson would take the job as president of USA Hockey in 1987. He would last there until 1990, when the lure of coaching Mario Lemieux and the Pittsburgh Penguins was simply too much.

Johnson would win his only Stanley Cup in 1991, fittingly, in the state in which Johnson was born. The Penguins defeated the Minnesota North Stars in six games to win Pittsburgh's first Stanley Cup. Johnson had finally summitted the hockey world, even if the route had been a tad more circuitous than planned.

Between being the reigning Stanley Cup champion head coach and his ties with USA Hockey, Johnson being named to run Team USA at the 1991 Canada Cup was an obvious choice. It was during that training camp, however, that Johnson was diagnosed with inoperable brain cancer. Pittsburgh doctors removed one tumour but could not remove another, prescribing radiation treatment.

Only ten days after being admitted to hospital, Johnson vowed to coach the Pens again. "The fire still burns in me to coach," he said. "It will be my greatest day in coaching."

Not fearing those brain tumours was a window into how Johnson never backed down from the mountain that was the Battle of Alberta.

"Bob Johnson loved the challenge of trying to beat the Oilers," Murdoch said. "He didn't fear the Oilers. He loved the challenge of trying to coach against them."

On November 26, 1991, the fire went out. Bob Johnson died, aged sixty, leaving behind his wife, Martha, five children, and nine grandchildren. "This was the one fight he couldn't win," Sather said that day.

Those Flames players from Johnson's time as head coach wore black armbands made from hockey tape at practice that day.

Presumably, they'd saved the white tape for one more outline of a hockey rink on the dressing room floor.

"He would always say, 'This is a great day for hockey,'" defence-man Neil Sheehy told reporters that morning. "Often guys would ask, 'When isn't it a great day for hockey?'

"I guess today."

5

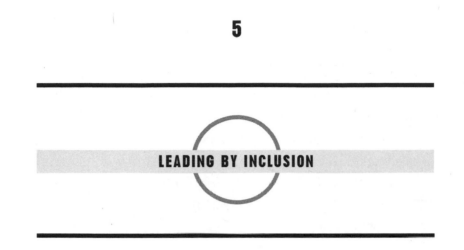

LEADING BY INCLUSION

Oiler Mark Messier's Subtle Direction

*"We were all mindful enough to realize
our teacher was right in front of us."*

Mark Messier is sitting across the breakfast table—"No coffee. Just orange juice, please"—and he's talking leadership. And the more you listen, the more it becomes clear that, to one of the greatest captains the game of hockey has ever known, leadership doesn't have that much to do with the leader at all.

"The need to give yourself to the team," he says. "It was very clear to me that, without that, there wasn't any chance."

Messier was born into hockey. His father, Doug, was on the road playing minor pro hockey for the first eight winters of Mark's life. When he returned to play senior hockey in Edmonton in 1969 and then coach the Junior A Spruce Grove Mets, Mark would be his stick boy, getting the time he'd missed with his father back in spades.

It was there—in the Edmonton city rinks like The Gardens or Jasper Place Arena or those small prairie rinks in Spruce Grove, Red Deer, Taber, or Drumheller—that the Mark Messier we now know was truly born.

"As a stick boy, I learned a lot of lessons in those rooms," he said. "The chalk talks, the inspirational speeches . . . You can't get that kind of education unless you're in there. It was tough hockey, a lot of intimidation in the game back then. It was a great education."

We've all seen the little Mark Messier before, the son of one of our buddies running around the beer league dressing room, fetching tape and hauling sticks to the bench. This Mark Messier, however, was Doug's son. This was no beer league room, for one. And when Doug Messier stepped inside a hockey dressing room, I am told, it wasn't going to be a place of jokes and merriment until the game was over and his team had won.

The Alberta hockey room, like one of those "Hinterland Who's Who" commercials, was the habitat of the Messier family. With the Mets, who went to two Centennial Cups, winning one, Doug coached, older brother Paul played, and Mark was the stick boy. Messier would never complete high school, but it was here that he earned his Doctorate in Hockey.

"I was allowed in on all of it—the speeches, the talks. I supposed there was a little bit of swearing, but nothing too bad," he recalled of his childhood. "But I'd been around the locker room when my dad was playing senior hockey before we'd even started coaching juniors. It didn't seem to be that big a deal."

Ask him for specific stories and Messier is left speechless. Ask him to talk about how, of all the quality characters who starred in the Battle of Alberta, he emerged as one of hockey's great leaders and he has an easier time talking about it. Because now the story doesn't have to be all about him.

"Someone once asked me, am I a dependent leader? Or an independent leader? Well, my initial reaction was, 'I'm an *in*-dependent leader. If something needs to be done, I'm going to go do it!' It was simple," he recites. "But, upon further reflection, it became obvious to me that, no, I was a *de*-pendent leader. That I needed everybody else around me for success."

While even Wayne Gretzky, the game's most generous passer, has a favourite he'll tell you all about, Messier does not. His mind, it seems, just doesn't work that way.

"When you really strip it all down, it's the journey that was really the interesting part. That took you all the way through, that forged the bond, the chemistry."

☆

Mark Messier's journey began on January 18, 1961—the day he was born into one of Edmonton's most prolific hockey families. The journey wound through junior hockey with the St. Albert Saints—as un-Saintly a group as ever you'll meet—through the old WHA and right on course into the Battle of Alberta.

His was a legend built on nights like May 8, 1990, at the old Stadium in Chicago, when Messier scored two-and-two in a 4–2 Oilers playoff victory. It was a heroic display of grab-'em-by-the-scruff-of-the-neck leadership and unalloyed physical dominance that harkened back to Maurice Richard and Gordie Howe. The kind of game you watch once and remember for the rest of your life.

Or on May 25, 1994, when, as a New York Ranger, Messier called the shot, guaranteeing a Game 6 Rangers win at New Jersey, with the Devils leading the Eastern Conference Final 3–2. New York was behind 2–1 on the scoreboard after forty minutes, but Messier scored a hat trick in the third period to deliver the victory that night. It was a performance that legends are built on, one that the New York media compared with Babe Ruth's famed "called shot" or Joe Namath's guarantee that the New York Jets would beat the heavily favoured Baltimore Colts in Super Bowl III.

When Messier arrived in Edmonton, however, he wasn't close to what he would become. He was a gangly kid who'd scored one goal in the WHA, drafted in the third round of the Oilers first-ever NHL draft, in 1979.

It was, by a thousand miles, the best third-round draft pick the Oilers organization has ever made.

"When I got to the Oilers," Messier said, "I wasn't as developed as a player. But I did have that deep understanding of what it took to be a team member. A very in-depth schooling in hockey from my childhood."

Mark Messier. In Edmonton he would come to be known as "The Moose."

★

Even a team as strong as the Edmonton Oilers had to stay fresh. You couldn't expect to come back with the same twenty players every year and keep winning. In fact, if you didn't create an atmosphere where the young players were pushing the older ones for roster spots, stagnation would set in. People would get comfortable, and at this level, *comfort* becomes a six-letter synonym for *lose*.

But think about it: you add five new players to a hockey team every year, and that means you're changing out 25 percent of your team. Even assuming there are twenty-five players who make reasonably meaningful contributions to the team, it's still 20 percent.

Get that turnover wrong, and you'll find the reasons why teams win just one in a row. Why players look back and say, "Man, we should have won more than we did." The ice, as it turns out, is the place where we see the finished product. But a hockey team is no different than a house or a great recipe. Get the foundation wrong—pick the wrong ingredients, the wrong mix of concrete— and your finished product doesn't stand a chance.

This is where Glen Sather did his finest work. Sure, he had all the great players at the top of his roster, the ingredients that would make a pretty good club down the road no matter what happened. But how to make a great one?

Sather knew that change was constant in the NHL. Hell, he had played for ten pro organizations, and his vantage point came from the middle to bottom of most of those rosters. His nickname, "Slats," literally came from riding the pine, so Sather clearly knew the value of the followers, having been one. He was a smart, observant teammate who knew that every great team required proper leadership at the top of its roster. The right someone. Someone to set the relentless culture that could win at all costs. A person who had hockey in his veins, the will to lead his team during the endless but crucial hours spent outside of the game uniform, and the skill and strength to lead once the puck was dropped.

So in the Oilers' first-ever draft, in the third round of 1979, he picked Messier with Edmonton's second-ever draft choice. (Edmonton's second-round pick had been traded to Minnesota for the rights to Dave Semenko.) Messier would become a captain whose glare was as sharp as his wrist shot, whose elbows and fists were as dangerous as his immense skill and fearless net-crashing. But before Messier would carry the Stanley Cup into The Bruin Inn, the teenaged drinking hole for every kid who grew up in St. Albert, Alberta, or ride with

Stanley down the Canyon of Heroes in New York, he had much to learn.

Luckily, Mark Douglas Messier didn't have far to go to school.

Doug Messier was an ornery minor-pro defenceman who never played an NHL game. But while the hippies spent the 1960s making peace and love, Messier went to war in the old Western Hockey League—an old professional league, not the junior one of today—his rights controlled, though never fully exercised, by the Detroit Red Wings. Messier Sr. wasn't a dirty player, but he was hard-nosed as a square-mouth shovel. Messier was known to be very, very tough if necessary, and, of course, he had The Glare.

"Was he crazy?" opponents asked. "Or is he just real intense?" Only the brave hung around to find the true answer. What Doug Messier was, however, was wise beyond the game. "He had more irons in the fire than just a hockey stick," said an old friend and opponent, Gregg Pilling, another Alberta kid who was busing around hockey's minor leagues about the same time.

While Doug was barnstorming through the Western Hockey League, mostly for the Portland Buckaroos with men like Tommy McVie and Connie Madigan, Mark was at home with his mother and three siblings. At age thirty-two, without ever having played an NHL game, Doug Messier came back home to Edmonton to play senior hockey for the Edmonton Monarchs and teach school. He'd play two seasons, the second as a player-coach, and then hang up his skates for good.

By 1969, Doug's first season coaching the Monarchs and last season as a player, young Mark was eight years old: the perfect age for a stick boy. At home, with his older brother Paul and sisters Jennifer and Mary Kay, Mark listened while his mother, Mary-Jean Messier, served up supper and his father dispensed the kind of hockey lessons one could only collect in that day and age.

Those helmetless years before corporations bought naming rights and players signed seven-year deals, a time when arenas carried handles like the Civic Arena (Seattle), the Edmonton Gardens, or the Cow Palace outside San Francisco.

"Many kitchen-table talks," Mark recalls, "where kids really get a lot of their knowledge about the game. In-depth knowledge. Stuff you can't necessarily teach [elsewhere]. I came through my minor hockey career with a great understanding of what hockey was, what it should be, and how to conduct yourself on the ice. What it meant to be a teammate, a team member."

Doug coached Mark in pee wee, then not again until junior with the St. Albert Saints, on a roster that included future 1,000-game NHLer (including playoffs) Troy Murray. Today there is a twin-rinks complex in St. Albert called Servus Place. There, the kids check the whiteboard in the foyer to see if their ice time is scheduled for Mark Messier Arena or Troy Murray Arena.

Messier was a sixteen-year-old on that Saints team, in an Alberta Junior Hockey League that included players up to age twenty, with names like Duane Sutter, Kelly Kisio, and Dave Babych. Messier would lead his team in both penalty minutes and assists — *at age sixteen* — testimony to the unselfish, courageous mindset that would endure throughout his days in the Battle.

Sather knew Doug, and had driven out to the old Perron Street Arena in St. Albert to watch his friend's son play for the Saints. The Oilers general manager believed in bloodlines, and while scouts from outside Alberta would gauge Messier's skills and physique, Sather already knew he had a heart the size of a buffalo's — because that's what his dad had. The next season Messier turned pro at age seventeen, scoring just a single goal in fifty-two WHA games for the Indianapolis Racers and Cincinnati Stingers. On draft day in the spring of 1979, Sather was waiting.

"Messier came from the WHA," Sather said. "Nobody [among the NHL GMs] really liked him."

As it would turn out, no one in that 1979 draft—not even the great Bruins defenceman Ray Bourque—would exceed Messier's 1,756 regular-season games played. Nor would anyone from that class come within 300 points of Messier's career total of 1,887. Messier would play just four games in the minors, sent down to the Houston Apollos of the Central League as a rookie, punishment for missing a pre-season flight.

As Messier readily admits, he was a raw piece of clay in those days, yet to be sculpted. So he fell in line with the rest of the rookies and young players, as is the pecking order in any dressing room, keeping his mouth shut more often than not. Sather, however, wisely surrounded his young core with the right veterans: Ron Chipperfield, Lee Fogolin, Colin Campbell (a current vice-president of the NHL), and goalie Ron Low, a streetwise veteran from Foxwarren, Manitoba.

"They didn't push us down or try to hold us back," Messier said of those vets. "They accepted the fact we were an expansion team and we were going young. They understood what their jobs were. Not only did they play well, but they guided us along the way."

Messier, as has been pointed out, never found the time to complete high school. Yet he is articulate and well spoken well beyond the average current or former NHLer. So, for that matter, is Sather, who was smart enough to turn relatively meagre earnings as a hockey player in the 1960s and 1970s into a largesse of Banff real estate and savvy investments. The two were perfect as teacher and prodigy. Doug had filled his son with guts and guile and passed Mark along to one of few hockey men who had even more of each. Sather was perhaps the perfect mentor to sculpt a raw, young St. Albert kid into one of the most feared and respected captains of his generation.

"Glen really punched home the fact that you had to be a team player, which was reassuring to me because that's what I had always learned," Messier said. "Nothing was ever about the individual. Everybody had to make sacrifices for the team."

The Battle of Alberta was a way of life for Messier, who required no introduction or explanation to what Edmonton versus Calgary was supposed to mean. In fact, it may have been the Battle itself that had never seen anything like Messier before.

"It was easy for me," Messier said. "Through my childhood, I grew up with the Eskimos and the Stampeders. I grew up with my dad playing senior hockey against Calgary and waking up in the morning, shaving with black eyes and lumps on his head. The Battle of Alberta was ingrained in me from a very young age. I was well versed in what it meant."

Messier was born, as we said, on January 18, 1961. Two months prior, the Eskimos and Stampeders had met in the CFL's Western semifinal, a two-game total-points affair won by Edmonton. The following November, in the West final, Calgary would win the two-game series by a single point. A rouge, as they say in the CFL.

When Mark was one year old, Doug won a Western Hockey League championship as a member of the Edmonton Flyers. They had rolled over the familiar-named Calgary Stampeders in five games en route to that final, which turned into a seven-game war against Spokane. So beating Calgary—or watching the local CFL team trying to beat Calgary—was a Messier family tradition long before Mark ever stepped on the ice. Now he was an Oiler, and the Flames were in his way.

In 1981, the Battle was headed in the wrong direction for the Flames, with one organization on its way up and the aging Flames needing a restart from the club that had arrived from Atlanta. The gap was widening because everyone could see the Oilers were only going to get better. Messier was the young lion, ready to take his place atop the pride, and the folks in Calgary's front office knew it. Their pride was led by older players like Ken Houston, Eric Vail, and Willi Plett, all of whom would be moved out within a season or two.

"If you had to put your finger on one moment, it was when Bob Johnson arrived [for the 1982–83 season] that things really turned for them," Messier said. "They understood that they had to build a team that could compete with us. And the second thing they needed to do was to make that team believe they could beat the Oilers. It's one thing to build that team, but it's another thing to make that team believe. All coaching, and all teams, once you have the talent they are all based on belief. And they did that. They brought in some amazing players, and built a team whose sole focus was to beat the Oilers."

Edmonton was firmly in the lead position, mostly because of the age of all of their future Hall of Fame core players. As a leader, Messier was passing from infancy into his adolescent years. He'd gone from Doug to Sather, and now Messier looked across his own dressing room at one of his peers—Wayne Gretzky.

But follow him . . . where? As great as Gretzky was, Edmonton had lost the final Avco Cup of the WHA's existence to Winnipeg in 1979, when Gretzky was eighteen. As nineteen-year-olds, Gretzky and Messier exited in three straight games in Round 1 to Bobby Clarke's Philadelphia Flyers, Edmonton's first-ever playoff series. The next year, 1981, they blew out the Montreal Canadiens in a milestone series for the Oilers, but the New York Islanders were too much in Round 2, and Edmonton exited in six games.

In Year 3, as twenty-one-year-olds, Messier and Gretzky found themselves in an opening-round best-of-five series against the lowly Los Angeles Kings, who had finished forty-eight points behind the Oilers in the Smythe Division that season. It was to be easy work for Edmonton, and the Oilers came out fat and sassy, losing Game 1 at home 10–8. That's right: 10–8. It took a Gretzky goal in overtime of Game 2 to avoid losing the first two games at home. Then came a game so famous, at once so memorable and catastrophic, it has its own title in hockey history: The Miracle on Manchester.

Messier opened the scoring in Game 3, and then Gretzky strung together four points for a 5–0 Oilers lead after forty minutes. In a fabulous show of immaturity, Edmonton would somehow blow that lead, with the unheralded Daryl Evans sifting one past Grant Fuhr just 2:35 into overtime to seal the win. A 5–0 lead had drifted into a 6–5 loss. YouTube it—it's something that needs to be seen to be believed. Despite a 3–2 win in Game 4, Edmonton was shaken and had let the Kings into their soft underbelly. Edmonton choked in the series finale, losing Game 5 at home by a 7–4 score.

Eliminated in Round 1, they had taken a step backwards. After having gone two rounds the previous spring and won their first Smythe Division title in 1981–82, the Oilers were first-round fodder. They had a team, and some great young players. But Edmonton didn't know how to win, and Messier still had not figured out how to haul his teammates over the hump.

"We didn't have anyone on our team who had ever won before," Messier remembers. "We were navigating our way through this by ourselves, trying to figure it out. Reaching plateaus and failing. Getting knocked back down. Then trying to reach past that the next year. Get knocked down . . ."

★

It seems contrived, that romantic tale of the moment in Oilers history when they finally learned what it took to win. That instant when Gretzky, Messier, and Kevin Lowe walked past the open door to the New York Islanders' dressing room on their way out of the Nassau Coliseum after being swept by the mighty Isles in 1983. When they gazed inside the enemy's winning bathhouse and were expecting to see a loud, bubbly celebration. Instead, the legend goes, they saw the New York players bandaged up, iced down, and eroded from having sacrificed at a level the young Oilers did not know existed.

Like Woodstock, more people claim to have been privy to that snapshot than possibly could have been there. I've walked past that very door many times, and though you can truly see into the Islanders room, could three or four young Oilers have actually stopped, poked their heads in, and drank in enough of that scene to generate the reams of copy and mythical tales of yore that ensued over the next thirty years?

"A million lessons along the way," Messier said, "and our best teacher just happened to be the four-time Stanley Cup champs because we had played them three times along the way. They were the perfect role model.

"When they beat us in '83, we realized we had to go back and play a much better, stronger team game. They dismantled us in four straight. We had gotten used to having our way, and we had pushed them before to six games [in 1981], and all that. But this was a real wakeup call that we needed to take our whole team game to a higher level. That was their fourth Cup in a row, and when you did walk by that dressing room, you did see the sacrifices that were being made in order to win. I mean, they were really banged up."

Four consecutive Stanley Cups. It is impossible to describe, in that innocuous four-word sentence, the pain, the blood, the self-lessness that a team must produce to win nineteen consecutive playoff series. They would have won twenty, those Mike Bossy–, Brian Trottier–, Billy Smith–led Islanders, but in the spring of

1984, after disposing of the New York Rangers, the Washington Capitals, and the Montreal Canadiens, from the West emerged Edmonton, back for more. A year older, a year hungrier, a year wiser. And a year better.

"It all *is* true. That *is* exactly the way it unfolded," Messier said of the dressing room walk-by. "We were all mindful enough to realize our teacher was right in front of us. They became our playbook. Our guide to the Cup."

It's about everyone else, it seems, when you talk to Messier about what makes a winner. (Not an uncommon trait, I found as I interviewed the various leading players for this book). And it makes sense because in hockey there is no Kobe or LeBron. Or perhaps even a Peyton. The top player on the team can play twenty-two, twenty-three minutes if he is a forward, maybe twenty-seven or twenty-eight minutes as a defenceman. So by definition, the most accomplished leader is the one who is not only a leading player on the ice but also does the most to raise the level of the lesser-skilled players that much higher.

Sure, Edmonton had so many future Hall of Famers. To a man, however, they'll tell you they would not have won all those Stanley Cups without the foot soldiers. For every Paul Coffey, there was a Charlie Huddy. For every Wayne Gretzky, a Dave Lumley. For every Messier, a Jaroslav Pouzar.

"The whole issue becomes, how does everybody else contribute?" asked Messier. "Not everybody is Wayne, so how does Pat Conacher contribute? How does Rick Chartraw contribute? How do these guys feel a part of the team, even when they don't have the same kind of responsibilities? Inclusion. That becomes the focus, the priority, inside the locker room."

Some teams win because they perform marvellously inside a short window: for example, the 2004 Tampa Bay Lightning or the 2006 Carolina Hurricanes. But the ones who keep coming back, they drill deeper into the well of success. Sure, it takes truly great players—and more than one of them—to win five Cups in seven years as Messier's Oilers did. But many great teams only win one Cup. One only has to look across the Battle of Alberta to find one.

There would be no surpassing Gretzky as the on-ice leader, not in the big picture. But if Messier was going to be the spiritual leader, the vocal chieftain inside this dressing room, he would have to meet a certain on-ice standard. Sure, Gretzky did things that no one else could do. But Messier, he did things that no one else *would* do.

Jamie Hislop first met Messier when he joined Hislop's Cincinnati Stingers in the WHA as a seventeen-year-old. The two would find themselves on the other end of the Battle years later.

"He played only forty games or so in Cincinnati and scored one goal," Hislop told my colleague George Johnson in 2005. "But you could just tell. He was already physically dominant. Great skater. Big shot. And mean. Even then, he didn't take anything from anybody. He set the ground rules early.

"I played with Mark at seventeen, and against Gordie Howe in the twilight of his career. When you look at them, and the way they were able to beat you so many ways, there's a lot of similarities between the two."

Messier did not quite match Howe's 1,767 NHL games played, but he did become in the eyes of many Howe's most recognizable prototype. Now a man of twenty-three, with a Cup disappointment from the previous year rubbing him the wrong way, Messier used the 1983–84 campaign to establish himself as a dangerous man when the chips were down.

Midway through season, on Boxing Day to be exact, Messier did what every opponent he'd ever played against feared he might do. "I just snapped," he would admit later that night. Calgary defenceman Jamie Macoun had belted Messier with a hard bodycheck in the second period and hurt Messier. Circling like a shark for the rest of the game, Messier exacted revenge later on. It was a different time then, a time before video review. As such, they spoke more freely about their transgressions in 1984 than players do today.

"I was going to go after him after the hit, but my hip and elbow hurt, and I had the wind knocked out of me," Messier told reporters that night. "I'd rather have done it at the time. The only thing I regret is maybe giving him an eye injury."

"I don't remember necessarily doing anything," said Macoun today, typically forgetting any wrongdoing he might have done that started things. "I played a tough game; I wasn't the biggest guy out there. If he thought something happened, it happened. Or maybe it didn't.

"I had skated by the bench, and he had come on the ice from behind me. He suckered me from behind. I was pretty groggy, getting suckered like that. He was a pretty big boy, north of two hundred pounds. To get caught from behind, it was a sucker-punch."

It was, at best, a vicious, vicious play, for which the NHL suspended Messier ten games. That was a pretty big suspension for the day, and a classic example of the kind of infraction that has been legislated out of today's hockey.

"It was different back then," Messier said. "I learned very early on that you had to be a player who was not going to be an easy target. Who was going to be around for a while. In order to do that, you needed to set some boundaries. That's the way the game was played back then.

"I'm not saying it was right or wrong. But those were the types of things you had to do as a player to ensure the likelihood that you could be healthy and playing for an extended period."

A few players stumbled into Messier's court of retribution along the way. Russian Vladimir Kovin was one. Calgary's Mike Eaves another. They often left on a gurney or, at best, with a teammate under each arm.

There is no exaggeration here. Messier played a brutal, relentless, and uncaring game and was suspended many times for it. That was simply how, by the knowledge he had accrued over all of his years in and around the game, the game of hockey was to be played. Like St. Nick, in Messier's world, 'twas always better to give than receive.

Did Messier ever regret any of his actions?

"Probably," he said now, as close to an apology as you'll ever get. "It's hard to say if *regret* is the right word. At that time, there weren't as many rules, it wasn't as closely monitored . . . It was just different. Whether it was right or wrong . . . you did some things that you felt were required to win, and to get room on the ice. However that's interpreted [laughing], I don't know."

He was no less dangerous with the puck than he was when the opponent possessed it. In Game 7 of the 1984 Smythe Division final, Messier knocked three Flames players out of the game with various acts of demolition—all during the decisive third period, no less. Paul Reinhart had long since been stretchered off; Mike Eaves lay crumpled like a discarded cigarette pack in a corner after being run over ("It was as if he got hit by a bus," recalled Oilers goaltender Grant Fuhr. "There were tire tracks running up and down his back"); and Al MacInnis exited early after being cut down by a knee injury. All courtesy of one man.

Carnage. Sheer carnage. Messier carnage.

"That Messier!" Flames coach Badger Bob Johnson would growl after that game. "That Messier! He knocked three of our guys out of the game! Three! That was . . . ," he stammered. "That was . . . ," he muttered. "That was . . . ," he repeated, his face changing to a look approaching awe, "Amazing!"

Where Gretzky was a points machine, averaging just fewer than two points per night throughout his career, Messier was like the Swiss Army Knife of leaders.

"Mark had all the tools to deliver whatever the team needed at any particular time," said teammate Craig MacTavish. "Leadership is about stepping up and filling voids in the team's performance, and Mark's game was so complete, he could fill any void. If you needed a goal, he could score you a goal. If you needed an elbow . . . If you needed a fight . . .

"There are very few players in the history of the game who had that amount of depth to their game. Combine that with an infectious personality . . . He was very inclusive of everybody—fun to be around. So guys naturally gravitated toward him. Even guys who we brought in from other teams who weren't necessarily viewed a winners, he would bring them into the circle, and treat them like winners. They wanted to perform for him. He just had the whole package. And a tremendous hockey player. Second overall in the history of the game in points and games played."

It was a time when leadership meant holding mandatory meetings at Edmonton's Grand Hotel, an aged downtown tavern that Messier somehow favoured, situated next to the Greyhound bus station. Maybe it reminded him of The Bruin Inn. It was a time before the Internet and cellphone cameras, so players could let their hair down in private.

"It was a fun era to play in back then, much more than it is today," said MacTavish. "No Twitter, no Facebook, no 'Gotcha!' [with a phone camera]. Less media. And the expectations . . . We'd practise and we'd be done. Now, you come, you have an hour of meetings, and an hour of practice, an hour of fitness. It's changed a lot."

Messier became married to left winger Glenn Anderson, who had the speed and skill to keep up with him and a net-crashing game that set Anderson apart from everyone else on the team. While Gretzky was fitted to the legendary sniper Jari Kurri, exactly the finisher that Gretzky's game required, Anderson was to Kurri what NASCAR is to F1 racing.

"We understood each other, and not everybody did. But Glenn did . . . and I loved his courage and his heart," said Messier. "When the chips were down, I knew I had a guy beside me who wasn't going to turn away. It's a comforting feeling, that you can rely in each other in the toughest spots."

In the Battle, a "tough spot" could have many definitions. It could be a Game 7 at the Saddledome. It could be a five-on-five at Rexall. It could be something off-ice, and yes, there were some hot times there as well for this Oilers team.

"All of that. All of it," Messier said. "It goes deeper than that, through to the whole team. But certainly the guy you're on the ice with every shift, for the better part of twelve years or more. He was a tremendous hockey player, a big-game player. But his courage, his 'No, compete,' was just off the charts. It was a perfect blend of styles."

Anderson, of all the Oilers, would take on the role of the closer. Only Kurri notched more playoff goals than Anderson's eighty-one in an Oilers uniform, and Anderson was behind only Gretzky and Kurri in playoff game-winners. His three overtime playoff goals were the most out of all them, as Anderson somehow channelled a sense of timeliness when it was needed most.

His expectation of winning was as ruthless as Messier's.

"What does it take to win? What do you need to do to win? I didn't want to have the feeling of loss in my gut, in my heart, in my soul anymore," he said. "So what did I need to become to be the winner? I became being the clutch guy. The go-to guy who is going to score the game-winning goal on a regular basis. The team would look at me and guys would say, 'Hey, this is your time,

Andy.' And I felt like, 'Yes. Give it to me.' I loved those moments in life."

Somehow the Oilers boiled down into pairs. Maybe all hockey teams do. But in Edmonton it was Gretzky–Kurri, Coffey–Huddy, and Messier–Anderson. Gretzky wore the C, but Messier was every bit as important a leader.

"You learn from your battles, your wars, and your losses more so than anything else," Anderson said. "As the Dalai Lama said, 'Never lose the lesson from a loss.' Mark read up on it. He developed his own mind so that he would be one of those guys who would not be beaten in any situation. But he just didn't learn it overnight. It was a period of losses, of championships, of heartfelt successes and heartfelt failures."

"Every year I was reminded of how hard it is to win," Messier told me, without ever being asked the question. He wasn't talking about the final game of the Stanley Cup as much as he was talking about the first pre-season game after a short summer off. In October when the games are for real, and the level rises again. Then again in late November, early December, when every player's timing has fully returned, and each team has a full grasp of how to execute its system.

"So what happens over time is you're playing [at the highest level] all the time. Because that's the only way you know how to play. So you become a winner," he says. "You don't just play winning hockey when it's time to play winning hockey. You play winning hockey all . . . the . . . time.

"Your mindfulness, your direction, the way you do things. You become a winner. Not only when you're at the rink, but in everything that you do. It takes a long time to settle in to that. And it takes a lot of good people around you."

Inclusion. It takes the right people up top, with the ability to include the group underneath.

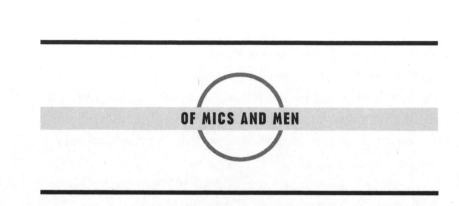

6

OF MICS AND MEN

Reporting from the Battle Press Box
*"The buildings had a certain crackling.
Always waiting for something to start."*

Old media men are no different than your father. For them, it was always better in the old days.

The reality is, however, that when it comes to covering the Battle of Alberta, it undoubtedly *was* better in the old days compared with what today's media endures. Better deadlines; better access; longer interviews with no bloggers hanging around, and fewer cameras; better players; better travel; better teams playing more meaningful games . . . And as such, better stories to write and report.

If you'll suffer a rant for a moment, all the Internet has done for hockey journalists is to allow them to file faster and with less hassle. And to communicate with fans and readers through social media. And to shoot video.

So today's editor wants more copy faster than yesterday's editor while demanding "Internet chats" with readers and plenty of tweeting. Oh, and because the Internet has crippled the newspaper industry, there are fewer reporters: "So can you file an extra sidebar after the game, and give me something off the morning skate?"

As legendary *Toronto Star* hockey scribe Frank Orr said to me recently, "Most of my contemporaries have gone to the big newsroom in the sky. I only hope they don't have to shoot video up there."

Okay, my rant is done. Seriously though, it isn't the increased workload that scares anyone off today. Almost to the person, the hockey beat journalists I've known over three decades in the business are not fazed by hard work, deadlines, or an extra sidebar. If anything has changed from the days of the Battle, it is that diminishing access and cookie-cutter personalities among the players have rendered the daily material to be simply not as intriguing or original as it once was.

For instance, both the Oilers and Flames were noted for having what us reporters called "good rooms" in the 1980s. They were full of characters with stories to tell about elements of life that didn't always involve a stick or a puck. Even Wayne Gretzky had played lacrosse and baseball growing up, while most of today's players have been one-sport kids since age eight.

Compared with today's dressing room, the opportunity to speak to those players of the 1980s—to really get to know them personally—was far, far better because the media relations staff didn't "close the room" and the players were happy to hang around and kibitz. The other difference? The old dressing rooms didn't have a labyrinth of hallways in which players can go but the media can not. They were small, and there were few—if any—boundaries.

"You just went into that dressing room, and you just sat down and waited for the guy you wanted to talk to. You knew he was going to come, and you knew he would talk to you when he did come," said Al Strachan, the curmudgeonly hockey writer with thirty-seven years in the biz. "Maybe he was having a shower or whatever. But you never had to wonder, 'Gee, maybe he's not talking to the media today.' Of course he was talking to the media today. They talked every day, for as long as you wanted, basically.

"And if you knew them at all, you could meet them after the game for a couple of drinks."

I'll never forget when "Planet" Al Iafrate would come through town, one of the all-time characters in the game. You'd see him in the room after practice, ask him to chat, and he'd say, "Meet me at the stick bench in a few minutes." You'd go to the workbench where players once doctored up their wooden sticks, and after a few minutes Iafrate would arrive, in sandals, shorts, and a T-shirt.

He had a cigarette in his hand, one behind his ear, and he'd hop up and take a seat on the table. Then he'd light one smoke with the blowtorch used to curve sticks, take a long drag, squint his eyes, and say, "What's up?" You knew you had Al's full attention for two smokes, or about twenty minutes, and if you couldn't mine a column out of Planet Al in twenty minutes, well, it was probably time to turn in your Professional Hockey Writers Association card.

Clearly, the walls weren't as high in the 1980s, just as they had been even lower in the 1950s when the Montreal Canadiens trusted Red Fisher to make up their quotes, to save everyone the bother of the post-game interview process. Or so went the legend.

The players on either side of the Battle got to know the various writers, partly because they didn't make nearly as much money and they were simply more normal folks and partly because there were a lot fewer members of the media in those days.

"I'd spent a year and a half backing up [beat man] Dick Chubey at the *Edmonton Sun*, so I knew all those [Oilers] guys," said George Johnson, who was on the beat with the *Calgary Sun* in the earlier years of the Battle. "I remember Gretzky—and he'll never remember this—but I remember him going out of his way to talk to me. And by doing that, he showed everybody else in that room, 'It's okay. You can talk to this guy. I'm talking to him. You can too.'

"I always felt like I could go into that Oilers room and get anything," Johnson said, looking across the coffee shop we had met at that day. "That lady over there having a double latte with chocolate sprinkles? She could get good stuff out of that room. It was a good, good room to work."

A journalist's goal is to tell the story as best one can—to bring the reader not only to the game but also to somewhere that the TV set cannot. It was about telling the reader who this Neil Sheehy character was, and why his whole Harvard Boxing Club shtick was such a ruse. Who was this Stu Grimson kid who'd taken Round 1 from big Dave Brown? How did it feel to be Steve Smith, who heard that Saddledome crowd croon, "Shoooot!" every time he picked up a puck behind his net for all those years?

Or when there was an issue either inside the greater NHL game or inside the team itself, it was far easier in those days to explore that issue with the names who mattered. That's where Gretzky was fantastic. He loved to sit and talk hockey, and after the formal stage of questions had passed he would ask reporters as many questions as we had asked him.

Remember, these were pre-Internet times, so if you'd come in from another series, players would want to know the inside scoop from St. Louis, or Vancouver, or wherever you'd been. It was an informal time when not everything was on camera or on the record. The scrum was small, and often everyone in it knew one another's name, wife's name, and how many children we all had. We trusted one another.

"I had left all of my laundry at the Westin in Edmonton," Al Strachan began, telling a story that occurred prior to Game 7 of the 1991 Battle of Alberta. "The Oilers, a bunch of them, used to go sit on the bench at the Saddledome an hour and a half before the game, just in their underwear. I used to go down there early and chat with them. There would always be six or eight guys just sitting on the bench with no one in the building.

"MacT says, 'What do you think happens tonight, Strach?' And I say, 'Well, I hope to hell you win because I left all my laundry up in Edmonton. If you guys don't win, I'm screwed.' MacT said, 'Don't worry, Strach. We'll get your gaunchies back for you . . .'"

Come playoff time, the beauty of the Battle was that, on a game night, it gave you a plethora of angles to explore. Then, on an off day with the proper opportunity to gather quotes and speak with players, the idea you'd brought to the rink could be adequately reported and written. It was a writer's dream—great drama, impeccable access, and the star power that sold newspapers.

As the Battle of Alberta simmered, both the players and the travelling hockey writers circled the games on their calendars weeks before puck drop. And during playoffs journalists came from far and wide to cover them. If your mission was to be at the epicentre of the game on an inordinate amount of nights, this was the place to be. And, of course, the greatest player in the game was here, which meant you could always sell your boss on a trip to cover Wayne Gretzky.

"It was different, and the buildings had a certain crackling. Always waiting for something to start," said Al Maki, the *Calgary Herald* sports columnist of the day. "Because you never knew what was going to happen, and it could happen on a variety of platforms. These were the things you came to the rink for."

It is a fallacy that there is no cheering in the press box. The true writer's rule is this: There is no cheering for your team. You can, however, cheer for your story.

So, let's say you predicted a breakout game for a player, or you'd written about how the one team's goalie wouldn't fare well against the other's shooters. You could pump a fist quietly when your story panned out or curse the goalie for making some saves. But whatever angle you might have had in your back pocket when you arrived at the rink for Flames versus Oilers, chances are you weren't going to need it anyhow.

When asked by his editor at 10 a.m., "What are you writing today?" then-*Journal* columnist Cam Cole's standard reply was, "An eff'ing column." Then he'd nod over to you and say, "The Lord will provide."

I'm not sure if Cammy prayed a day in his adult life, but the Battle did indeed provide like a golden goose, for him and the rest of us, for most of a decade.

"Even as a writer or an observer, you got caught up in the wave of emotions," said Maki, whose nickname, of course, was Chico, after the old Chicago Blackhawks player Ron "Chico" Maki. "This game, you had no idea what you might see. Great artistry? Sure. It was always competitive. Bad coaching? Great goaltending? But the game, it spoke for each city. 'We're better than you are.' 'No, you're not, 'cause our hockey team is better than yours.' 'No, it's not.'

"It made it hard, years later, when both teams had lost their way. Both were losing, and missing the playoffs, and you were starting to sound like an old grandfather: 'Remember those old days . . . ?'"

Let's face it: A good, solid spear in the nuts made for great copy. And the fallout? There would be mayhem on the ice, and reams of quotes afterwards about the heathen from the opposing team, while our poor boy was just standing there, minding his own business . . .

"I remember when Carey Wilson lost his spleen in the '86 series," began the *Edmonton Journal*'s Jim Matheson. Wilson had his spleen removed in the hospital after Game 6, and the Flames wanted everyone to know that it was the fault of Oilers defenceman Steve Smith.

So a Flames assistant coach escorted a few writers inside their video room to witness the heinous spear of Smith. After watching the video, however, the reporters emerged unsure if there had been any serious spear at all. The messengers were ready and willing to deliver the message—it would have been good copy, and likely got them down to the lobby bar that much quicker once the write was complete. But you can't report on something you're not sure even happened, and the next day when Wilson himself came down to look at the game films, he found out that it wasn't Smith's stick that had injured him at all.

"Turned out it was Charlie Huddy, later on in the game. A crosscheck in the back." Matheson chuckled. "Back in those days they were fast and loose with the facts."

Few businesses have changed like the media between the pre-Internet years of the 1980s and today, when everyone is connected 24/7. In the early days of the Battle, newspapers were yet to have their monopoly impinged upon. In 1982, a reasonable percentage of the population still awoke without knowing the score from last night's game, a percentage that is infinitesimal today. Newspapers weren't only pertinent, they were necessary, and the better the hockey teams, the more well read the sports sections.

If you were a Flames fan on an off day, you got literally 100 percent of your Flames news from the *Calgary Sun* or *Herald*. In

Edmonton, what the *Journal's* Jim Matheson and the *Sun's* Dick Chubey printed was taken as gospel. Cam Cole's *Journal* columns were the first pieces that much of the male population of Edmonton read each morning.

There was no Sportsnet or TSN breaking stories in those days. Scoops were the sole property of the newspapermen, with the odd play-by-play announcer like Peter Maher or Rod Phillips breaking a story along the way.

I delivered the *Journal* as a kid and grew up on Jim Matheson's "notebooks," his daily collections of notes, quips, predictions, and touts strung together on an inside page. Nobody in the Edmonton market cobbled together a notebook like Matty, while in the Calgary market, George Johnson and Eric Duhatschek worked across the street from each other at the *Sun* and *Herald* respectively, two highly talented beat men who have forged long, distinguished careers in the local and national market.

And those men held sway in those dressing rooms, to be sure. Like the time the notoriously grumpy Robert Reichel decided early in the season that he would boycott the media that year.

"He announced at the beginning of the year that he wasn't talking to the media," recalls Al Strachan. "The Flames had Frank Musil, the Czech defenceman, and he was a real nice guy. A great guy. And Reichel decides one day that he *will* talk. So Frank comes over to Eric in the dressing room, and he says, 'Robert has decided that he will talk to the media now, and he'd like it if you'd go over and have a chat.'

"Eric, very politely, says to Frank, 'Tell Robert that I'm not talking to *him*, and my ban lasts all year. He can go *$@# himself.'"

I ran into Reichel a few times, from covering the Flames and the other teams to which he was moved. He was as advertised: a bit of an aloof jerk. Perhaps he'd have been a nicer guy if he'd ever produced in the clutch. Alas, we'll never know.

"The Oilers played Calgary so often, all the Flames players knew us Edmonton scribes by name," Matheson said. "Neil Sheehy? We became like best friends. He had no problem telling you what he was going to do to Wayne Gretzky. In those days, they didn't care if you knew what they were going to do. Sheehy made no bones that he was not a very good player, and that he was going to get under Gretzky's skin any possible way. And for the most part, not legally.

"Really, the Saddledome was almost like a second home," Matheson said. "You knew the security guys when you were coming in the back door at the rink. You knew Bearcat, Al Murray, Bobby Stewart . . ."

Matheson started on the beat for the *Journal* in 1973—Year 2 of the World Hockey Association. He has literally seen it all in the Big E, from Jacques Plante tending goal for the old Alberta Oilers in the Edmonton Gardens to attending the meetings in which the Oilers were accepted into the NHL.

"They were held at the St. Regis Hotel in New York City," he remembers. "They'd been talking for several years that some teams from the WHA might get into the NHL, but it was a war of attrition as teams tried to last until the NHL finally did let them in. There were only four teams left when the Oilers got in."

Matheson worked for years on the Oilers broadcast with Rod Phillips. Together they met owner Peter Pocklington's plane on the tarmac in Edmonton to break the story of a kid inside that plane who would sign a twenty-one-year personal services contract with Peter Puck. His name? Wayne Gretzky.

From there, Matheson, Phillips, and Dick Chubey pretty much joined the Oilers themselves, watching Glen Sather mould a championship team from their seats on the plane, the bus— whatever mode of transportation the team was using at the time.

"The same media guys travelled all the time. It was me for the

Journal, Chubey for the *Sun*, and Rod," he said. "You became a part of the travelling circus. We were like part of the team. They'd let you travel on the bus with the players, to the rink and back. It's probably not right, but you did it.

"Back in those days, Pocklington would go out to dinner with the scribes," Matheson said. "Me, Dick, Rod, he and Slats, and Tuele would come to dinner with us." (And usually Pocklington would pick up the tab.)

Together, Phillips and Matheson were introduced to that Bobby Hull–led Jets team that would serve as Sather's template for the NHL Oilers.

"He watched them play, as an Oilers player and a coach, and he just loved the style they played," Phillips said. "That's the kind of team he wanted to have, and once all of these guys showed up, their whole offensive attack was based on what he had seen with the Winnipeg Jets.

"We're going to wind up, do some circles, and we're coming at you. Coffey was coming up hard, and there was always five guys."

Those eyes have seen a lot of goals, plenty of records, and perhaps more fights than Ferdie Pacheco. Only once, however, can Matheson recall a night when things went too far — that back end of a home-and-home in 1990, when Dave Brown tangled with Stu Crimson.

"Dave was beating him up, and didn't seem to want to stop. It made me a little squeamish. I mean, the whole idea of telling us, 'Don't be going for coffee,'" Matheson said. "The rest of the time, there was a lot of theatre. Guys jumping into dog piles, punching somebody in the face. It was as much theatre as it was a game. But that was not Stampede Wrestling or make-believe. That was very real.

"You don't get that much anymore, where a guy can say, 'I'm going to get him next game.' Today, the NHL would step right in. Collie Campbell would be in the stands at the next game. Back then, though, you could do it."

Phillips was equally sympathetic to poor Grimson: "Ach. They were both enforcers, tough guys," he said. "One enforcer had won the first fight and there was going to be another one. Simple as that."

The Battle was fought, by and large, in the days before sports radio. Your market might have had a nine-to-midnight show, but there was no two-hour hockey shows on at lunch-time, or surely no all-sports radio stations in the province the way there are today.

Hell, a fan couldn't even get all eighty games on TV back then. If Calgary went out on a five-game road trip, two of the games might well not be televised. If the Oilers played a Saturday matinee in Boston or Philadelphia, it simply would not be shown on TV. Saturdays were for CBC's *Hockey Night in Canada*, and CBC only showed the games that started at 8 p.m. Eastern.

This was also the time before the dais. Before coaches held "availabilities," with strategy sessions beforehand between coach and PR man, sussing out the line of questioning that could be expected. Sather did his press scrums right in the dressing room, in front of the stick rack, where the players could hear his message. The crowd of reporters was smaller, and as such, a journalist could pursue a line of questioning. If it was a good one, and the juicy quotes were forthcoming, the group often knew enough to let the soloist continue. They were all going to harvest the quotes anyhow, so why get in the way or change the line of questioning?

Today's general managers might make the odd media appearance during a playoff series or speak to their local media once every month or so. But it will be well staged, generally taking place only if his team is losing and in need of some kind of edge. In 1986, Cliff Fletcher came to practice on most off days and was more than approachable. Glen Sather was both coach *and* general manager. They were both available on game days, and off days, and thus the pot stirred with more centrifugal force than today, when the Internet, the sheer mass of media, and those damned podiums all combine to sanitize the access that the reader/viewer gets.

There was, however, a different atmosphere surrounding both teams. Their collective personalities mirrored their two leaders, Johnson and Sather.

"Badger Bob had that college mentality," said the easily perturbed Strachan. "They were always meeting, those people. Sometimes you had to wait three hours for another one of the Flames meetings to finish. MacTavish used to call it, 'Paralysis by analysis.' The only time the Oilers had a meeting was at noon, and that coincidentally coincided with the arrival of the pizza [for the players]. So they'd have their alleged meeting, and after twenty minutes they'd open the room back up to the media—once the pizza was consumed."

It was the military precision of Badger's Seven Point Plan versus the creative freedom of Sather's bunch. Tactics versus freelance. It extended away from the rink.

"Badger, when he had an eight o'clock bus, well, that bus left at eight o'clock," Strachan continued. "The Oilers bus left when people got there. If they got there. Sometimes they had to go back into the hotel to get people, and sometimes it was a coach. I remember one time, they had to go back in and get [assistant coach] Bob McCammon out. But nobody worried about things like that with the Oilers."

All beat writers travelled closely with their teams in those days. There were no charter flights in the NHL back then, so the team would book their beat people on the same commercial flights they were on, and the same went for hotels. Then they'd send the newspapers the bill.

Covering the Oilers meant an annual trip to the home of Pocklington's buddy, former U.S. president Gerald Ford. I was lucky enough to enjoy one of those trips, and it came with a round at Pebble Beach. I can't imagine today either a newspaper allowing their reporter to accept this type of hospitality or a team willing to offer it.

"That was Pocklington," said Matheson. "After golf we'd all go out to dinner at a place called Wally's Desert Turtle. We'd eat, and then Gerald Ford would make a speech about the U.S. economy or the government. It was over the head of most of the players, who were mostly Canadian."

Then the party would adjourn, Secret Service men and all, to the Fords' lovely Palm Springs home. I can say that I've shaken the hand of President Ford and met the former first lady Betty Ford at one of these. Even made friends with the Ford's dog, a spaniel as I recollect.

"I was there the night Rod Phillips was talking to Betty Ford," Matheson recalled. "He missed his mouth with his drink and it went all the way down his shirt. She had been talking about the Betty Ford Center, and she puts her arm around Rod and says, 'Maybe you should come with me . . .'

"I remember being in Gerry Ford's office and putting my feet up on his desk, just thinking I was a big shot. Dave Hunter, he went to the bathroom and plugged the Fords' toilet. He was so embarrassed, he didn't know what to do or who to tell."

The Oilers and their media ended up on the set of *M*A*S*H* one day, meeting Alan Alda and Loretta Swit, and spent an evening at the home of Muhammad Ali, where the aging heavyweight conducted a magic show for his guests. Eventually, Ali would end up at the old Edmonton Gardens, fighting Dave Semenko in a charity bout.

Through it all, there were many relationships forged. Those

former players and managers, almost to the man, greet the reporters today with a smile and a handshake. They had spent nearly a
decade of their lives travelling the same road, seeing one another
more than they did their own families during the season. As a
scribe, you never cheered for a team. But as objective as I am
proud to say I am, the biggest test of one's sympathies was not to
cheer for some of the really good guys you've met along the way.

Hockey players tend to be good people. For every Reichel,
there are ten Pattersons or Peplinskis. For every Glenn Anderson,
whose relationship with the Edmonton press was always a tad
strained, there was a Gretzky, whose generosity knew no bounds.
Like in this very book, Gretzky's words lent gravity to all of our
columns over the many years. He knew that, and always had
time to answer a question.

In turn, for a guy like Maki, watching Gretzky's final shift at
the Saddledome is a moment he'll never forget.

"When Gretzky came through Calgary with the Rangers in
1999, there was this sense that this was it. This was the last time
he'd be coming through the Saddledome," Maki recalls. "He
went for a faceoff, deep in the Calgary end. The crowd starting
cheering, cheering. . . Now they're standing and applauding.
And the Calgary centre skated away [from the dot]. Gretzky
looked like he was going to do something, and a linesman skated
over, and you could see he was telling him, 'Just enjoy it.'

"Gretzky acknowledged the fans, and eventually they resumed
playing. But after all these years—and no one knew for sure that
he was retiring—it was very nice. Everybody knew, this was the
last time they would see him.

"The Battle of Alberta had changed."

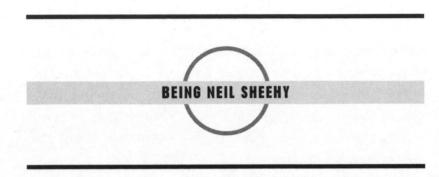

7

BEING NEIL SHEEHY

The Battle's Most Hated Villain
*"I figured it out: if they do something stupid, and I don't fight
them, then they'll do something even more stupid.*

"Neil Sheehy is on the phone, trying to characterize how—
among all those villains over all those years—the black hat of the
Battle of Alberta had found his head.

"So here's the thing," he explains. "I was there to be a pest. To
be an annoying SOB, okay? Listen, I understood why the guy
[Wayne Gretzky] would despise and hate me. Because I was an
annoying prick, you know? Okay?"

Of all the players that people loved to hate in the Battle, it was
Neil Sheehy—"The Butcher of Harvard"—who became
Gretzky's personal hate valet. He would be the first man in the
Battle to introduce turtling as a successful survival strategy, and
upon his retirement Sheehy would have the nerve to write a posi-
tion paper—entitled "The Systematic Erosion and Neutralization

of Skill and Play-making in the NHL"—on how players who play the game the way he had were ruining the game of hockey.

It took a lot of nerve, in the big picture, to take on the role of trying to eliminate The Great One from the game when an arena full of fans and hundreds of thousands across the country had tuned in to see Gretzky entertain. On a micro scale, Sheehy had no shame. He would stir up as much trouble as possible, refusing to fight his battle the way we had become used to seeing it fought.

And the worst thing of all? His shtick worked. It actually worked very well.

"Neil saw an opportunity to make a bit of a name for himself, to get under Gretzky's skin," said former Flames defenceman Jamie Macoun. "I'm sure if you talked to Wayne, he hated Neil Sheehy. He was always buggin' him. Then, because it was the Battle of Alberta, the media built it up. Suddenly you had all these Neil Sheehy stories about Gretzky. It just took on a life of its own. But everything about Calgary and Edmonton took on a life of its own."

Over the years, Calgary general manager Cliff Fletcher and coach Bob Johnson had devised as many schemes as they could to neutralize Gretzky, and few if any had worked. Until one day in 1983, when Flames assistant coach Pierre Pagé walked into Team USA's pre-Olympics camp to take a look at a centreman named Joel Otto.

"Joel and I used to do battle drills in front of the net, and Pierre liked that," Sheehy recalls. "We practised and battled every day together."

"Neil Sheehy was a big man," Macoun said of his teammate. "He reminded me of that picture of Bobby Hull. The one with his shirt off, throwing the bale of hay? Neil Sheehy had big shoulders, big arms—he was a thick man. If you went to fight him, you had yourself a tangle. He could grapple with ya."

He arrived on the scene like an old-time wrestler. He had attended Harvard and told everyone that he'd been the heavyweight champion of the Harvard boxing team. You almost expected him to knock Gretzky out one day by pulling a foreign object from his trunks or bashing him over the head with a folding chair.

"First of all," said former *Calgary Herald* columnist Al Maki, "there was no Harvard boxing team."

"There was a club," counters Sheehy. "But it was educational. They *learned* how to box, but they didn't really box per se. Was I the heavyweight champ at Harvard? Yeah. But how many boxers go to Harvard?"

He was a character unlike any other in the Battle, and the rivalry was richer for it. Looking back, it must have taken a near genius to figure out how to eke 379 career NHL games out of the meagre level of talent with which Sheehy was blessed.

"He was a very bad hockey player. Like, barely-able-to-play bad," said veteran Calgary sports writer Eric Duhatschek. "But why Wayne still let him get under his skin, I don't know."

Sheehy did not arrive in Calgary earmarked to be Gretzky's personal irritant. He evolved into the role, the same way a tasty leftover roast beef can evolve in the back of the fridge into a green, smelly mess. "On the ice," Sheehy observed, "our relationship was one of hatred, on his side. On my side, it was a love affair. Because he was the reason why I had an NHL career."

Sheehy, whose choice of colleges would earn him the nickname "Harv," was yet another of those undrafted NCAA gems unearthed by the Flames, their counterpunch to Oilers chief scout Barry Fraser's out-of-his-mind drafting run in the early 1980s. Sheehy's older brother Tim had actually played three seasons for the WHA Oilers in the mid-1970s, alongside then player/coach Glen Sather.

Neil was the last of nine children born to Larry and Kathleen Sheehy, who lived in International Falls, Minnesota. When the town's hospital closed down, the last seven of the Sheehy kids were delivered in the hospital about a mile and a half away, up in Fort Frances, Ontario.

He was a border baby whose dad sold real estate, ran a gas station, was a mechanic, sold insurance . . . whatever it took to keep the groceries rolling in to feed a family of nine. But merely feeding those kids wasn't Larry's only goal.

"My dad was one of twelve," begins Neil. "He grew up during the Depression, in a town called Cass Lake, Minnesota, and quit school so he could support the rest of his family. When he married my mom, who was a college graduate, he said he wanted all of his children to go to college. We all worked summer jobs, we took loans, and each and every kid funded their own way. It was expected: 'You're going to go to college. Nothing comes easy— you've got to work for it.' That's what each and every one of us did.

"I had a brother and sister go to Marquette University. I had a sister at University of Minnesota. I had three brothers at Boston College. I had a sister at St. Scholastica College in Duluth and another one at St. Cloud. I was the ninth one, the baby of the family, and I chose Harvard."

Sheehy's route to an Ivy League school was really the same gravel road that he would travel throughout his journeyman NHL career. But Harvard? Here was the ninth of nine kids, paying his own way, and he picks an Ivy League school?

"I was contacted by an alum who told me to think about Harvard. And when I was contacted, I thought, 'Harvard? Well, I could never do that.' Then I got my chest up and I said, 'Wait a sec. Why can't I do that? How cool would that be?' My brothers were at Boston College and they told me, 'You ever get the chance to go to Harvard, you go.' So, when I got the chance, I took it."

Sheehy is clearly intelligent, possessing the grades to gain entry into Harvard and the wherewithal to graduate with an economics degree. He would attain a law degree after hanging up his blades, and today he is part-owner of ICE Hockey Agency, which boasts of such clients as Ryan Suter, Matt Niskanen, Nate Prosser, and Lubomir Visnovsky, among others. In 1983, however, Sheehy was a mangy-looking twenty-three-year-old long shot who showed up at the Calgary Flames training camp as an afterthought.

"He'd gone to training camp in his first year," said Duhatschek, who had moved from the *Calgary Albertan* to the *Calgary Sun* in 1983 and would complete the circuit when he worked at both the *Herald* and the *Globe and Mail*. "There were seventy-one players invited to the camp that year, and he was given sweater No. 71. He knew right from the beginning what he needed to do to make an impression, so he went and beat up a guy named Greg Meredith."

As we've said of Sheehy, he was no dummy. He knew that Meredith had come out of Notre Dame, so he hadn't fought much. And he also found out that Meredith didn't have a lot of backing in that training camp—very few friends, if any—so there would be no residual effects from Sheehy's challenge.

"Meredith was a cerebral guy on a team of rockheads, and Neil found out that he didn't have a lot of friends on the team, anyone who would stand up for him," Duhatschek said. "So he beat Meredith up. He knew he was going to have to make an impression because he was wearing No. 71."

It would be a theme that Sheehy would live by: Look like you're making it up as you go along when in reality there was a plan afoot.

"In order to play, I had to have a certain amount of madness, but what I had was a method to my madness," Sheehy said. "I was never a guy who lost control. I never lost my head. There was always a purpose for what I was doing."

In the Battle, Sheehy would convince a goodly part of the hockey world that he was some slug whose only worth was to subtract the skill and speed from any given hockey game — particularly against the high-flying Oilers. He was, in the end, a lot smarter than we all had thought. He was of average skill, at best, notching just eighteen goals in a career that spanned 379 games. He was never drafted, never wore a letter, and his presence likely never sold a ticket to an NHL game in any of his stops through Calgary, Hartford, Washington, and then Calgary again before it ended unceremoniously on a Slovenian League team, cavorting through Eastern Europe with former Flames teammate Colin Patterson.

"When I got to Calgary, I was going to make it by being a rough-and-tumble-type guy. I knew, the only way I was going to play was if I brought toughness to the lineup. The game changed in the 1990s, where you just had your nuclear warhead; your big guy who just goes out and fights the staged fights. [Back then] I was a guy who added to the team toughness. I could fight if I needed to fight or stand up for other players who were getting taken advantage, but back then you had to go out and play. Nobody got to sit on the bench for all but two minutes then go out and fight, like what happened after they brought in the instigator rule."

As was a theme in the Battle, Sheehy's weight class and structure within the rolling of lines landed him a fairly regular dance partner in orange and blue. Sheehy was a tad small for Dave Semenko, and didn't find himself on the ice as much against Mark Messier. Somehow Kevin McClelland became his opposite number, which could have something to do with Sheehy's pacifist leanings as the Battle waged on.

"We were always trash-talking each other, and he's saying to me one night, 'C'mon, Neil. Let's fight,'" Sheehy remembers. "I say to him, 'Kevin, if I fight you, I'll get fined.' So he says, 'I'll pay it. Let's go!'"

It was during his many hostilities with McClelland, a very tough and plenty eager middleweight who patrolled the wall as a third-line right winger for Edmonton, that Sheehy realized a higher calling in the Battle.

"I fought him several times. But then I realized, I didn't have to fight these guys," he said. "If I just kind of poked and prodded Wayne, they would have to fight me. I knew what my job was, so I figured it out: if they do something stupid, and I don't fight them, then they'll do something even more stupid.

"I always knew I would get hit in the face, and did so every game several times. But my hope was, it would draw two or three penalties, and we had the best power play in the league."

Sheehy wouldn't fight when the Flames were ahead or when the momentum was in their favour. Why would he? He only had that momentum to lose. But if the Oilers were ahead and he could stir things up, well, the Harvard boxing champ would step into the ring. "I was more of a situational guy, an analytical guy. Like, 'How do we gain from this situation?'"

It was always about orchestrating a scenario that was favourable for Sheehy. Give him credit—he knew that if he relied solely on God-given talent, his career would have been a short one. So he created this persona that set him apart, beginning with the Harvard boxing club shtick.

"When you're in the Battle of Alberta, the whole thing is about hype," he said. "If your competition has any doubt about who you are and what you are about, that can be an advantage. And Calgary needed every advantage because—let's face it—those Oilers teams were great, great teams, and we were just trying to close the gap. When Bob Johnson showed up in Calgary, we didn't have a team that was even close to Edmonton. Then we started signing those undrafted college guys, who had unfettered enthusiasm. Guys who were willing to sacrifice for the unknown. Well, at that time, the unknown was beating the Oilers."

If that was "the unknown," then the unheard-of was getting Wayne Gretzky off his game. He either made you look silly when you tried to hit him, or if you did catch him, you had to deal with one of the Oilers looking to punch your lights out.

Sheehy, always searching for an angle, analyzed Gretzky from the bench for a few games, then realized what The Great One could do for him. Ice time! That's what Gretzky turned out to mean for Sheehy.

"What happened was, I watched [Flames defenceman] Paul Baxter. He was the guy who was always out against Gretzky, and whenever he would get physical with Gretzky there would be fights, and guys would come after him. But then I'd always see in the paper where he was being praised for getting to Gretzky. Then he got a lot more ice time.

"I just said to myself, 'I need to get ice time.'"

Against Edmonton, Sheehy would take a short shift to throw off the rotation of the defencemen. Eventually he'd find himself on the ice with Gretzky, even if that hadn't necessarily been the game plan of assistant coach Bob Murdoch. But when opportunity came knocking for Sheehy, he answered the door with plenty of preparation on hand.

"I always knew that he would be by himself in the opposite corner, and I knew the Oilers had a tendency to rim the puck around the boards and the puck would come to Gretzky on the opposite side all alone," he said. "Rather than stand in front of the goal and cover nobody, I'd just go stand by where he was in the opposite corner. Then, when the puck was rimmed around, I was standing there."

But wait, as they say in those Slap Chop commercials. There's more!

"Now, I knew that I would get a penalty if I did anything cheap. So I'd keep my hands down low and I'd slam him into the boards. If I came up to the chest area, I'm getting a penalty every time. Because the league would protect Gretzky. So I'd push him, then right away the big guys would come after me. I'd say, 'What are you going to do to me?' and then I knew the punch was coming.

"As they caught me, I would turtle."

Sheehy became more effective the less he fought, something never before seen in the Battle. This was the psychological warfare, and at that point in the Battle, the Flames needed all the help they could get.

So the pest was born, and despite the fact that Edmonton had a player like Ken Linseman on their side, the role of the pest is always more valuable to an underdog. As Shakespeare taught us, what's the point of having a protagonist if there is no antagonist?

"Their big guys, they wanted to kill me," Sheehy laughs. "I just recognized, if I didn't fight the top guys and they took penalties, it drove the skill guys nuts. Because I wasn't being accountable. There is always supposed to be accountability in the league, so if you touched one of their skill guys, you'd end up fighting one of their tough guys.

"When I broke in, I fought their tough guys, and after analyzing things, I realized there was a better way. That I could hurt them more by drawing penalties. Now, the only way that strategy works is if you have a great power play, and at the time Bob Johnson always had the best power play in the league."

That was another factor here—the Calgary power play. Johnson was such a magnificent tactician, and the one place where a coach can really put his stamp on a hockey team is on special teams. In interviewing for this book, I can't tell you how many times I heard someone say, "If Badger had Gretzky, Coffey, and the boys to work with, that power play would have won Stanley Cups by itself."

And so Johnson's power play became Sheehy's bodyguard. He could ply his trade, turtle when he wanted to, and the fear of that Calgary power-play unit was like police protection for Sheehy. And Lord knows, he needed it.

"Kevin McClelland was constantly trying to get him, and Sheehy would do his thing," said Edmonton heavyweight Dave Semenko. "That was the agitating thing about him—he wasn't going to fight anybody. Mac would go after him, and he'd end up taking a penalty. Mac tried, but it wasn't happening, so it became personal. I'm sure I made my attempts, but he was just going to skate away or cover up. You were just going to take a penalty.

"I probably should have gone after one of their small players, but I couldn't see myself purposely running over one of their players. Just didn't sit right for me. If someone else did it, then I could get involved," mused Semenko. "But [Sheehy] frustrated not only the star players but also the guys who were supposed to prevent it. He just said, 'I'm not going to fight you guys, but I'm still going to do this . . .'"

It was the act of a marginal player who had found a niche that would earn him an NHL paycheque, and he was ready and willing to exploit that. No different than the fighters—I mean, does anyone really want to bare-knuckle fight on skates for a living?— Sheehy was doing something distasteful because it worked.

"Most people didn't want to take punches to the head, or get suckered by guys. I was willing to do that," he said. It was about the cause, about the Battle. Guys did things in Calgary versus Edmonton that they wouldn't necessarily do for Washington–Pittsburgh, or Detroit–Minnesota. "During the 1980s in the Battle of Alberta, we hated each other," Sheehy said. "It was tale of two cities, and Edmonton–Calgary hated each other, and that carried on to the ice. Back in the day, when we went into a bar and there were any of the Oilers in there, we just turned around and walked out. We'd go somewhere else."

Eventually, Sheehy earned the nickname "The Butcher of Harvard," which he loved. And, yes, he even earned the grudging respect of Gretzky, who finally met a player who had taken up residence in his kitchen. "It must have been frustrating for Gretzky, that somehow he couldn't shut out this ten-minute-a-game defenceman," Maki said. "There were points in a game when Gretzky would just slash him on the ankles. Or Semenko would come over and step in.

"Was it really working? On some nights, yes. On others, Gretzky was just going to dominate, and you were just going to watch."

And when the Battle was over, Sheehy versus Gretzky waged on elsewhere.

"He took two separate roughing penalties on me in the same game once, in Washington. He was playing for the L.A. Kings and I was playing for the Washington Capitals," laughs Sheehy today. "But the one time, I was walking out of Northlands Coliseum, and Gretzky was right behind me. We had just beaten them [in 1986], and he was very gracious. He just said, 'Great job, congratulations, and good luck the rest of the way.' He was such a class act."

Sheehy also took his circus act with him when he left.

"Neil was the last player to wear No. 0 in the NHL [with Hartford in 1988]," said Maki. "He figured, if Gretzky was 99, I was one better. Zero.

"I asked him once, 'Why do wear the number 0?' He says, 'It's for my family. Our original name was O'Sheehy.' Of course it never was."

Today they all look back with a smile. The punches don't hurt anymore, the comments have long since ceased to dig in.

"I say this with a great deal of respect," Gretzky said, "that the guys I hated playing against the most were the guys I wanted on my team. He was a smart player with tremendous mobility for a big guy, and he knew how to get under the skin of myself and a guy like Jari Kurri. He did it as well or better than anyone in hockey.

"So, when you've got a guy who wants to win and will do anything, at all costs, to become a champion, as Neil Sheehy wanted to, then you become fearless. Neil Sheehy played against us fearlessly. He knew that if he was going to run myself or Jari . . . he'd have to deal with a guy like Semenko, or McSorley, or Dave Hunter. He took those hits. He didn't back down. The fact he played with that emotion, and that kind of guts, made him a tough guy for our team to compete against. He did that job as well as anybody."

As mentioned, Sheehy would go on to become a successful player agent in Minnesota, the State of Hockey. He walked away from hockey after that 1993–94 season in Slovenia, but somehow ol' Harv still had something to say. This Ivy Leaguer had more thesis paper in him, and so he penned a treatise called "The Systematic Erosion and Neutralization of Skill and Play-making in the NHL."

That's right, folks. Neil Sheehy, decrying the fact that pluggers were neutralizing the superstars and taking the skill out of the game. "I am writing this article knowing that I will be criticized for having the audacity to write it," was how Sheehy opened his paper, going on to decry how the league had handicapped the Oilers by changing the rule that once saw coincidental minors result in a four-on-four situation, changing it so that teams played five-on-five hockey instead.

"Coaches," he wrote, "want their players to agitate opponents and draw penalties. 'Agitate, but don't fight,' they say. This was a novel idea in the '80s, but now it is the norm and our overall game is suffering because of it. It neutralizes skill and frustrates the very players that make hockey the greatest game in the world."

Huh? Really?

Thirty years later, Neil Sheehy is still agitating.

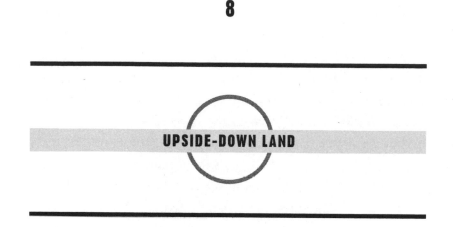

8

UPSIDE-DOWN LAND

The Flames Capture the 1986 Battle

*"It was the Stanley Cup for Calgary,
it really was. Unfortunately, there happened
to be some teams left. Bastards."*

In their own minds, the Calgary Flames were making up ground
on Edmonton in 1986. They had scored the second most goals
in the NHL that season, behind Edmonton, and Calgary had
the second most points in the Campbell Conference, behind
Edmonton. The 1985–86 Flames were finally tapping on that
glass ceiling that had seen them finish second to the Oilers in
the Smythe Division in three of the past four seasons.

Calgary could beat everyone else, but their primary issue
remained: Calgary still couldn't beat Edmonton. So on April 4,
1986, as the teams arrived at the Olympic Saddledome for a meaningless Game 78 of the eighty-game regular season—Edmonton
and Calgary cemented in the one–two spots in the Smythe, a

chasm of thirty-two points between them in the standings—the season series did not exactly reek of parity. In the seven games played thus far that season, Edmonton had gone 6–0–1, outscoring Calgary 37–24.

Wayne Gretzky would end up with twenty-four points in eight meetings between the teams that season, and these hollow, late-season affairs were right up his alley. In that final meeting on April 4, he would register point No. 213, breaking his own mark from four years prior en route to that famous 215-point season that still stands today as the most productive campaign in NHL history.

Normally, NHL players began to dial it down this close to the post-season when the two points really didn't matter. There was nothing to gain and plenty to lose if someone got injured a week away from Round 1—especially for two teams planning on a two-month run through the post-season. In this game the new kid, Mike Vernon, would be in goal for Calgary, after Edmonton had scorched Reggie Lemelin for five consecutive losses in 1985–86. The teams hadn't seen each other in two months. . . Really, this one was a formality for both sides, right?

Well, as it turned out, it depended upon what side you were on.

Something happened that night in Calgary that gave pause to the Battle. The Flames, after having beaten Edmonton—wait for it—just once in the previous twenty-four regular-season games, *crushed* the Oilers 9–3 that night.

"It was the first time we'd beaten them by any margin," recalled Calgary winger Colin Patterson. "Hey, any time you could beat the Oilers it was good for your confidence."

Peter Maher, the radio voice of the Flames, looked down on a scene he'd not witnessed in the Saddledome in ages. And as the goals went in, he could feel—at least for one night—the air coming out of that Oilers mystique. The Flames were playing the way Bob Johnson wanted them to play, executing the vaunted Seven Point Plan to perfection.

That much was satisfying, that the Calgary players were finally able to take all of Johnson's Xs and Os and execute them successfully on Saddledome ice. But the fact that Johnson's agenda was really working on Edmonton, for the first time in about three seasons . . . ? That was what gave Maher a different feeling that night.

"It was the game that Gary Suter had six assists. Tied the Flames record," he said. "I look back at that 9–3 game, and that had a lot to do with giving the Flames confidence. Because they couldn't beat them all year."

The game went all but unnoticed in Edmonton, with the general opinion being that Calgary had won a game that didn't mean anything. Big deal, right? If the Oilers were ever accused of being cocky, this was hard evidence of a dismissive attitude built on years of besting the Flames.

As expected in a six-goal game, this one ended in a huge brawl. Marty McSorley fought Joel Otto. Kevin Lowe went at it with Jim Peplinski. Semenko, Patterson recalls, "fought, then was on the loose and the refs tackled him.

"We'd played really well, and I remember the big brawl, with four or five minutes left. I do remember it being a turning point for us, and gaining some confidence."

After the two teams disposed of their Round 1 opponents— Edmonton in three straight over Vancouver, Calgary in three straight over Winnipeg —Johnson seized that Game 78 result in the lead-up to what would be the third Battle of Alberta in a four-year stretch.

"It's like when you broke par on a golf course—shot 69. You know it can be done because you've done it!" he crowed, the media gathered round after a Flames practice in Calgary. "It's like batting practice. It's four hundred feet down the left-field line. If you've never hit one out in batting practice, how the hell can you hit one out in the game?"

In Edmonton, they'd written that 9–3 loss off by the time they got off the plane at the downtown Municipal Airport post-game. They were still rollicking in their years of dominance over Calgary. Years that were, unbeknownst to them, about to come to an end.

"Calgary seems to have such a complex about our city. I don't know why," Oiler Dave Lumley told reporters prior to the series opener. "We've only got the Oilers, the Eskimos, West Edmonton Mall . . . The only thing they've got is a nickname. You can have Cowtown though."

Yuk, yuk, yuk. While Johnson was showing his team film of that 9–3 game, reaffirming that his plan, when properly executed, could fell the giant, the Oilers were aloof. They'd won two straight Stanley Cups. How was that going to change?

"There was one game we lost late in the season, we lost 9–3 in Calgary," recalled Glenn Anderson, unprompted. "Not only should we have learned from that game, we should have countered out attack and revamped our own system against that team. Because they'd done that to us.

"Bob Johnson revamped their whole system to play against us. How to beat Coffey how to beat Gretzky, how to beat Kurri. He started matching guys up. He implemented is system, and we didn't counteract it."

★

The CBC had to change its broadcast plans even before they'd dropped a puck in the 1986 Battle of Alberta. Mother Corp had planned to sequester the Battle to Alberta and British Columbia, and treat the rest of the country to the mighty Toronto Maple Leafs' second-round series against the St. Louis Blues. It was typical CBC — giving Westerners in Saskatchewan and Manitoba a crappy, fifty-seven-point Leafs team against an American opponent rather than the two-time defending Cup champs against a provincial rival, either of whom could have mopped up the Maple Leafs using wrong-handed hockey sticks.

Inside the CBC's Jarvis Street offices, however, whatever was happening out in the colonies was only a sidebar to the daily drama at Maple Leaf Gardens. It was partly Toronto's self-importance and partly ratings-based decision making. But as the disparity in the quality of hockey grew — Edmonton's 119 points to Toronto's 57 in 1985–86 — so too did the level of ridiculousness surrounding a Canadian broadcaster believing that Canadians outside of Leafs Nation would share their Toronto bias.

"People outside the province, I don't think they understood how good the hockey was," said Flames winger Colin Patterson, a native of Rexdale, Ontario. "You'd have to ask [producer] John Shannon, but I'm pretty sure that 1986 series cost him his job with CBC. He said, 'We're not leaving, and we're not going to show *The Pig and Whistle*, or whatever the hell was on at the time. That's how you knew, people didn't know about the Battle.'"

There was so much blowback from hockey fans on the prairie, when Saskatchewan and Manitoba fans found out they were going to be shown the Norris Division series, CBC knuckled under. "We decided to change that distribution when it became apparent that viewers in Saskatchewan and Manitoba preferred the Calgary–Edmonton series," CBC spokesperson Glenn Luff said diplomatically. That it would take angry phone calls to lift the CBC brass's heads out of their cauldron of Toronto-centricity was quintessential CBC.

Calgary and Edmonton had only been in the NHL for six and seven years respectively, and among Canadian NHL owners in Vancouver, Montreal, and Toronto, there was still some bitterness that the Alberta teams (and Winnipeg) had bitten into the Canadian TV pie. National TV money that not long ago was shared three ways was now being split six ways, even though in those days before the Saturday night double-header, *Hockey Night in Canada* was still exclusive ground of the Leafs and Habs out East.

The TV landscape, compared with today, was antiquated. While today Rogers has the ability to air seven Canadian teams simultaneously on seven different channels—and TSN has five or more digital channels from which to choose—in 1985 there was one English and one French CBC channel. *Hockey Night in Canada* games were shown regionally across the country, all at the same 8 p.m. Eastern start time on a Saturday night. So the Jets' home game would go at 7 p.m., Edmonton and Calgary at 6 p.m., and the Vancouver Canucks at 5 p.m. local.

Sometimes, if your game ended early, CBC would switch you to another one that had three or four minutes left. Other times, if the national news was up, the CBC would not. It was analogue television—prehistoric by today's technical standards—a time when people bought satellite dishes that wouldn't fit through the garage door once assembled.

As such, while prairie fans watched the Oilers rewrite the record books throughout the regular season, fans in Ontario were treated to Alberta hockey only when the Leafs were playing either the Flames or Oilers

When the Oilers and Gretzky would roll through Toronto for a Saturday night game, it was hockey's version of The Beatles coming to town. Tickets were so hard to come by that, one night, Gretzky did not have a ticket for his own father. He sent PR man Bill Tuele into the streets outside Maple Leafs Gardens an hour before game time, brandishing one of No. 99's famous white and red Titan sticks, signed, to be traded for a pair of tickets to the game that night. That's how they rolled in the 1980s, a time before cellphones and the Internet.

So, in April 1986, Albertans were amped up as another edition of the Battle approached. And those CBC types who were immersed in it, like producer John Shannon, who produced "every Oilers–Flames game between 1979 and 1986," knew damned well that it was going to be the kind of hockey that every Canadian should see. Even ESPN took notice.

"The Battle was Red Sox–Yankees every night. Regular season and playoffs," Shannon said. "Because it was Gretzky, ESPN was here a lot. Wayne drove so much of Western Canada . . . he was the icon who drove the sport. They talk about what he's done for the Sunbelt markets, he did it first for Western Canada—whether people in Calgary like it or not."

The difference in 1986 was that Calgary was ready to compete. They'd lost in five games in 1983, seven games in 1984, and now the Flames were back for another kick at the Oilers can.

"It was a growing, a maturing as an organization and a team. We could play with the Oilers, and if we played to our level of ability we could win," said assistant coach Bob Murdoch. "We had toughness; we had our Seven Point System; we had our left winger back; our power play firing full throttle. We not only had the answers to what the Oilers were throwing at us, but we had some things going where they had to worry about us.

"I think the Oilers were so arrogant—not in a negative way—but so confident that they could beat us under any circumstances. They [thought they] could turn it on and turn it off."

Johnson knew one thing, and it would turn out to be prophetic: "The longer the series, the better the chance we have." Truer words, it would turn out, were never spoken.

Game 1 was, of course, up north at the Coliseum. It took Lanny McDonald eighty-seven seconds to score the series' first goal, and six minutes after that Gary Suter made it 2–0. Calgary won the game 4–1 and had now outscored Edmonton 14–4 in their last two meetings. Confidence? You bet. Edmonton, meanwhile, was nervous, and if you weren't sure about that, their lineup changes for Game 2 were the greatest tell.

Into the lineup went Lumley, who had played just once in the past six weeks, and out came McSorley. In went veteran defenceman Don Jackson, out came rookie Steve Smith. The more defensive-minded Raimo Summanen replaced Esa Tikkanen. Johnson, it seemed, had Sather on the run just sixty minutes into the series.

But Calgary had its own problems. Mike Vernon was injured in Game 1, Reggie Lemelin lost Game 2 in overtime, 6–5. Lemelin was a good goalie, but Edmonton was his nemesis. He just couldn't keep them under five. Still, the Flames had scored first again and led the game 4–2 after forty minutes, and as Calgary made its way south for Game 3 the Flames' level of confidence had never been this high. Not only had they scored nine goals in Edmonton, they had limited Wayne Gretzky to two measly assists — one each night.

"You started playing, and you'd get in those moments in the game, and you weren't panicking," Colin Patterson said. "All of the sudden we could feel ourselves not panicking in situations where we'd have been a little tense [in the past]. Now we're starting to get that feeling, 'Yeah, this *is* the year we can do it.'"

Remember, Edmonton had gone through all of those lessons in losing. The Oilers were more battle-hardened than Calgary, after being upset by Los Angeles in the Miracle on Manchester in 1982, losing to the Islanders in 1981 and again in the 1983 Stanley Cup final. Then Edmonton had gone ahead and won two Stanley Cups, while Calgary had never made it out of the Smythe Division since Johnson took the reins in 1982.

So in the evolution of the two franchises, Edmonton was far ahead of the Flames in the spring of 1986 when it came to staring down adversity with their season on the line. Now Calgary was banging on the cell door, and the hand that held the keys was beginning to shake. Calgary won Game 3 at home on a Joel Otto goal, 3–2. Then Edmonton punched back on a Gretzky hat trick and five-point night in a 7–4 win.

Calgary came up to Edmonton and handled the Oilers 4–1 in Game 5. It was their third lead of the series, and now it wasn't just the Flames who believed. It seemed like the entire city of Calgary was on the bandwagon when the Flames landed back home that Saturday night.

"It was eleven-thirty, twelve o'clock. The airport's jammed," said Otto. "They're screamin', high-fivin' us all the way through the terminal. We don't get home for a couple more hours because the parkade is so packed we can't get out. And that was only Game 5! We hadn't even won the series. I'm in my second year, going, 'Oh my God . . .' That was my baptism into this rivalry."

Of course, the quotes coming out of Calgary on that off day were staid. A quiet confidence pervaded the Flames dressing room, having won two of three at Northlands, their only loss coming in overtime. "We haven't won anything yet," said Jim Peplinski. "We've gained a little respectability, but we're not anywhere yet. We're still trying to get there."

The biggest shot in the Flames' collective arm was their newfound ability to get pucks past Grant Fuhr. This was brand new in the Battle—Fuhr entered the series with a 16–1–4 regular-season record versus Calgary—and couldn't have possibly had anything to do with those two practice goalies, Al Hryniuk and Jamie Bowman. Could it?

The Flames were silently convinced that they had discovered the long-sought-after formula, and to a player they were ready to put the hammer down Monday night at the Olympic Saddledome. However, any writer worth his notebook knew that the best practice day quote that Sunday would be found in Edmonton.

"I don't think I'm speaking out of line when I say, if we don't win, there will be changes made on this team next year," said Wayne Gretzky that day. "Not only are we playing for the Stanley Cup this year, but for our lives and jobs next season. We'd better win, it's as simple as that."

Okay, so Gretzky wasn't fooling anybody. He wasn't really playing for his job. But his message was, "Nobody here should feel safe." Even if, coming off two Stanley Cups, there were clearly ten or eleven guys who weren't going anywhere.

Among those players, however, there had been little production thus far in the series. Jari Kurri had scored sixty-eight goals that season, but under boa constrictor–like checking from Colin Patterson, Kurri had one goal on just thirteen shots through five games. Mark Messier hadn't scored yet. Nor had Paul Coffey. Fuhr wasn't playing as well as he needed to play to beat the new and improved Flames.

The Seven Point Plan was unfolding like a flawless map to the top of Bob Johnson's mountain. The Flames, for the first time in the Battle of Alberta, were better.

"Maybe we caught Edmonton off guard in Game 1," allowed Otto. "And then Edmonton won Game 2, and maybe kind of got comfortable again, and we won Game 3. They won again in Game 4, and maybe they got comfortable again in Game 5.

"But we knew, 'We can get these guys.' We started to believe in ourselves. We weren't there 100 percent skill-wise, for sure. But we were strong enough to match them in a bunch of areas. We could play with them."

The mystique crumbled that spring, and the regular-season results over the remainder of the Battle of Alberta's pertinent years proves it. The next time Edmonton would win a season series over Calgary was 1996–97, long after the air had been let out of this rivalry. Edmonton surrendered the one intangible that had been most valuable that spring; the singular element that Johnson had coached, and coached, and coached to try to eliminate. It was the aura. The belief that Edmonton was just too good for Calgary to defeat. All that flashy skill, that dominant toughness, the superior goaltending, and the winning depth that made Edmonton the big brother in this rivalry disappeared that April.

"Badger was ahead of his time," Otto said. "He went over stuff I'd never seen before. Locking wings. Understanding that the Oilers would come up their right side because they had Coffey and all these left-handed shots. He was on top of a lot of stuff we tried to expose against Gretzky's line . . .

"It was a great series, a physical series, and we got a break."

"We got sloppy," Kevin Lowe admits, looking back. "We were a little more selfish in our play and less committed to the overall team game. That was the difference. Their tenacity was getting to us. We weren't as disciplined in reacting to it, and we weren't able to play with the lead enough to really get our swagger going.

"They had closed the gap," Lowe revealed, "and we needed to be even more disciplined than we ever had been. We weren't in that series."

Before the puck dropped on Game 6, scalpers outside the Saddledome were getting $500 per ticket, big money in the pre–StubHub days of 1986. A homemade sign behind Mike Vernon's net read "Champagne for the Flames, Whine for the Oilers." In Calgary they were fixated simply on beating Edmonton, while the *Edmonton Journal* headline belied a bigger picture concern up north: "Oilers' Cup Crown on Line."

With back-to-back Cups at stake, it wasn't as much about being the best in Alberta. In Edmonton, it was about being the best—period.

The visitors came out on fire in Game 6, outshooting Calgary 14–3 in the first period. But Vernon, who was enjoying his coming-out party as a legitimate NHL No. 1, kept the game scoreless. Then, in a 1:22 span of the second period, goals by Joe Mullen and John Tonelli gave Calgary a 2–0 lead. It was then, however, that Fuhr's legend held true. The Flames peppered him with chances, yet he simply refused to allow that third goal—that next goal that would have made the deficit insurmountable. If there is one thing they all say about Fuhr in his retirement, it is that he always knew when to slam the door, as he did that night in Calgary.

Esa Tikkanen, like he would five years later in the last, and perhaps greatest, Battle of Alberta, slipped an awkward goal in behind Vernon to give Edmonton a spark. Messier followed up, checking in with a short-handed goal, and the Oilers were in business, tied at two after two.

On his locker room stall that night, Gretzky had taped up a picture of his mom, Phyllis, with her arm around him as he clutched a bottle of champagne after a Cup victory. Why? Why not? His mom and Stanley each had a piece of No. 99's heart, and he came out flying in that third period, bent on ensuring Johnson's prophesy of a longer series.

Gretzky set up Anderson on the power play, then Mike Krushelnyski for an empty netter. Craig MacTavish ripped a late one home for a resounding 5–2 win, and the series would head back to Northlands, where Edmonton usually won. There we would have a Game 7, which the hockey world fully expected Edmonton to win.

How would the Oilers approach Game 7? "Scared to death, I hope," Gretzky said back then. "The fact we came back from down 3–2," Lowe remembers, "we were really confident. 'We're on home ice. We're going to win.' I would think, maybe we were overconfident."

The Flames, meanwhile, would travel north without centre Carey Wilson, who had to have his spleen removed after Game 6. Bleated general manager Cliff Fletcher, "It was a direct result of him being skewered [by Steve Smith]!"

It was a style of bygone days, to be sure, as no edition of the Battle was complete without a couple of honest spears. "There were a lot of other spears in that game," Johnson told the travelling press. "They speared more than we did."

The Flames showed the video of the Smith spear that would leave Wilson holed up at the Holy Cross Hospital, and the printed response was, "It didn't look that vicious." It was simply the way hockey was played back then, and with the Flames pushing the Oilers to the brink, it was expected that the level of violence would run concurrent with the level of desperation. Later, we would discover it was a Charlie Huddy crosscheck that cost Wilson his spleen, not Smith's spear. There was so much more stickwork in those days, who really could tell which infraction was responsible for the removal of which organ?

Game 7 would be, looking back over all the games played between these two rivals, the single most memorable of them all. It was played under a fog of nervousness in Edmonton, with Hakan Loob scoring the lone first-period goal and Peplinski adding another early in the second period. As they had the entire series, the Flames were calling the tune in Game 7.

Edmonton got equalizing goals from Anderson, now shifted up to play next to Gretzky and Messier, who had spent the last two games with Kurri on his right side. That's how messed up the

Oilers were, courtesy of Johnson and the Flames. Sather had split up the two most dominant forward duos in the NHL because somehow that was supposed to help the Oilers beat Calgary.

It did not.

Just past five minutes into the third period Perry Berezan dumped a puck into the Oilers zone and went for a change. Smith pulled up behind the Oilers net, gathering up a puck left for him by Grant Fuhr. The Oilers defenceman took one stride to his left and rifled a pass back through the empty slot aimed at Krushelnyski, who was touring up along the right-side boards.

The puck never made it to Krushelnyski. In fact, it never made it through the Oilers crease, catching the back of Fuhr's skate and ricocheting into the Edmonton goal. The Oilers had three-quarters of a period to right that error, and they could not. In the end, the shots were 6–6 in that final frame, and with just a few ticks left on the clock, one final faceoff in Calgary's zone lay between the Flames and the top of their mountain.

"I still remember the faceoff, to the left of Vernon, with about four or five seconds left," said Maher. "They dropped the puck, and Kurri's shot went just wide . . . That's when I yelled out, ' 'Yeah, baby!' for the first time. 'The Flames have climbed the mountain!'"

"They'd caught up," said Maher's counterpart, Edmonton radio man Rod Phillips. "Smitty's goal is what people remember most from that series, but the Oilers had a lot of opportunities to win that hockey game and they didn't. The last shot of the game, Jari had a chance to tie it up and he missed by that much. The clock ran down, Calgary won the series, and I think they deserved to win. They played better than the Oilers in that series."

Said Lowe, "It just seemed we didn't have it. You know? We didn't have it. We didn't have the horsepower, the next gear we'd always had against them previously."

The celebration at Northlands was one of those visitors' parties where you could hear the whoops and hollers of the thirty-man Flames contingent above the silent disbelief of 17,498 patrons. It was no different than when Calgary would win the 1989 Cup at the Montreal Forum or Edmonton's celebration in 1990 at the old Boston Garden.

Inside the CBC's mobile unit, however, another battle was being fought, this time between John Shannon and his superiors in Toronto. It was a time when the sanctity of *The National* news program took precedence over the revenue-generating *Hockey Night in Canada*. CBC, in the same wisdom that would have host Dave Hodge tossing a pencil in the air a year later (they left an overtime game for the news that night), wanted Shannon to get off the air so the news could start on time.

"We had a rule at that time at the CBC, where you had to be off the air four minutes after a game," said Shannon. "Well, the Flames win, and the celebration on the ice alone is three minutes. You had commercials to run, the network is demanding that I get off the air, and I'm saying, 'I'm not going off the air until we get a Flames interview, an Oilers interview, and the handshakes.'"

Shannon had watched the Battle from the time he started producing games as a twenty-three-year-old in 1979, when Edmonton emerged from the World Hockey Association. He was a kid from the Okanagan who had not been touched by the Toronto bug, despite his employer's leanings. So on the most historic night of the Battle of Alberta, Shannon put his job on the line for the sake of the story—as any good journalist would (or should) do.

"We got Lanny right after the game, and he was bawling," he recalled. "Then I got suspended for the next two games. At the end of the playoffs that year I was relieved of my duties. Because they 'couldn't control me.' I was right, to this day.

"Give me better television than that."

When Shannon finally relinquished control of the airwaves, CBC switched Alberta viewers to the all-important alternative to the Battle of Alberta. An episode of *Star Trek*.

While Shannon was having a good day, anyone associated with the Oilers was watching their dynasty crumble. Remember, this was the day of the true dynasty. The Montreal Canadiens had won four straight Stanley Cups from 1975–79. Then the Islanders took over, winning the next four. Now Edmonton had the baton, and they'd just watched their two-year run come crashing to a halt.

"I threw up in a garbage can after the game. I was so sick, so wrapped up, so sick to my stomach," said equipment man Barrie Stafford. "Losing to Calgary, of all teams. It was devastating."

"I'm not sure that our psyche was as strong as Calgary's in that series, at that point in the series," Gretzky said. "You looked at the paper, and you'd finished eighteen or twenty points ahead in the regular season [actually thirty]. All of the sudden you're in a Game 7, and you're thinking, 'How can this be?' Well, Calgary was simply a better team than the regular season indicated. They had a better coach than the regular season indicated.

"Maybe, after two straight Stanley Cups, going into that third period of Game 7, maybe we didn't have the same hunger or fight that they did. It's not to say we didn't want to win. But maybe their fight was a little bit harder, their energy a little bit higher than ours was in the third period of Game 7. That's all it took."

The story had ended the same way for so many years, on so many nights. The Big Break had always fallen north of Red Deer, whether that break was being the first to get a new rink in 1974, thanks to money from the Commonwealth Games, landing Gretzky, or drafting a raft of Hall of Fame players while Calgary built in the same incremental fashion as all the other teams. Edmonton always got the Big Break.

On this Wednesday night, April 30, 1986, when Steve Smith went back to retrieve that puck, and Grant Fuhr nonchalantly retook his position in the Oilers crease, the Hockey Gods smiled on Calgary. Maybe for the first time ever in the Battle.

"Preparation," Otto said. "All of the sudden we got put in a position [to succeed]. Guys were blockin' shots, doing whatever it took. Could have been the Hockey Gods. I don't know."

Smith would become the scapegoat, but not a single player or management type I've ever spoken to who was involved in this series has ever subscribed to that theory. Stafford summed it up best: "I see that picture of him on his knees, by the net, and it put chills on my back now. How devastated that poor guy was, and how bad he felt about letting the entire organization down. We still had time to win. We could have come back.

"But in the tradition of a great franchise and great players, Steve Smith faced the music. He took responsibility, he stood in front of the media. He took the heat."

I was still working for the University of Alberta's newspaper, *The Gateway*, that spring, and thanks to the generosity of Oilers PR director Bill Tuele I had been accredited with a pass for the entire playoffs. I was in the Oilers room that night the moment the door was opened and I witnessed Smith's fate. The Calgary room, much smaller and immeasurably more jubilant, was another scene I will never forget.

By the time I made my way down there, the interviews were well underway. The visiting team's room is always more cramped than the home team's room, and there was a table in the middle, further limiting the room to manouevre. Two things I remember: Cliff Fletcher, finding me blocking his way as he roamed the room, put both arms around me from behind and steered me to the side of his path with a huge smile and a bear hug. He did not have a clue who I was at that time.

And Jamie Macoun. By the time I arrived in the Flames room, the real newspaper reporters from the *Calgary Herald* and *Sun*, and the sidebar guys from the two Edmonton papers, had worked the room pretty hard. I was catching up, and with no real deadline the next day, I'll admit it, I was really just in there for my own personal experience. I saw Macoun sitting in his stall, with faraway eyes, looking like a man who couldn't even hear the din that was going on all around him. He was lost in thought, in the realization that he was sitting there at that moment. In Edmonton. A winner.

I approached him for an interview, and he very politely said, "Would you mind if I just enjoyed this for a moment?"

I let him be.

One thing I did not see that night, nor have I ever witnessed in all the playoff series I have since covered, was something that has been obscured by history: an unheard-of visit into the Flames room by Oilers owner Peter Pocklington and coach Glen Sather.

"Slats and Pocklington walked into the Flames dressing room after Game 7, and the place went as silent as a grave," said *Calgary Herald* scribe George Johnson. "It was like, 'What are *you two* doing in *here?*' But you know what? That was real classy. All this Slats's arrogance, with the smirk and everything. He came into the other army's bunker, and who does he bring with him? Pocklington! We're doing the interviews, and we all stopped mid-sentence. I thought I was hallucinating.

"It kind of humanized the Battle. Because before that, Sather was this ogre who had been kicking their rump all the livelong day. And he went in and said, 'Congratulations. You guys deserved this.' To have the two of them walk in there, with all the bad blood built up between those two organizations, was really something."

"They were very polite," confirmed Fletcher. "They came in and shook hands with us, congratulated us for winning the series. Both of them."

Truly, this was Upside-Down Land for the Flames. Everything they'd known about the Battle had changed, and every emotion they'd felt when playing Edmonton in big games was now completely opposite. From the feeling in the post-game dressing room, to walking out the bay doors to the waiting bus on the ramp, the Alberta spring night was a breath of fresh air after a sweaty, steamy dressing room.

"I remember so many games, walking out of Northlands and having lost 7–0. Six to one," Maher said. "That's what I remember about that night, leaving Northlands in 1986, thinking, 'How many times have we walked out of this building having lost by an overwhelming score? Tonight we're walking out of here, and we're on top of the world.'"

Of course, there was the little matter of a Campbell Conference final to be played, with Game 1 against the St. Louis Blues scheduled for the night after next. That's right—one off day to enjoy the greatest victory of many of these players' NHL careers thus far—and then they strapped their gear back on and faced the Norris Division champs from St. Louis.

Sadly for the Flames, there would be no memory created that spring that would surpass April 30 in Edmonton, even though they eked out a seven-game win over St. Louis and finally brought the Flaming C to a Stanley Cup final against Montreal.

"We had finally built a team that could beat the Oilers, and we thought we were finally able to win a Stanley Cup," Murdoch said. "But the Stanley Cup was almost secondary to getting through the Oilers. We'd already won our Stanley Cup. When we went on to play the St. Louis Blues, we should have finished those guys off in four games. Montreal had finished [the New York Rangers] off in five games, and they were waiting for us.

"We beat Montreal the first game, then we lost in overtime the second game. After that, you could have taken a cattle prod and you couldn't reach our guys. Our guys were so goddamned exhausted, so mentally and emotionally spent, they had nothing left. They'd left it in Edmonton."

Speaking of leaving Edmonton, that's exactly what the Oilers players did. You've heard of getting out of Dodge? Well, Lowe and Coffey were on a plane to Phoenix the next day, bruises and all. They'd heal up in the Arizona sun—anywhere to get away from what had transpired against the Flames.

"I went into hiding. Didn't want to be seen anywhere," Lowe said. "Not that I felt shame, I just didn't want to talk about it. Got to Phoenix as fast as possible. It was as if the season was over for everybody because it was over for us.

"You would get out of town, put two or three weeks between the loss and the next time you've got to face someone, you know?"

What do two guys do when they're alone in Phoenix, tired, worn down, and looking to avoid running into anyone who may know them?

"We were in the back of a bar shooting pool, no one else was there. The TV was on, and the Flames game came on," Lowe said. "I couldn't . . . None of us could bear to watch hockey—and even more so if it was the Flames playing. And I suspect they felt the same way about us.

"Coff went over to the TV, and he pulled the plug."

9

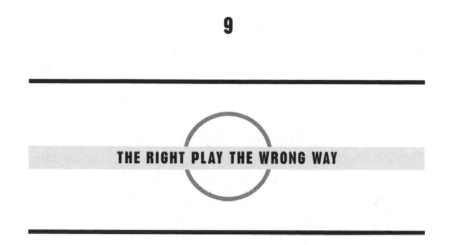

THE RIGHT PLAY THE WRONG WAY

Oiler Steve Smith's Unforgettable Goal

"It was human error. I guess I've just got to live with it."

"I got good wood on it," Oiler Steve Smith said moments after that fateful Game 7 that he would wear like a tattoo for the rest of his playing days. "I thought the puck went in fast."

Not an hour removed from what remains today the worst experience of his life, Smith was having a laugh at his own misfortune. Why not? A young defenceman's first playoff run isn't supposed to end that way, but on a team full of future Hall of Famers, Steve Smith—born on April 30, 1963, twenty-three years to the day before his errant breakout pass snapped Edmonton's run of Stanley Cups—was never supposed to play a leading role in the Battle. He hadn't ever dreamed that he might one day become a chapter in the book, and really, Smith never was the kind of guy whose game was meant to stand out.

Smith was the personification of why the Oilers and the Flames managed to stay on top for an entire decade: another mobile six-foot-three defenceman who could fight and play coming out of an Edmonton farm system that—as barren as it has been in the 2000s—simply belched talent in the early 1980s. He had arrived on the scene after a couple of years seasoning in the American League, a gangly, twenty-two-year-old defenceman who took nothing for granted. He wasn't good enough to feel any entitlement as he walked into the dressing room of a team coming off back-to-back Stanley Cups in 1984 and 1985.

"I felt there was an opportunity, but my road to junior and the NHL wasn't an easy one," Smith said. "It wasn't like I was a highly touted [prospect]. I was the last guy to make my junior team. I was never drafted in junior."

Smith was born in Glasgow, Scotland. He was two and a half years old when he and his parents packed up and came over the pond, typically with not much more than what was on their backs and in their pockets. They settled in Cobourg, Ontario, a blue-collar town that lies an hour and a bit up the 401 from Toronto, along the shores of Lake Ontario.

The Smiths settled into some rich Ontario Hockey League country, with Oshawa, Peterborough, and Belleville each within an hour's drive. But Rae Smith had to find work before his boy Steve—and the two brothers who would soon arrive—would play any hockey.

"My father came over, and on my birth certificate it still states that he was a 'lorry driver.' A lorry driver is a truck driver. Says it on the bottom of my British birth certificate," Smith chuckles. Rae Smith only drove truck for a short while, though, before finding himself working at a juvenile home in Cobourg known as the Brookside Training School. "He was responsible for juvenile delinquent kids who needed counselling. It was a social-work type thing, for kids who had been in trouble with the law."

You can imagine that the Smith boys stayed on the straight and narrow. Or at least young Steven kept his disobedience to the hockey rink, where he was good enough to get an invite to the London Knights camp. As he said, he wasn't drafted, and that first season, even on a team that would post a medio-cre 20–48–0 record, head coach Paul McIntosh wasn't sure about the Smith kid from Cobourg.

"My first year, everyone else was put into billet homes early on. I remained in a Motel 6 until just before Christmas, before they finally got me off Cheeseburger Row and moved me in with a family," said Smith. He was doing anything he could to stay with the Knights, playing right wing on a line with Basil McRae and Dave Simpson, the older brother of Smith's future teammate in Edmonton and current Rogers hockey analyst, Craig Simpson.

There are some players who arrive in junior knowing that the NHL lies in their future. There are a lot more, however, who secretly can't believe they've made a major junior roster and do not even dare to dream of a lucrative career in the professional game. For those players, there is often a moment—a singular accomplishment or occurrence—when they realize, "Wait a second here. I might actually be good enough to do this."

Was there an "aha! moment" for Smith?

"I've gotta tell you, I'm not sure there was one. Not early on in junior," he said. "I remember my first training camp in London, [marvelling] that I would ever have an opportunity to play at this high pace. That quickly changed in my second year of junior. I went back with a lot more confidence."

Only fifteen players from Smith's 1981 NHL draft class would go on to play more games than the 804 logged by that lorry driver's son from Cobourg. None would retire with more Stanley Cup rings than Smith's three. But back then he was a nobody. As Dale Hawerchuk went first overall to Winnipeg, Steve Smith wasn't even the first Steve Smith to have his name called at the draft. Philadelphia picked a defenceman with the same name at sixteenth overall, out of the Sault Ste. Marie Greyhounds. He would go on to play a grand total of eighteen games.

"It's amazing," Smith said now, looking back at how the cards fell. He didn't get drafted until the sixth round, 111th overall — right between Jim McGeough (Washington) and Rod Buskas (Pittsburgh) — the eagle eye of Edmonton Oilers head scout Barry Fraser still in its very prime. What seems obvious today, however, was never quite so noticeable when Smith was plugging up and down the right wing on his way to a sixteen-point season in his first year of junior, his draft year. He hadn't played in the Ontario Hockey League as a sixteen-year-old, like so many others.

"I think, in all honesty, that's what gave me my chance. Just knowing how hard I had to work every game. Knowing that I was afraid for my job every day made me a better player, a better person," Smith reckons. "It made me drive harder for an end goal, which eventually became the goal of making the NHL. Knowing how hard I had to work to stay [in London] was a key component."

The Knights were a middle-of-the-road club, but getting drafted took Smith to the next level: the Moncton Alpines, another collection of less than notable hockey hopefuls. Except for one, who would later be immortalized in the movie *Slap Shot*.

Bill (Goldie) Goldthorpe was one tough bastard, a surly left winger out of Thunder Bay, Ontario, with minimal skills but tougher than a five-dollar steak. He played for ten minor-league teams and another four in the old WHA. While Smith was a young, impressionable, up-and-coming player with a chance, the man who would be characterized as Ogie Ogilthorpe in the 1977 classic movie *Slap Shot* would play one final game with

Moncton that season. It was a game that Smith will never forget.

"We were in Halifax, back when John Brophy was coaching Halifax. He had all these tough guys on his team, and I remember Goldthorpe saying to me before the anthem, 'Hey, kid, watch this.' He got off our bench, skated down the boards to the other bench, and I see him literally pointing at each one of their players as he's going along. Boom, boom, boom—right out of the *Slap Shot* movie.

"He comes back to our bench and he says, 'Now, watch this.' Maybe ten seconds before the anthem ends, every one of their guys sits down," Smith remembers. "I say, 'What's that?' And he says, 'I told 'em it was my last game, and whoever was the last guy standing up? That was gonna be my guy.'"

While Smith was percolating on the farm, the big team was winning Stanley Cups in Edmonton. His rookie NHL season was the 1985–86 campaign, and it was a blur. Smith played fifty-five games, mostly on the five–six pairing with Randy Gregg, scoring twenty-four points and collecting 166 penalty minutes. He was plus-thirty, as good or better than every other defenceman except for Lee Fogolin and Paul Coffey, who was an amazing plus-sixty-one.

The Oilers rolled that season, going 56–17–7 to win their second Presidents' Trophy. They stomped Vancouver in the Smythe Division semifinal, winning in three straight games with an aggregate score of 17–5.

After having beaten Calgary in five games in 1983, and seven games in 1984, the 1986 Smythe Division final was, in a way, an odd place for Smith to find himself. Everyone else had so much invested in the Battle, but Smith was more concerned with his own standing. He didn't even have any promises that he'd be in Glen Sather's lineup every night—he would dress for just six of Edmonton's ten playoff games that spring.

Smith's hockey intuition told him, however, that something wasn't necessarily right. This team had won games for fun all season long, but even before Game 1 at Northlands Coliseum that April, he could sense that something had changed.

"I'll always remember that feeling," he said. "We always felt like we were going to win games, but I remember going into that series with Calgary thinking, 'This is really a solid team. This is a team that could beat us.' They were really, really well coached. They were in the right spots all of the time. They were taking away, being physical against our top players, and we were taking penalties against the Baxters and Sheehys of the world. And they were scoring on the power play. They had a wonderful power play.

"They had all the components to win games, so there was always a feeling they could beat us. They were a fast-moving team, they moved the puck really well, they were a physical team, they were an intimidating team . . . And, of course, the emotions of the Battle of Alberta just tightened everything up."

Fast-forward to Game 7. Smith had been in and out of the lineup, but he'd been practising with the team every day and was around the dressing room on game nights whether or not he was dressing. Even a rookie could sniff the air and know there was a whiff of something new in the Oilers' room. Something he'd not smelled before in there.

In hindsight, what Smith likely smelled was fear.

"Overall, there was a real uneasiness about the team," he said. "It was almost beyond being a quiet confidence about that team when I arrived in Edmonton. They had won a couple of championships . . . and there was a confidence—nor arrogance, for sure—but a confidence that was around that squad. And it seemed like that confidence wasn't there as we went through that series. It was like, 'Wow, these guys are better than we

Glenn Anderson and Mark Messier celebrate one of Andy's 498 career goals. "The hardest things to beat," said Anderson. "The heart, the mind, and the soul."

Glenn Anderson on a fly-by through the slot, with Al MacInnis. "As the Dalai Lama said, 'Never lose the lesson from a loss.'" —Anderson

"It's a great day for hockey" was Badger Bob Johnson's motto.

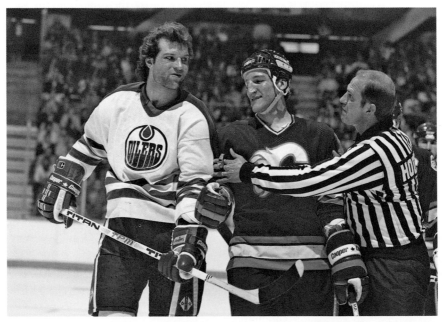

Dave Semenko and Tim Hunter discuss the weather as linesman Bob Hodges adjudicates. "I hated every single guy on the Oilers, 'cause they all hated me. It wasn't about having a relationship with anyone from the Edmonton Oilers. It was about The Battle." —Hunter

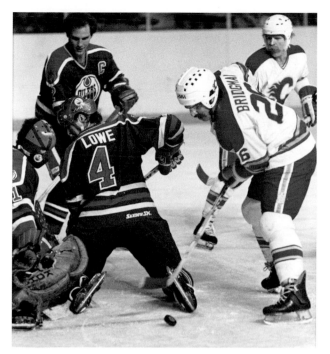

The men in this picture—from left: Mel Bridgman, Kevin Lowe, Grant Fuhr, Lanny McDonald, Lee Fogolin—played a combined 5,134 NHL games.

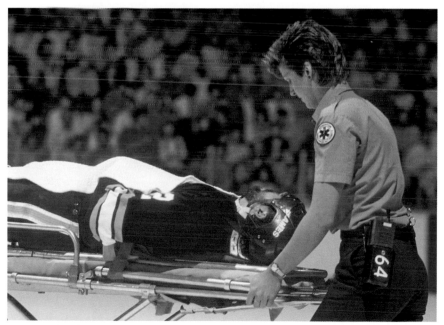

Mike Bullard leaves on a gurney after being speared by Marty McSorley in 1988. "Nothing like being in the wrong place at the wrong time," Bullard would say later.

Always more fun to score against Edmonton. Gary Suter, Tim Hunter, and Lanny McDonald silence the Northlands Coliseum patrons.

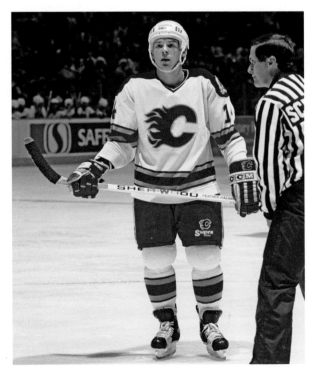

A young Theoren Fleury looks so innocent. "In order to get room out there, I had to become this f— hatchet man. And I had no problem f— cutting your eye out. Wouldn't have bothered me a bit." —Fleury

"I knew how big this Edmonton–Calgary rivalry was," Fleury said. "And I knew that if I played real well against the Oilers it would go a long way to me making the Flames as a regular. From that moment on, I played some of my best hockey against the Oilers."

Doug Gilmour was one of three Calgary players acquired by GM Cliff Fletcher who would be enshrined in the Hockey Hall of Fame. Joe Mullen and Lanny McDonald were the others.

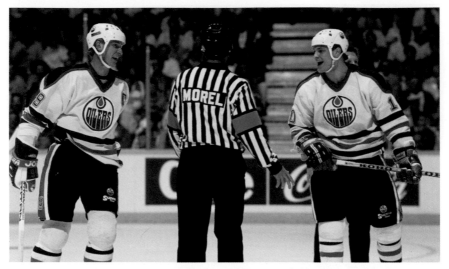

"Wayne understood our job very well. He always worked with us. The mutual respect between him and I was perfect." —Referee Denis Morel

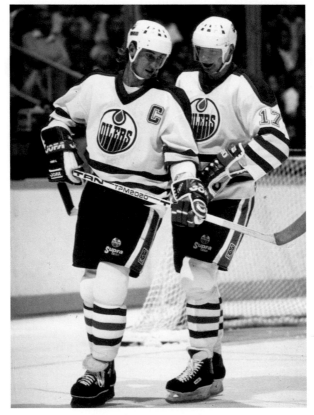

"He and Jari Kurri . . . they were lethal. A match made in heaven." —Flames winger Colin Patterson

This photo, taken shortly after the 1988 Stanley Cup, marks the last time Gretzky donned an Oilers uniform. He would be traded to Los Angeles on August 9, 1988.

Gretzky and Coffey in 1985. Edmonton went 16–3 that spring, and 10–0 at Northlands.

The only two members of the 800 Goal Club: Wayne (894) and Gordie (801).

"I was never knocked out. I was never knocked down and couldn't get up. I came out relatively unscathed, and I was probably the guy who fought the most against the Edmonton Oilers." —Tim Hunter

thought. These guys are good players. They've caught us a little bit off guard.'

"They were a very, very disciplined hockey team, and we just didn't have the answers."

The score was 2–2 after forty minutes. In Game 7, with less than twenty minutes to play, everybody is thinking the same way: don't make a crucial mistake because one more goal will probably be enough to get a team to the finish line.

That's what Calgary's Perry Berezan, an Edmonton native playing for the Flames, was thinking when he gained centre ice and dumped the puck into the Edmonton zone before turning and getting off the ice. The puck took a path along the boards, sliding slowly around the corner and settling on to the stick of Grant Fuhr, who had hustled behind his net to set the puck up for his defenceman.

Smith was that defenceman, and in that very situation—with the Flames changing on the fly at their bench up the left-wing boards—the Oilers had installed a quick breakout into their scheme that called for the defenceman to look up the right-wing boards for a long pass.

"You just went back and you almost didn't look," said defence man Kevin Lowe. "You just forced it up to the spot." The centre-man and whoever was available were expected to be near where the blue line meets the boards, across the ice from the changing Flames. Maybe even as high as the penalty box doors. A long pass would spring them, and the changing Flames players had eighty feet of ice to travel to get to the puck carrier.

"Fuhrsie was a little lazy getting back in the net, and Smitty just tried to cut the corner a bit," Lowe said. "He was firing it to that [far] blue line. That's how he hit Fuhrsie in the back of the foot. Grant was kind of meandering back to the net, and Smitty was trying to be quick . . . on that quick-up play."

The late Don Wittman, the CBC's Western-based play-by-play man whose voice provides the soundtrack for so many moments in this rivalry, was caught in mid-story, talking about how Mike Vernon and Fuhr weren't afraid to leave their crease to challenge the shoo—

"Oh! They scored!" he blurted. "Oh! Steve Smith! In attempting to get it out of his own zone, *put it into his own net!*"

It was a surreal moment at Northlands that those of us who were there will never forget. Wittman, as always, was right on the play. But so many people in the rink that night had used the Berezan dump-in to take a breath, to grab a couple of seconds in a game so tense you could have parcelled the collective worry and angst and sold it in loaves.

The people in the end of the building behind Fuhr could see the puck in the net. The folks at the other end could see the red light, but most didn't have a clue why it would be on at this point. On Writers Row up in the press box, there was a cacophony of noise, metal chair legs scraping on concrete as the scribes pushed their chairs back, stood up, and gathered under the televisions that hung every twenty feet or so.

The video showed Smith in a moment you wouldn't wish on anyone: a young player who, with a flick of his wrists, had stepped into ignominy. He'd only just arrived, and in a blink of an eye he was infamous. A pass that couldn't be recalled, a play never to be taken back.

Alas, Smith saw exactly what happened in real time. And as 17,498 patrons, in the days before there was even a video replay screen above the ice in Edmonton, looked for some explanation of what had just occurred, Smith took his first dejected stride toward the Oilers bench. He would not take a second one, his legs simply folding underneath him in disbelief, dejection, and embarrassment.

"At the time it was devastating," he says now.

I can honestly say that in a quarter-century of covering the NHL I have never seen a man fall to the ice as Smith did that night, burying his head in his hands. After the final buzzer sounded? Sure. We've all seen that many times. But with fourteen minutes and forty-six seconds to play in a 3–2 game?

Smith rose to his knees, and the merciless camera of the CBC focused on his face. Was he crying yet? If not, he soon would be. There would be more tears later on in the handshake line, and in the post-game dressing room.

Happy birthday.

Today, Smith takes full responsibility for the play. Doesn't duck his fault in the goal for a moment. But as Lowe points out, he didn't make the wrong play. He made the right play the wrong way.

"The play that I made was a play we were working on as a team. Get the puck, and they were forechecking real hard so we were trying to get the puck up as quickly as possible," he explains. "I remember thinking afterwards, 'What was I doing? Why would I do that? Would I do it again?' And that was something we were working on: quick-ups. I take ownership of what I did, but it was something we were trying to do to alleviate some of the fore-check pressure Calgary was bringing at us.

"I went back for the puck, and as I went back for it I knew I was being forechecked pretty quickly. I think it was Mike Krushelnyski I saw heading toward the penalty box. I turned, pulling the puck back away from the net toward the bench side, and went to force a seam pass across the ice.

"At that point in time, you're looking at your receiver. You're not looking at where the puck is or whether it's on your stick or not. You're looking up-ice. Obviously I didn't see Grant or his leg. It went off of him.

"If I look back on my career and ask, 'Did I make a lot of bone-head plays in my career?' Well, everybody does. Everybody makes mistakes; everybody does things that they would take back. That was a natural play for a defenceman: take the puck, get yourself a stride away from the net, and get the puck up-ice. It was a common occurrence in the game. It was a catastrophic result. But it wasn't [a mistake borne] from thinking the game incorrectly. It was just the result that made it a memorable play.

"If that's in the middle of December, nobody remembers that."

There isn't a player on either team who'll tell you that it was Steve Smith's fault that Edmonton lost that game, or the series. On Calgary's side, they had worked for five years toward this victory. Bob Johnson's boys had climbed their mountain, and you'd better be ready for a fight if you were going to walk into that visiting team's dressing room and suggest it was all really a fluke, handed to them by a rookie defenceman.

"Whoever got a break was going to win it," Calgary assistant Bob Murdoch said matter-of-factly. "The puck went in, and it was a break for us. It was our day."

In Edmonton's room, they knew that no seven-game series was ever decided on a single play by a single player. And even if you did blame Smith, that 1985–86 Oilers team recorded the second-most goals ever scored in a season (426), second only to the 446 Edmonton scored in 1983–84. (Perspective: Chicago led the NHL in 2013–14 with 267 goals.)

The highest-powered offence in the history of the NHL still had most of fifteen minutes to score a goal after Smith's gaffe and it failed, offering up just six third-period shots in total.

The news cycle, however, does not rely on common sense or big-picture thinking. Steve Smith would be *the* story for the collective media when those dressing room doors opened that night in Edmonton and the media questioned him mercilessly.

Under Glen Sather, and aided heroically by long-time public relations director Bill Tuele, the Oilers had always taken media access—and the responsibility of players to speak to their fans through the media—extremely seriously. Ask any of the national newspapermen of the day, Al Strachan, Scott Morrison, Frank Orr, or Red Fisher, the Edmonton room was known industry-wide as a place a journalist could get good work done. You could sit and talk to players. Get to know them. Talk for ten minutes on the record, and another five or ten afterwards with the pen and notepad having been put away, a time when you learn things that truly help a writer paint the picture for the reader.

Had Steve Smith had his misfortune today, there are teams that would shield him from the media. Or, at least, try to. But not this team. It was not Edmonton's style.

First, though, they needed to find this twenty-three-year-old around whom history had turned. He wasn't in his stall taking his gear off like everyone else was that night.

"I went to look for Steve Smith," said equipment man Lyle (Sparky) Kulchisky. "He isn't in his stall. He isn't in the washroom. He isn't in the players' lounge. I can't find Steve Smith. We had an equipment room in behind the coaches' room. You had to go through the coaches' room to get to it. And Smitty was in there, devastated. Crying. I just wanted to say, 'Smitty, it's not the end of the world.'"

If it truly wasn't the end of the world, Steve Smith could see it from where he sat at that moment. When he emerged, both Randy Gregg, the picture of calm and maturity, and owner Peter Pocklington, for whom the loss of at least one more round of home gates (and likely two) meant losses of well over $1 million, instructed Smith to face the media.

"They looked at me and they said, 'Handle this right. Go out there, like a man, and talk to the press.' I made the decision that

I would go out into the locker room and take my lickin' then."

I was in the first wave of press that swarmed into the Edmonton dressing room as soon as Tuele gave the doorman the okay. I was a kid of twenty on a press pass for the University of Alberta newspaper, *The Gateway*. Because I did not have the same "buzzer beater" deadline responsibilities that the real newspapermen had, I got a jump down the stairwell to ice level. I didn't know much about the trade at that point, but I knew enough to realize that the story would be sitting in the stall belonging to Edmonton defenceman No. 5.

Several photographers had pushed to the front of the media pack, which was rare, as a still photographer seldom attended the post-game dressing room. When they ran down the corridor (never get in between a good shooter and his preferred photo position), they found Smith in his stall, awaiting them. Before the reporters could assemble to begin the interview process, the photographers mercilessly set upon him with their motor drives. *Click, click, click, click, click . . .*

As *Edmonton Journal* writer Ray Turchansky penned that night, "Steve Smith's stall in the Edmonton Oilers dressing room was no longer a comforting cubicle. It was a witness box."

"It was human error. I guess I've just got to live with it," Smith said that night before managing a faint smile in self-deprecation. "I got good wood on it. I thought the puck went in fast."

Today, Smith is comfortable in his own skin, a long and successful career behind him. He is an assistant coach for the Carolina Hurricanes as I write this, and still, when someone makes a real bonehead play, his phone will ring. Not as much now as before, though.

"One of the things you decide upon when you play this game, and I hate to use the cliché from *The Godfather*, but this is the business that we chose," he said. "If I didn't want to have the possibility of being exposed, this was the wrong business for me. I should have been an accountant. I should have been a doctor. Something behind closed doors where nobody knew what I was doing. I decided pro hockey was for me. It was the game I wanted to be part of, and I understood the risks that were involved."

He didn't play another shift after the 5:14 mark of the third period that night. Sather would likely have trusted the pre-goal Smith to play again, but the player he had seen on all fours on the ice, tears streaming down his face? This was no place for that person.

The play was a life-changer for Smith, as it would have been for anybody. Not everybody, however, would be able to say that the effects of that night have been almost entirely positive, as Smith can say. Like Stu Grimson, who told himself after that terrible beating by Dave Brown, "If that's the worst I can suffer, and if I can bounce back from that, then I've got nothing to fear," Smith has become a more compassionate soul since that day at Northlands.

"It taught me humility. I came into Edmonton as a brash young guy. It taught me to cheer for people," he said. "To expect—and want—good out of people as I moved forward in life. Never did I spend another minute cheering against someone, whether it was an opponent or not. I always wanted the best for everybody, and always felt that, if I was going to be part of a winning team, I wanted the other team to be at their best, and we were just going to be better that day.

"When you're young, you don't think that way. You just want to win at any cost. Certainly that's an admirable trait, but from that day forward I always had a sense of cheering for everyone. I never wanted anyone to have the day that I had that day. And that's something I have stuck to pretty closely for a long,

long time. I am a much more positive person now than ever."

How much courage does it take to relive a moment, a period of his life, that was as painful as this was? Smith generously spent forty-five minutes on the phone for the interview, baring his twenty-three-year-old self, then extrapolating those emotions on to the man he is today. It would have been so much easier just to bury the experience. Not to pick up the phone.

"It's something I'll always be remembered for," he said, "but it certainly doesn't define me as a player or as an individual. That, I can tell you for sure."

Most of his teammates will say that they've never spoken to Smith about "The Goal." In a professional dressing room, unearthing negative feelings or experiences is taboo. Digging at a wound is something you might do to an opponent, but never, ever to a teammate.

Did anyone ever reach out to Smith? Did he receive any counsel on how to deal with that experience?

"No," he said, after thinking for a while. "No, to tell you the truth. There was not, other than the support from my family. My father and I, my brothers and I, were very, very close."

His family was bitter toward an Edmonton media that was not nearly pragmatic enough in dispensing blame for a Stanley Cup reign that had been snapped. Smith, mature beyond his years, could have become bitter toward the media, like Philadelphia Phillies pitcher Steve Carlton or NHL goalie Tom Barrasso.

"I spent a lot of time trying to take that portion away from [his own psyche]," he said. "Guys were reporting what they were reporting. In my mind it was a different story, but that was irrelevant. It made me a more humble person, and quite frankly adversity, when dealt with correctly, certainly makes you a better person. It makes you a better player and makes you stronger as you go forward.

"Would I look back and say I wish it never happened? Absolutely. But that can't be changed, It doesn't define me. It was just part of my history."

We all know that part of Steve Smith's history. But I bet you didn't know of this little addendum to that goal in 1986:

After 1986, every visit to the Saddledome was like a string around Smith's finger, reminding him of that clearing pass that never cleared in '86. Every time Smith gathered a puck behind his goal, lifted his head, and looked up-ice, Flames fans would yell in unison: "Shooooot! Shooooot!" It had long since ceased to be funny, yet it was a tradition that Flames fans just felt compelled to uphold.

One day, several Septembers into his career, Smith rolled into Calgary for a preseason game, an established defenceman with more skill than you'd expect from a D-man with that much sandpaper. He'd heard it from Flames fans for long enough, and knew he'd be hearing "Shooooot!" again that night. So before the game he wandered over to goaltender Bill Ranford's dressing room stall. Smith had a plan.

"I said, we're going to have a power play at some point tonight, and I'm going to carry the puck up-ice. If no one is around me, I'm going to swing around at the blue line, I'm going to turn around, and I'm going to take a slapshot.

"Then I said, 'And you'd better fuckin' stop it.'"

And that's exactly what Steve Smith did. After all he'd been through, he did something you might never see in a lifetime of watching hockey.

"I came out of the zone, I turned around, and I fired it," he says, smiling at the memory. "I put my stick up to the fans and waved, and the whole place stood up and gave me a standing ovation. It was kinda cool. For the most part, they left me alone after that."

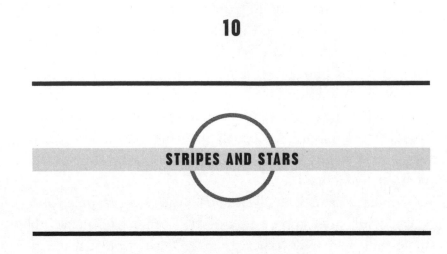

10

STRIPES AND STARS

Reffing the Battle of Alberta
"You couldn't give those games to a rookie.
You had to have a guy who had experience."

Kerry Fraser was across the ice at the old Chicago Stadium penalty box, leaning in to speak through that little bank-teller hole in the glass to inform the official timekeeper of his latest penalty call.

"The Oilers are getting spanked in Chicago, and with a couple of minutes to go Kevin Lowe, frustrated as hell, took a pole axe shot on a Blackhawks player. I gave him a penalty for slashing," Fraser recalls.

The clichés about a ref being blind, or needing glasses, always omit the fact that a good official exercises all of his senses when he's working a game. It is not only about what you see but also what you sense, what you feel, and, on this occasion, what Fraser heard. A rise in the Stadium crowd told him there was something going on behind him that required his attention, and so he spun around to see the Oilers amassing at the rear of their bench area, trying to get at a fan or fans seated on the other side of the glass.

"All the Oilers players, and Glen Sather, were standing up on the Oilers bench. The players all have their sticks raised, and they're clubbing at the glass, with a fan. And I'm thinking, Aw, ——!"

Referees are like cops. They'll hand out a ticket, or a minor penalty, with relative ease. It's about maintaining control of the situation, a tenet of both refereeing hockey and policing in general. But when you start talking match penalties and game misconducts, well, it's like the difference between a warning and taking a suspect in for booking.

The latter comes with a lot of paperwork, and really, these guys didn't get into the business to become secretaries.

"From my end, I just want to get this game over with, and I didn't want to have to write reports about players and coaches going after this fan. That's a lengthy process after a game, and we want to go for a beer," Fraser says. "So I skate over, I tug on Slats's pant leg, and I get his attention."

Fraser told him to rein in his players, and Sather did so immediately.

"He was like a symphony conductor. He raised his arms and had all his players sit down. Like an orchestra," marvelled Fraser. "I said, 'Glen, you want me to get security and get this fan out of here?' And he says to me, 'Naw, we're okay, Kerry. The guy said that the penalty you just gave Lowe was a horseshit call, but we stuck up for you.'"

★

There was a third team in the Battle of Alberta, and to them, the games were every bit as special as they were to the players.

For a Theoren Fleury or a Glenn Anderson, they would know they were going to play against their arch rival eight times a season, a couple or few times in the pre-season, and perhaps six or seven more times in a playoff series. For an official, however, it was completely different.

"When you received a game of that magnitude in your assignments," said Hall of Fame referee Bill McCreary, "you knew that you had the respect of your peers. And that [the head of officials] had enough confidence in you to handle one of those hockey games."

The temperature ran pretty hot in the Battle of Alberta, but it wasn't the only rivalry in the NHL. Boston–Montreal was good, or Habs–Nordiques. St. Louis–Chicago, Islanders–Rangers, or Rangers–Philadelphia—all were divisional foes in a much more violent time in the game, when stickwork was not only more prevalent but also, to a certain extent, within the rules.

The difference was, none of those other rivalries were producing a Stanley Cup finalist every year for eight years running like the Battle did. So, as the years passed, the pedigree of official required to work the games was upped as well.

The late John McCauley was the referee in chief for much of the 1980s, succeeded in 1989 by Bryan Lewis, who had come off the ice after a refereeing career that spanned from 1967 to 1986. It was back in the day of the one-referee system, and clearly not a place for a nervous person.

"You couldn't give those games to a rookie. You had to have a guy who had experience," said Lewis. "I used to call them 'the any referee.' Any game. Any time. Any place. Anywhere.

"He could do Philadelphia–Washington. He could do Philadelphia–New York Rangers. Chicago–Minnesota in those days. Chicago–St. Louis. And then you had Calgary and Edmonton."

Denis Morel was one of those "any refs," and he got the call in Montreal to come out west and work some of those games. He'd done his share of the Battle of Quebec during the season. How much tougher could Edmonton–Calgary be?

"When I was coming back to Quebec, they would always say to me, 'Oh, that rivalry between Quebec and Montreal. You guys have a lot of pressure.' I would say, 'Pressure? When you go out west, between Calgary and Edmonton, the pressure is double.'

"You'd do the first or second round between Edmonton and Calgary, it was like doing the Stanley Cup final."

The officials were the transient members of the Battle. A referee would never worked both ends of a regular season back to back, though the linesmen team of Randy Mitton and Swede Knox—who both lived in or around Edmonton—did so frequently. The intensity of the Battle commanded that only the top referees drew the assignments, so the cast of referees didn't change much come playoff time. The linesmen, however, were always sent to the other conference in the post-season, so Knox and Mitton never got to work the Battle when it burned the hottest in April and May.

One by one, however, the various zebras forged the relationships during the regular season that would be counted on when the sticks hit the fan come playoff time. And it worked both ways—a Battle of Alberta game in January was like a playoff preview for any official assigned to the game.

"Simply, it was just mean. They were mean, and they really hatred each other with a passion," Mitton recalled. "But the people from Edmonton hated the people from Calgary. And vice versa. It was just mean, and it was scary. There were obvious bench-emptiers from teams that weren't rivals, per se. But this was different. This was just meaner than anything else. I don't know how else to describe it."

"As a referee," Lewis said, "our assignments were always done by game numbers. So if you got game No. 312, and you looked it up and it was Edmonton and Calgary, you knew. You didn't need [former referee in chief] Scotty Morrison to call you and say, 'You'd better be ready.' The style of game alone said, you'd better make sure you got to town early. You'd better make sure you got your rest. You'd better have a half-decent pre-game meal, and then get a good rest before the game. Because you knew: You were going to have three hours of hard work.

"So, when I started doing the assignments, I had to have the same mentality. I couldn't give that game to a lesser experienced guy. I had to give that game to a Kerry Fraser, an Andy Van Hellemond. A Bill McCreary. Because they were an 'any ref.'"

As a fan, or a viewer, we tend only to see the interaction between officials and coaches, or officials and players, when a contentious issue has arisen that requires direct communication. Then the camera pans in. Those moments tend to unfold predictably: the player or coach wants a call to go in favour of his team, and the referee is either mediating or explaining the situation.

What a referee will tell you, however, is that if you wait until a moment like that to have to forge a relationship with a coach or a player—when everyone is hot and a referee's call is about to have a major impact on the game—you've waited too long. It's when the camera is trained elsewhere that the respect between coach and zebra is earned or lost.

Linesmen and coaches don't talk a whole lot. But it behooves both the referee and the head coach if they can see things eye to eye. It's funny, not every referee I interviewed for this chapter had the same opinion of the various characters inside. It is a simple fact that some guys get along better than others, and that's no different inside an NHL game than it is in the dressing room of your beer league team.

Kerry Fraser and Glen Sather seemed to find that middle ground. For them it became a battle of wits, the veteran referee and longtime Oilers coach each trying to get the last laugh.

"He was the coach with the most wit I ever saw, and it was fun to try to match wits with him," said Fraser, who refereed more than two thousand NHL games in total and thirteen Stanley Cup finals. "Slats had this unmistakable voice. It was squeaky—a voice that was very high-pitched, especially if he got excited. Glen was like a father to those young guys, but he could also be one of them, a child with them. He was a pretty modern-thinking guy as an older man coaching boys."

One night at Northlands, Fraser was readying for the puck to be dropped by one of his linesmen, poised in that universal position of the zebra—bent over, hands on his knees, head forward in full observation mode. His back was to the Oilers bench.

"I heard Slats yelling at me. I just rotated my head and upper body, and I put my fingers to my lips. Like, 'Hush.' He plays innocent. Puts both his hands up like he's saying, 'I surrender.' His eyebrows are raised, and he says, 'Kerry, it wasn't me.' And he points at a photographer who's shooting between the benches."

The next night the Oilers are in Vancouver, and so is Fraser. So before the game begins, as the anthem singer is leaving the ice and the arena staff are picking up the red carpet, Fraser skates over to Edmonton's bench.

"I skated over to him, and I said, 'Listen, Glen, before I start this game tonight, I wanted to know if we were going to have any trouble with that photographer tonight?'

"And Glen says, 'No, we left the sonofabitch at home. He couldn't keep his mouth shut.'"

Then there was Denis Morel, who had a completely different viewpoint when it came to Sather.

"Glen, he was a tough cookie, and in those years, the intimidation was working with some officials, no doubt about that," said Morel. "When you stepped into that building, it was a different feeling. But if you didn't stand up in front of Glen, Glen would chew you up. Chew you up very well."

It was no different being a referee, as it turns out, than being a reporter. Sather's act was to break in anybody with whom he wanted an edge. It was like you were a newly saddled horse, and his power and position provided Sather with the necessary intimidation. The solution for the referee was the same as it was for us reporters:

"If a referee let him go an inch, he'd take a foot. Then a yard. Then after that, who knew? You were losing control," Morel said. "If you were willing to face him, he would back off. This guy, he was willing to do anything to win. He'd play with the rules, and if you let him go, he'd take even more. If you prove you can stand your ground, he was okay with that."

Fraser was, as we said, one who loved the debate. In that classic Game 6 in 1994, when the New York Rangers captain Mark Messier scored the hat trick after guaranteeing a win at New Jersey, there is a fascinating close-up of Fraser debating Rangers coach Mike Keenan about a call. Coming out of the commercial, the game is literally delayed while Fraser and Keenan go back and forth in heated, but respectful, dialogue.

Though Flames coach Bob Johnson appeared to take part in the gamesmanship less, the Oilers coach was always ready to test a zebra's courage in conversation.

"Slats had an amazing personality," said Fraser. "He could be sarcastic in his comments, but he was a needler. He enjoyed the banter, and if he could pull a referee into his world with his banter and maybe get him a little bit off his game, make him think about maybe owing him one, that was his win.

"I loved it, the game within the game that Slats played."

Behind the Flames bench, the scholarly Johnson was far less animated. It was as if he'd concluded that tactics when the puck was still moving were the ones on which he would focus his attention. Once the whistle blew and the puck stopped moving, it wasn't Johnson's time. Johnson's Xs and Os were superior to Sather's, but he did not possess the intimidation game that Sather had.

"Bob was so calm. He'd never say much behind the bench," said Morel. "But he was in the game, you could feel it. The old Badger, he'd talk to you smoothly. Like (speaks slowly), 'What do you think about that call, Denis?' He'd say calmly, 'I think you made a mistake there, Denis.'"

For Mitton and Knox, Northlands and the Saddledome were equal parts their home rink. They'd do thirty or so games a year — about 40 percent of their season — between the two Alberta cities. But where the referees interact with head coaches, captains, and players who feel they've been wronged by a penalty call, the linesmen have a completely different perspective. They deal with the centremen when they're dropping pucks for faceoffs, forwards who find themselves frequently going offside, and defencemen on icing calls. And they're the ones grabbing the puck out of a goalie's glove after he's made a save or hauling it out of the net after a goal has been scored.

The difference was, where the referee is mandated to interact, a linesman can — for the most part — keep his mouth shut and quietly do his job.

"I never got too close with any of the players or staff. I didn't care if they liked me, as long as they respect me and the job I did," said Knox, the latter thought echoing almost to the word what Mitton and other officials have said. "I don't think you can do that job if you're worried about who likes you. Every call you make, someone is going to be pissed off at you, right? Fifty percent of the people are going to be pissed off at every call you make."

Let's face it, though: working on the same sheet of ice over all those years, opinions form. You like some people who you work with, while others . . . Let's just say, not all of these guys are Facebooking each other when their birthdays roll around.

"[Craig] MacTavish and I simply didn't get along," Mitton said of the former Oilers centre and key faceoff man in the latter half of the 1980s. "He never did a faceoff cleanly, even once, in his career. He was the biggest cheater. And he simply didn't like me at all. He hated me. Thought I was crazy. But he had to do what he needed to do, and I had to do what I needed to do. And that was conduct a faceoff properly."

How many fights did Knox and Mitton break up in the Battle? Who possibly could have kept track?

"The big guys were one thing, but sometimes the small guys were the worst ones," Knox said. "The guys who very seldom got into fights, when they get in one they'd go cuckoo. Grimson, Semenko, Brown, they were all pretty good. They knew their job and they did it.

"[Paul] Baxter? He never stopped talking," Knox continued. "The other guy was [Theo] Fleury. As talented as he was, he was just a shit disturber. He'd come in and start mouthing off, then everyone would congregate and all of the sudden you don't see Fleury anymore. Now it was all the big guys.

"He was 'Yap, yap, yap, yap.' And not just to the opponents. To us too. But he had a job to do. He made our job more difficult, but he was doing his job too. Constant talking, constant bickering. But he was one of the best at that."

I won't lie to you. When you sit down over a cup of coffee with a guy like Mitton—who worked 2,109 regular season games, 156 playoff games, the 1987 Canada Cup, two All-Star games, and a Cup final—the memories all haze together a bit. I'm asking him about things that happened thirty years ago, and it's no surprise that some of the dates have slipped through the cracks. What is amazing, though, is some of the minutiae that he does recall. And he remembers like it happened last week.

On Theo Fleury: "When Theo was going through his issues, there was a period later on in his career [with the Rangers] when he was thrown out of six out of ten games, or something like that. I had the game in Edmonton, and he got into it with a referee and he was going right off the wall. I took him right off the ice because he was thrown out and he was going to try to get back. He wasn't that big, and I'm not either, but I had a good hold of him.

"So I said, 'Theo. Don't make it worse.' And he looked at me and he said, said, 'Okay, Mitts.' And he went off."

The Fleury Whisperer. Who knew?

Or this one, on a faceless linesman's relationship with the great Wayne Gretzky:

Mitton recalled a game in which Gretzky had taken a long pass, and as he crossed the blue line he left the puck sitting right on the line. Then Gretzky went deep into the offensive zone, knowing that Jari Kurri would be coming to gather up the puck he'd left behind. Of course, the entire puck has to be over the entire line for the play to be onside. Mitton knew this. Gretzky, strangely, did not.

"Maybe two seconds passes, and Kurri picks up the puck and brings it over the line. So I blow the whistle: offside. It's an easy call," Mitton said. "Gretzky comes by and he's screamin' at me, givin' it to me, and I give him an unsportsmanlike conduct.

Well, afterwards in my town, [the Edmonton suburb of] Leduc, people are saying, 'How can you give Gretzky an unsportsman-like conduct?' It's easy. He yelled at me and he embarrassed me.

"Well, some days later we're in L.A., and we used to drink—players and officials—in a place called The Melody Bar [an old haunt from the days of yore. Drank there myself]. Gretzky was around the other side, and I walked around to talk to him. I told him that story, and he said, 'I didn't know the entire puck had to be inside the zone?!?' He sent over a couple of beers and it was all good.

"Gretzky reacted to the officials but not maliciously. He did it because he was so intense," Mitton said. "Other guys, they were just jerks. Mario Lemieux? I don't really remember him ever saying anything. Joe Sakic? What a gentleman. Dave Semenko? I don't even remember what Dave's voice sounded like. He just never said anything."

The officials never had any trouble remaining impartial. Honestly, I have met and drank with many an official, and I've never met a ref who cared—or remembered for more than a day—what the final score was in a game. The toughest part, sometimes, was not breaking out in laughter when one player really burned another with a verbal shot.

The choicest remarks were seldom if ever aimed at the striped shirts. Why waste a good line on an official when there was an Oiler or Flame on the other side of the faceoff dot to spend it on?

There are ten skaters on the ice at any one time, give or take the power plays, and sometimes the tough guys and the skills guys would discuss things. Dave Semenko, for instance, is known to be one of the wittiest former Oilers, his dry sense of humour emanating from behind a serious mask. It makes for the perfect delivery, from a truly sharp and funny guy. To this day, with Semenko serving as a pro scout for the Oilers, fellow scouts who join Semenko at the pre-game meal or for an intermission coffee almost always walk away with a joke to be told a few nights later, in another press box in another NHL town.

Flames tough guy Nick Fotiu was another who was as quick with a verbal jab as he was with a left hook. He was a sharp-witted WHA survivor, who still carried the accent one gets by growing up in Staten Island, New York. He would end up with more than sixteen hundred penalty minutes as a pro, and lose one testicle to the Battle, an excruciating story he told me about one day long after.

("Pain?" Fotiu asked in his New York accent. "Fuggedaboudit . . .")

"He was a big guy who didn't play very much," Fraser began. "And he always caked his face with Vaseline [so the punches would slide off]. There was a scrum, it was in Calgary and right in front of the Flames bench. Glenn Anderson was involved, and he was down on the ice. When Andy got up, Nick Fotiu stood up on the bench, right in front of him. He was taunting Anderson."

Anderson's nickname was "Mork," from an old Robin Williams character in a sitcom from 1978 called *Mork and Mindy*. Mork was from outer space, and in many ways, so was Anderson, it seemed. He didn't fit the mould of the everyday hockey player — he wasn't the ultra masculine type and spoke with a bit of a lisp. He was obviously a hell of a player, and the king of the "accidentally on purpose" high stick delivered to the chops of some opponent. But in this culture, at that time, if you didn't conform to the group, a player would hear all kinds of things that would be considered totally unacceptable today.

(For instance, Morel, one of the top refs of his day, was fondly nicknamed "Kermit" by his fellow zebras.)

"Now, Anderson, there was speculation that he was a bit of a different sort," continued Fraser. "He had that lisp when he talked. So Anderson said to Fotiu, in the crowd of players with me and the two linesmen around him, 'Aw, Nick. Why don't you just go put some more Vaseline on your face?'

"So Fotiu, right out of the hopper says, 'Well, at least I don't shove it up my ass, Anderson!' That's the kind of stuff that went back and forth. It's not politically correct, but everybody laughed. And Anderson laughed as well."

If it was a different time when it came to political correctness, so was it a different era of NHL officiating. First off, it was the one-referee system. Secondly, it was that era when coaches would yell, as an opposing puck carrier moved through the neutral zone, "Get a stick on him!" The era of the great rodeo was about to begin, as coaches like Jacques Lemaire devised systems that slowed the game down to a crawl. In fact, Johnson's "left wing back" system is seen by many as the forebearer of the left-wing lock.

"The standard," as officials refer to it, was in a totally different place in the 1980s than it is today. Early on, Edmonton was allowed to skate, and they dominated the NHL. As Johnson figured out how to slow them down, so, too, did every other coach demand that their team clog up the neutral zone and hook and ride every chance they had against competition with superior skill.

Everybody began to figure out that if you let Paul Coffey hit your blue line in full stride, you were dead, so eventually the hooking and holding began. When the Battle really started cooking in the playoffs, that meant a referee would make more "non-calls" that affected a game than actual calls.

"You were rewarded for non-calls that helped to control the hockey game," explained Bill McCreary. "You were still challenged to make the calls that kept the game fair and safe. That's the way I always reffed a game: if you kept the game fair and safe, the players would respect that."

Billy was a true pro, and he learned along the way from the best in the business. I've known him for a long time, and he was one of those guys: If he says it, and it's about refereeing a hockey game, you can take it to the bank.

"You were never told or directed [by his superiors] not to call penalties. I don't know where that fallacy ever got started, but it wasn't true," McCreary said. "But, you *were* credited with controlling a hockey game without calling marginal calls. Without interrupting the flow of the game.

"John Ashley [a Hall of Fame referee from the 1960s and 1970s] used to say, 'If the team of horses is getting away on you, you have to pull the reins in a bit.' Matt Pavelich [the first linesman ever inducted into the Hockey Hall of Fame] used to give direction: 'Don't let it get out of control on you in the first period because you'll never get ahead of it by the time the third period starts.'

"Frank Udvari [a referee from the 1950s and 1960s] used to say, 'If you're going to make a call in the first period, make sure you're willing to make that call in the third period.' He always talked about consistency. So there was a lot of direction to make strong calls but not marginal calls. Nobody wanted a marginal call. Coaches didn't want them, general managers didn't want them, and the players didn't want them."

Bill McCreary, like those select few players in the Battle, would become over the course of his nearly two-thousand-game career the singular best referee in the game. He was chosen to work the Olympic gold medal games in 1998, 2002, and 2010, and also was assigned to four separate Game 7s in the Stanley Cup finals over the years.

When he thinks of the games he worked in Alberta between the Flames and Oilers, "I think of mean, I think of tough," he said. "I think of a game that would border on mayhem. Right away, I think of Joel Otto, Lanny McDonald, [Jim] Peplinski, [Mike] Vernon,

[Jamie] Macoun, Hakan Loob, Fleury. And on the other side, it wasn't just Wayne and Mark. It was Charlie Huddy, Randy Gregg, Dave Lumley. They had a cast of characters who could play the game."

In a one-referee system, and before the help of video replay on goals, there was simply no way to be cognizant of what the puck was doing and also keep complete track of what was happening behind the play.

"First of all, you tried. Second of all, it wasn't possible," he said. "It became a trust factor. From a trust factor comes respect, and is the players respected you, how far would they go until you had to get involved in it and slow it down?

"Could you catch everything? Absolutely not."

Like the time Marty McSorley speared Mike Bullard in Game 3 of the 1988 series. Kerry Fraser was working that game. He saw it and issued McSorley a spearing major and a game misconduct. That didn't mean it was such a big deal though.

"I saw the spear, and it was pretty solid. Didn't come out the back end of him, but it was put in there pretty good," said Fraser. "When I first started, I was about twenty-one, and we had a rules session at training camp. Scotty Morrison was going through the rules, and back then we had the ability to call a two- or a five-minute penalty for spearing. I asked Lloyd Gilmour, 'What's the difference between a two-minute spear and a five-minute spear?'

"He said, 'Well, kid, if they stick the stick in, that's two. If it comes out the back, that's five.'"

Gilmour worked games for nearly two decades in the *Slap Shot* years, retiring in 1976. He'd worked such games as the time the Soviet Red Army visited the Philadelphia Spectrum to get absolutely beat up by the Flyers, a disgraceful day for North American hockey when Bob Cole coined the phrase, "They're goin' home! They're GOIN' HOME!!"

The violence had gotten a little sneakier by the time the mid-1980s rolled around. But that just meant a ref had to have his head on a swivel that much more.

"A guy like Kevin Lowe, you'd have to watch. He was vicious with the stick," Morel said. "Paul Baxter, you never know what could happen when Bax was on the ice. He'd use his stick or throw a punch for no reason. Start a brawl for nothing. Hunter, he was a guy who was ready to fight at any time . . ."

Working the Oilers and the Flames, as we've stated, meant you were one of the best. And for Morel in the 1988 Stanley Cup final, that meant working "the blackout game" at the Boston Garden. It was a Game 4 in which the power went out in the old Garden, and the two teams had to come all the way back to Edmonton for the Oilers to complete their series sweep.

"Boston was my first final," Morel remembers. "Andy Van Hellemond said, 'Imagine a first-year referee seeing the Stanley Cup [get awarded].' And when Edmonton scored the goal to make it 3–3, I thought, 'Oh boy! We will see the Cup tonight!' We knew Edmonton was too strong for Boston that year. And when they scored that goal, I said, 'All right. I will see the Stanley Cup on the ice.' Then I'm ready to drop the puck, and poof! Lights out.

"[Bruins general manager] Harry [Sinden] pulled the plug. He didn't want to see the Cup there."

There was justice, however. Morel worked Game 6 in 1989 — when Calgary became the first-ever visiting team to win the Cup on Montreal Forum ice.

11

CONTAINING THE GREAT ONE

Like Trying to Hug Fog

"This is art. Hockey history right before our very eyes."

"It's the best goal I've ever scored."

When Wayne Gretzky is saying that, you know there is more to it than simply a nice shot or a deke that left the goalie sprawled four feet from the puck and a wide-open cage to accept the puck. To be Gretzky's all-time favourite from more than 1,000 regular-season and playoff goals, it would have to have come at an important moment, against a championship-calibre team, in a game that had some gravity.

Clue No. 1: There is a slim chance that there would still be snow on the ground when Gretzky's all-time favourite goal was scored. Clue No. 2: It is a pretty fair bet that the Calgary Flames would be his victim. Both were true of the slapshot he unleashed on April 21, 1988, at the Saddledome, the one you've seen so many times on that *Hockey Night in Canada* intro.

It was a game-winner in overtime, scored short-handed. A rare, blistering slapshot by No. 99, labelled for and perfectly delivered to the top-right corner over Mike Vernon's left shoulder. Why wouldn't that be Wayne Gretzky's favourite? If any of us had ever scored a goal like that, even in our beer league, it would be our favourite, for sure.

"The one thing I was really never known for was being a guy with a hard shot who could score from the wing very often," Gretzky said. "I will say, it was one of the hardest shots I have ever taken. I picked my spot once I got over the blue line. I knew exactly where I was shooting it. In my mind, I'll say it again, it was the best goal I ever scored in the National Hockey League.

"Or, it's my favourite goal I've ever scored in the National Hockey League."

★

If there was one tangible element inside the Battle that exemplified why Calgary was so often in the chase position, it was Wayne Gretzky. The Flames had plenty of fire power, but so does a small Eastern European country. It doesn't mean they take on the United States in battle.

"Edmonton played hockey the way you're supposed to play hockey. It was just 'Let 'em loose, Bruce,'" said Mike Bullard, who had a 103-point season for Calgary in 1987–88, his best NHL season. "Gretzky, Messier, Coffey, Anderson, Simpson . . . What it came down to was, their top guys were better than our top guys, when you looked at the stats. And we had big stats. But my 103 points to Gretzky's [149 that year]? Sorry. Just a little off. Gretzky was just in his own world."

Gretzky was, truly, on a higher plane than everybody else. There were only two seasons during Gretzky's nine NHL seasons with Edmonton—from 1980 to 1988—that the Flames' leading scorer came within ninety points of Gretzky's total. In five of those seasons, Gretzky's seasonal production surpassed the combined total of Calgary's *top two* scorers.

It was on the back of these seasons—from his entry with the Oilers into the NHL in 1979 until Gretzky was traded/sold to the Los Angeles Kings on August 9, 1988—that Gretzky's ownership of the NHL record books was built. His sixty-one NHL records and four Stanley Cup rings all came from the same place: his prime, spent in the blue, white, and orange silks of Edmonton.

It was incredible to see, the most gifted offensive player in the history of hockey, reeling off the feats that would make him a legend. Scoring ninety-two goals in 1981–82, including a never-to-be-matched fifty goals in thirty-nine games. Fifty in forty-two games the next season. Fifty in forty-nine games the next year . . .

He set the record for assists in a season in 1980–81 with 109, then proceeded to break his own mark in each of the next four seasons, finally settling on 163 in 1985–86. He broke his own record for points in a season twice as well, and along the way, Gretzky could turn a Tuesday night in Hartford into a game you'd be telling your grandchildren about forty years later.

"There were times when we would sit back, maybe one in ten games, and say, 'Here we go!'" said trainer Barrie Stafford. "This is art. Hockey history right before our very eyes. The other nine games he'd get a goal and two assists, or whatever. But I mean, the guy had a hundred points at Christmastime in 1985."

Craig MacTavish arrived just in time for Gretzky's greatest season, his 215-point campaign in 1985–86, slotting in behind Gretzky and Messier as Edmonton's No. 3 centre. That meant he was almost never on the ice with Gretzky, other than the odd penalty kill. What MacTavish saw from the bench on a nightly basis, however, he still marvels at to this day.

"Incredible drive. Unreal drive," said MacTavish, who would go on to be the Oilers head coach and then general manager. "A lot of guys in today's era, if they had three points and there are ten minutes left, you're up by four [goals], they don't care if they don't play. Wayne had his foot over the boards. He wants four [points]. Always looking to get one more goal or one more assist. He was never, ever satisfied."

Down Highway 2, the Calgary Flames coaching staff were burning the midnight oil trying to game-plan against Gretzky. That exercise was equal parts utterly impossible and absolutely necessary, but what the Flames didn't know was, Gretzky's own teammates were dissecting his game as well—off the ice. Mark Messier, for one, was doing his reconnaissance, almost from the first day he laid eyes on the kid from Brantford, born just eight days after Messier in 1961.

"In a funny way, we all watched Wayne," Messier said. "We were all the same age, but he was so far ahead of us from a preparation standpoint and a mental standpoint. I was asking myself the questions 'Why? Why is he this good? What is he doing that makes him this good?' You were always looking at the established, veteran guys. But here was this phenom . . . and you quickly realized he was good for a reason. He was the hardest-working guy and putting the most into it out of any of us."

Part of what Messier saw was what we all could see: the God-given, Walter-cultivated talent that Gretzky displayed nightly. "Never go to where the puck is; always go to where it's going to be," as his father, Walter Gretzky, taught. But Messier knew to look deeper. That, as with his own father, the well waters swirled far below the surface. Messier watched Gretzky when the spotlight was turned off. When Gretzky, like any great artisan, was preparing, working ahead. Tending to the minute details that would allow the talent to flow when the TV lights flicked back on.

"The obvious was there for everyone to see," Messier said of Gretzky. "What people didn't see was the commitment. The drive to be the best. When you were with Wayne every day and saw how committed he was to be the best, to carving his name into history, the drive was incredible. It was a message for all of us: If you wanted to be the best, there was a price to be paid. And here was the best, paying' that price. It was easy to follow Wayne."

Of course, Gretzky was ahead of the play. He has been under the microscope since well before he scored 378 goals as a ten-year-old in Brantford—in a single season.

"I always knew the players were looking at me. I knew I had to be as hardworking in practice as anybody, and my preparation for a game or a series had to be as sincere, as strong as each and every guy on the team," Gretzky says today. "So there were no shortcuts with our team. The one thing we always had which was overshadowed: we were a good, talented team . . . but it was a group that was extremely dedicated to becoming a successful, unselfish team. I always felt it was most important that the captain show the team that winning was most important, and that being unselfish was the key to the success of any group. That was the key to being the captain of that team."

There was a special set of rules for Gretzky, which goes against the accepted tenet that everyone on a team should be subject to the same set of regulations. The reality was, Gretzky quickly became a superstar, and the NHL needed to "borrow" him from Edmonton once in a while. The rigours of fulfilling those obligations—lengthy off-day travel, very few days spent completely away from the sport—usually took more of a toll on Gretzky than did the practices he missed on his Oilers teammates.

Messier, who had been indoctrinated with the realization that even the best player on the team had to think of others before himself, soon learned that there would be times when the team had to support their superstar.

"We learned that Wayne was a special player. He needed special attention, and needed to be treated differently," Messier said. "It was for the benefit of the team, so nobody ever looked at it like he was being treated differently than the team, or that it was a burden. In fact, it was, 'How can we contribute to the process?' And that is not always the case [on other teams].

"There were more demands on him. His schedule was different. We'd go on a twelve- or fifteen-day road trip back then and he would fly home with the team on a seven a.m. flight, then fly back to Toronto to do some selling of the game. Sometimes after games he would fly with [owner] Peter [Pocklington] somewhere to do something. No one ever looked at it like he was getting preferential treatment. It was necessary."

The one ritual where Gretzky was neither given any preferential treatment, nor did he request any, was when it came time to play the Calgary Flames.

Toughness was a prerequisite in the Battle, and often there was so much mayhem out on the ice that there simply would not be enough time to defend the skill players like Gretzky whenever a liberty was taken. His teammates tried, but there were times when their hands were full, and the skill guys would just have to figure it out themselves.

"We knew we were a pretty tough team, with Semenko, and McClelland, and Donnie Jackson, and Messier and McSorley, and Lee Fogolin. And they were tough, with guys like Peplinski, Baxter, Tim Hunter, Sheehy. . .," Gretzky said. "We had sort of an unwritten rule in our locker room. If the tough guys were going to be tough, if they were going to battle all of these guys, then guys like me, and Kurri, and Coffey had better take hits to make plays.

"I remember Kevin Lowe saying one time, how much he had hacked and whacked that Hakan Loob, and how Loob just kept coming back. It was like nothing had happened. What made the series intense was, not only were the tough guys tough, but the so-called elite guys understood their responsibility of getting their noses to the grindstone also. Because if you didn't, you weren't going to be part of the group. You'd be weeded out."

There was, it seems, a proportional line drawn between how much offence one produced in the Battle versus how much of the fisticuffs one would be expected to partake in. Translation: Score more, fight less; Score less, fight more. Gretzky, of course, wasn't expected to fight at all. Nor was his trigger man Jari Kurri, or Loob and Nilsson on the Flames end. Messier voluntarily opted out of the equation. But the spirit of being *in* the fight spiritually was as important as being in one literally, as MacTavish noted, "Everybody had their toughness challenged. That's what it was all about. Peplinski was a very tough guy, and he challenged Mess. And Mess was a very tough guy. McSorley–Sheehy, Hunter–Semenko . . .

"It's a good game to reflect on," MacTavish said with a wry smile, "but not so good to prepare for. But the last thing you wanted was to be in a dressing room at the end of a game where everybody was into it but you."

That last line sums up a hockey team. Being the only guy in the post-game dressing room without need of an ice bag was a poor visual. A scraped-up face from a fight was no different than a bruised hip that came from taking the hit to make a play. The Battle was no place for a perimeter player—even when your last name was Gretzky. No one wanted to be that guy who was deemed "unwilling to pay the price," especially in those early years before 1986, when the Battle was still a fairly lopsided series. That meant early Oiler leads and games that inevitably eroded into confrontation.

"I think they [the Flames] knew themselves, over an eighty-game schedule, chances were that we were going to finish first and they were going to be second," Gretzky said of the pre-1986 Flames. "But they were gearing up for that second-round matchup, that seven-game series. [Flames general manager] Cliff [Fletcher] brought in a coach in Bob Johnson who really was one of the best Xs and Os coaches who ever lived. They built a system, a strategy, for their group that would work against the Edmonton Oilers."

That meant building a system that could control Gretzky. Good luck.

There was an old line: "You can only hope to control Gretzky, but you'll never totally shut him down." I don't know which coach said it first, but they all did eventually. It has become a cliché in Alberta press boxes, trotted out now when a Luke Gazdic or Deryk Engelland somehow puts together a two-point night. "You can only hope to control Luke Gazdic" some smart-ass scribe will say to get a laugh from the ink-stained. It is said in jest today, but not when Gretzky played.

Wayne Gretzky retired with a career average of 1.9 points per game, higher, of course, than anyone who ever played the game. His production was even higher, however, during his Edmonton years. As an Oiler, Gretzky averaged an astounding 2.4 points per regular-season game, settling at 1.9 points per playoff game. So, if the Flames could figure out a way to hold Gretzky to only two points a game, in theory they were keeping his performance needle below "average."

"You never had total success against Wayne Gretzky," said Johnson's assistant Bob Murdoch, with a variation on the old theme. "In all fairness, he was so good, you could never really neutralize him. We did to a point, comfortably enough so we could play, and try to get the game so we could still win it."

Calgary's biggest problem was that there were so many places and situations from which Gretzky could derive offence. His "office" behind the net, of course, was the place that drove opposing coaches the most crazy.

"He'd go behind the net with the bloody puck, and he'd have two defencemen chasing him there. He'd just dish it out in front and the guy would tuck it in," said Murdoch. "If you took away all his receivers, you had a chance of shutting him down. Wayne Gretzky behind the net wasn't dangerous. It was the two defencemen and two wingers who were dangerous. Again, take away his targets to eliminate him."

Of course, that often meant you would have a ninety-two-goal scorer walking out from behind the net with the puck, lending a new meaning to that old hockey tenet "leave the shooter to your goalie." But it illustrates what Johnson and the rest of the Flames coaches went through in the film room. No coach, since the day Gretzky played his first game at age six on a team comprised of ten-year-olds, had figured out how to stop Gretzky. Very few even slowed him down, in his prime.

"Hit him every chance you get!" was an oft-chanted mantra that has followed Gretzky all the way up from pee wee hockey. Brad McCrimmon, the Flames defenceman from 1987 to 1990 who died in 2011 in the tragic plane crash of the Lokomotiv Yaroslav hockey club (he was the team's head coach), had some advice for those who thought that possible.

"Trying to hit Gretzky," McCrimmon once said, "is like trying to hug fog."

"People always say, 'Why didn't you hit him?'" said long-time Flames winger Colin Patterson. "Well, the one thing that made him great was his lateral movement. He wasn't the fastest guy, but he had the best lateral movement of anyone. And smarts. He moved the puck before you could hit him. It was always too late, he was by you anyways, and you're making a fool of yourself. Stuff you could do against a normal player, you couldn't do against him.

"He and Jari Kurri, and whoever they had on that line. They were lethal. A match made in heaven."

Murdoch was Johnson's assistant coach in the early days of the Battle, but even before that he had been an NHL defenceman himself, manning the Flames blue line in Atlanta and Calgary during Gretzky's first three NHL seasons. "If you overplayed him, he would just make a fool of you. He saw the ice so well, he would draw two or three of you in and dish it behind you because you'd left your position to chase him. Kurri or whomever would be there, and they would just pick you apart."

As odd as it sounds, the Flames' plan was to force the game's best one-on-one player into one-on-one combat. "Try to isolate Gretzky after you'd taken away his receivers," Murdoch repeats. "Gretzky didn't like to try to beat you one on one. He just lured you out of position, the bugger. You had a better chance of shutting down Wayne Gretzky one on one," than giving him outlets to pass to.

When Johnson and his staff went for dinner on the road, the table was inevitably cleared and the salt shakers and ketchup bottles would be used as markers in a defensive scheme meant to beat Edmonton. When he went to bed at night, Johnson lay awake thinking on how to "climb the mountain" against Edmonton. Of course, containing Gretzky was Johnson's base camp.

Sometimes, in the ebb and flow of the Battle, Calgary would enjoy some success, gain some territory. And so it would be the turn of the Oilers coaching staff to ask for more from their troops.

It was a constant back and forth, a small Flames gain countered by an Oilers push. Then the playoff series would come around, and the added intensity would mix with those strategic moves like fire and gasoline.

"Some of the greatest meetings that we ever had as a hockey team, whether they were organized by management, the coaching staff or the players, all happened in Calgary," MacTavish remembers. "The most dramatic moments I remember in the dressing room happened in Calgary. There would be probably, three of those."

The one that Gretzky recalls was in 1984. The Oilers had walked over Calgary in the 1983 Smythe final 35–13 in the five-game series. A year later, there they were in the visiting team's "bath house" at the Saddledome, as former *Edmonton Sun* beat writer Dick Chubey liked to call it, packing their bags for a Game 7 showdown back home.

The Oilers had jumped to a 3–1 lead in the series, but rather than fold as they had right from the start in 1983, the Flames punched back. They won Game 5 in Edmonton, costing the Oilers a nice playoff break before Round 3 had they won the game, and then Calgary had the audacity to win Game 6 on a goal just 1:04 into the overtime period. "Lanny McDonald," Gretzky remembered correctly.

"Glen held a meeting after that game. It was a 'Come to Jesus' meeting."

Most coaches will tell you that words spoken immediately after a game are more often wasted. Players are in wind-down mode and emotions are high. Many general managers forbid themselves to trade a player within twenty-four hours of a loss, while just as many coaches will save their spiritual gathering for the morning light, when cooler heads are present.

Glen Sather was both coach and general manager of the Oilers, not to mention president of the club as well. He had seen his team lose the 1983 Stanley Cup final to the New York Islanders, then claw its way back into position for another chance at the dynastic Isles. Suddenly, just getting out of the Smythe Division had fallen into question. In case his players had not been aware of the gravity of the situation, Sather would drive that very serious topic home with a sledgehammer that night in Calgary.

"It was a pretty emotional meeting," remembers Gretzky. "But I think what put pressure on the team was that Calgary had built their team for a playoff run. They didn't build their team to get 120 points in a season. [*Note:* In 1983–84, Edmonton won the Smythe Division with 119 points. Calgary was second with 82.] They weren't really concerned about that. They knew they were going to get into the playoffs, and Bob Johnson was such a positive motivator that he'd built his team to beat us in a seven-game series. Simple as that."

Sather's sermon was a powerful one that night, marking another milepost in what would become a classic match of two coaching fortes: Johnson's Xs and Os versus Sather's ability to motivate the very best performance out of his admittedly superior players. In Game 7, back at Northlands Coliseum, the game was played on Edmonton's terms. Gretzky had a goal and two assists, Kurri had a pair of goals, and Edmonton broke open a game that was tied at four late in the second period, winning 7–4.

Remember: that Oilers team had not won anything yet. We think of them as a dynasty today, but in the spring of 1984 they were still trying to figure out exactly what it took to win. The Islanders had swept the Oilers in the 1983 Stanley Cup final, and now Calgary had improved to the point where getting out of the division was more than just a little problematic.

It would be no different when they next met in 1986, a series so memorable that we've reserved an entire chapter for it in the book. Then again, in 1988, when the one Wayne Gretzky goal that still finds it way on to your television screen today—more than any other—was scored.

Gretzky and the Oilers had gone on to win their first Cup in the spring of 1984, with Messier winning the Conn Smythe Trophy as the most valuable performer in the playoffs. It was a seminal moment, as the balloons rained down on the Northlands ice surface with seconds still ticking off the clock in Game 5 of that final. It must not have felt that way in Calgary, however, where Flames fans watched their bitter rivals celebrate. But the fact was, the Stanley Cup would reside in Edmonton that summer, the first time in Alberta hockey history that had happened—and only five years after the province's first NHL team had arrived in Edmonton.

The Oilers would win again in 1985, and we would see a disturbing trend begin that saw the Calgary Flames actually lose their first-round series to the Winnipeg Jets in both 1985 and 1987. Somehow, the team that was built to beat the Edmonton Oilers had found its second-greatest challenge in that other, quietly strong Smythe Division team, the Jets.

In 1984–85, the Jets had in fact finished two points ahead of Calgary, riding home-ice advantage to a first-round win. Edmonton, Winnipeg, and Calgary had finished one–two–three in the Campbell Conference, now known as the Western Conference, that season, and in the league's overall standings, Edmonton finished second behind Philadelphia while Winnipeg was No. 4 and Calgary No. 5. That's how strong the Smythe Division was in those days.

You might think that because Sather had patterned his young Oilers after the creative, high-flying Jets team that won the final Avco Cup in the WHA, the Jets would be a tough matchup for Edmonton. In fact, the opposite was true. The Oilers beat

Winnipeg for fun in the playoffs, with Gretzky and Kurri racking up huge numbers. Through five playoff meetings between Edmonton and Winnipeg in the Gretzky years, Edmonton never lost a series. In five series meetings, Edmonton won by an aggregate of eighteen games to one.

It was a Game 3 win in the opening round of the 1988 playoffs where the Jets finally beat Edmonton, with Daniel (The Bandit) Berthiaume tending the twine for the Jets. But Edmonton quickly won out, while in Calgary the Flames were disposing of the Los Angeles Kings in five games. It would set up a scenario that nobody recognized at the time: How could they have known that, four months later, Oilers owner Peter Pocklington would sell Wayne Gretzky to the Los Angeles Kings and owner Bruce McNall?

That 1987–88 season was also the first year that Calgary had ever finished ahead of Edmonton in the regular season. It was Calgary's first Presidents' Trophy, having led the entire NHL in points, and if you consider the arc of each team, 1988 was likely the apex of the Battle. The two teams were as good as they were ever going to be, with Gretzky still in Edmonton, Coffey having moved on, and the Oilers on their way to a fourth Cup in five years.

Calgary had been to the Cup final in 1986 and would finally win it in 1989. This series was quite possibly the most hotly anticipated of any of their five meetings between 1983 and 1991. Yet somehow it would turn out to be the shortest.

"We were the Presidents' Cup winners," recalls Bullard, "and the whole thing was, everyone knew that whoever won this series would win the Cup. So I get a knock on my door before the series, and it's a landscaper. He says, 'I'll landscape your whole property if you give me your tickets to the series.' So I go to my wife, and I say, 'We can get our place landscaped, a couple of trees . . . I can always get tickets. Should we give our tickets away?'

"She says, 'Hell, why not?' That's how devoted the people of Calgary were to seeing that series."

With the series ready to drop its first puck, Oilers defenceman Steve Smith told the *Edmonton Journal*, "This may be the toughest series we've ever had. Maybe for the first time since the Oilers beat the Islanders in 1984, we're going in as underdogs."

If only they'd known. The Oilers, opening at the Saddledome for the first time, won Game 1 by a 3–1 score. Normally, to list Game 1 as a turning point in a series would be absurd. But when the team that loses the first game never manages to even get a nibble of the series . . .

"I remember reading the paper the next day," Gretzky said, "and Bob Johnson was saying, 'It was one of the best games we'd played all year. And Edmonton was really not in the game, and somehow they won.' And that really was the case. They were the better team that night, our goalie [Grant Fuhr] stood on his head, and somehow we found a way to get a couple of goals. Had they won Game 1, the series would have been completely different."

Even though they had swapped Game 7 victories in their last two meetings, and Calgary had finally passed Edmonton as a regular-season team that season, Calgary was still the little brother in this relationship. Edmonton had three Cups by this point. They had the greatest player in the world. In the 1987 Canada Cup played prior to the 1987–88 season, Edmonton had put five players on Canada's roster to Calgary's none (three Flames played for Team USA).

"I believe that the best team that Calgary ever had that *didn't* win the Cup was that team of 1988," Gretzky declared. "They were flying. We were coming off of three Stanley Cups in four years, but we'd stumbled during the season a bit. We didn't play our best hockey, but we were good. We snuck through the first round because our goaltender was so good."

Game 2 went to overtime—a typical mid- to late-1980s offensive classic—in a game Calgary had led for most of the way. But Jari Kurri walked through Paul Reinhart and, with Hakan Loob hooking him for all he was worth, still managed to blast a slapshot off the right wing past Mike Vernon to tie the game at 4–4 late in the third period.

That set up the goal that, among 1,016 lifetime goals in the NHL both regular season and playoff, to this day Wayne Gretzky refers to as "the best goal I've ever scored." And it began with a mistake, an overtime penalty by Mark Messier.

It was a blatant trip of Joey Mullen in the offensive zone, with still 150 feet and four Oilers between Mullen and Grant Fuhr. But Messier's penalty helped to create a magical goal, as Gretzky unleashed the best slapshot of his career over Mike Vernon's shoulder.

Of all the goals in all the big games, why was that one Gretzky's favourite?

"One, Vernon was playing as well as Mike Vernon had ever played at that point in time. So the opposition, the game was really strong," Gretzky said. "Two, the team in Calgary was the best team they'd put together in a lot of years. A tough team to beat, to say the least."

In Game 1, Gretzky had come down on Vernon, not quite as close to the boards and at a better scoring angle, and very nearly blown a similar shot past the Calgary goalie. But Vernon got the tip of his glove on the shot, and the puck cartwheeled off of the post and stayed out.

This time, Gretzky had hopped the boards with just over twenty seconds left in Messier's penalty, circled back inside his own blue line, and, as always, Gretzky accurately read what was going to happen next before anybody else on the ice could even consider the possibility. The puck squirted out of the corner to

Jari Kurri near the right faceoff dot, and before Kurri had even reeled the puck in, Gretzky was flying out of the zone up the left-wing boards.

Kurri instinctively banked the puck off the boards with Gretzky in full flight. The linesman hopped up on the dasher boards to allow the puck to slide under his skates uninterrupted, and as it passed a churning Gretzky he didn't even bother to touch it with his stick for a few strides, knowing it would be there when he needed it.

The 1 to 1.5 seconds that Gretzky's instincts had bought him back in his own zone was now the distance between him and a chasing Flames defenceman, Gary Suter. That buffer allowed Gretzky the time to settle the puck, lift his head to set his sights one last time, then bury his head and unleash the slapshot every Canadian kid tried to make on that outdoor rink near the school grounds, winter day after winter day.

"For a team that, over the years, had not had home-ice advantage against us, to finally have earned home-ice advantage against the Oilers—but all of the sudden look up and be down two games to nothing?" Gretzky stated. "Our team was on a roll. We were in a good position to win that series and obviously go on and win a Stanley Cup."

The goal was shown across the land for the next two days, and so it should have been. They don't come any sexier—blazing down the wing, dropping his head, slapping a puck high over Vernon's shoulder. The "ping!" off that bar in the back of the net. When you dream of scoring a game-winner, that's what a kid dreams of right there.

Unless that kid is Bullard, who had the panoramic view of Gretzky's shot.

"Every goddamn time I see that highlight of me coming back late into the zone," Bullard says. "Got caught back late, just like everybody else."

It broke the Flames' back, that goal. They'd gone from a power play in overtime to a road trip up Highway 2, trailing a series they were supposed to lead by two games. Edmonton would sweep the series, likely the most unpredictable result in Battle of Alberta history. Many picked Edmonton to win but not in four straight games.

The Oilers would win another Cup that year, and then Gretzky would be sold away. He could have won more had he stayed, but one thing that Gretzky took with him from his time in Edmonton is the knowledge that his Oilers left nothing on the table.

"One hundred percent," he said. "That's one thing I would never waver from, about that group. It was a really unselfish group that was motivated by winning and being successful. The preparation of the team—not only for being ready for every game during an eighty-game season—but playing the best and being the most ready you could be for each and every series we played in.

"Unfortunately for our club, we faced a very good team in the Calgary Flames. They were a well-put-together group. Cliff was one of the most respected people in the game, with Bob Johnson, and they put together a package with an elite team that wanted to win as badly as we did.

"Are we disappointed we lost to them in 1986? Sure, but we respected them because they were such a good team. But the one thing I will go to my grave saying is that we did everything we could to beat them each and every time we played them in the playoffs. Just, sometimes, teams are a little bit better than you are. That's not to say you left something on the table. It's a credit to how badly they wanted it also."

In the end, the Flames should get some credit for an Oilers team that won four Cups in Gretzky's final five seasons in Edmonton.

"We really rebounded after 1986 and became a better team in playing in the finals in 1987 and 1988. Our team was a better

team in 1987 and 1988 for what we went through in 1986,"
Gretzky said. "You know, we said the same thing about the New
York Islanders. You learn from teams that beat you. They make
you better. The Islanders made us better because we respected
them, and Calgary made us better because we respected them as
a team, and how hard they played."

12

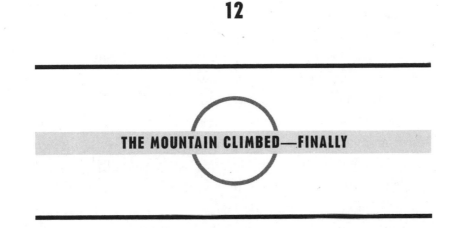

THE MOUNTAIN CLIMBED—FINALLY

The Flames' Lanny McDonald Hoists the 1989 Stanley Cup
"Thank you very much. I am out of here."

Lanny McDonald was thirty-six years old and at the end of the line in the spring of 1989. He uses the word *we* today, but you can be sure, then a part-time player, in his own mind he was thinking first-person.

"We all knew," he said, "if we didn't win it in 1989, we likely weren't going to win at all. That window of opportunity, all of a sudden, goes by you."

In a career that spanned 1,111 regular-season games, McDonald had only played in one Stanley Cup—a losing cause with the Flames in 1986. Now he was back, and almost certainly in the harvest days of a long, bountiful career. He had done most everything, including that trademark overtime goal as a Maple Leaf—Game 7, 1978, against the New York Islanders.

McDonald had been moved on to the hapless Colorado Rockies the following December, and after a couple of years there they shipped the native of Hanna, Alberta, home to play for Calgary. In a time when Canadians got one televised NHL game a week—*Hockey Night in Canada* on Saturday night—Lanny's time with the Maple Leafs had made him a household name. But it was that iconic, walrus-like moustache that set him apart, sitting on his lip like a tumbleweed, under friendly, weathered eyes and an ever-rising forehead.

Truly, when McDonald grew a playoff beard, all he needed was a mule and a pickaxe to pass for Klondike Mike, the old prospector. Behind the moustache and the personality, however, resided an elite goal-scorer. The Maple Leafs had drafted him No. 4 overall out of Medicine Hat, and no one out of that 1973 draft would score more goals than McDonald's five hundred career goals. He had sixty-six one season for Calgary—twenty more than the next closest Flame—after consecutive seasons of forty-six, forty-seven, and forty-three goals in Toronto. When he was dealt to Colorado, Toronto fans gathered outside Maple Leaf Gardens in protest.

On this night, however, inside Canada's other hockey shrine of the day, the faithful had arrived at the historic Montreal Forum to witness Game 6 of the 1989 Stanley Cup final. Dressed in dinner formal, the way so many did when attending a Habs game, Montreal fans were expectant of a Canadiens victory. They always won big games here. In fact, no team other than *les Canadiens* had paraded the Stanley Cup around the Forum before or since. Surely this expansion team, relocated from Atlanta to Calgary less than a decade before, would not deign to be that team.

The Canadiens had run away with the Eastern Conference, then lost just three games over their first three playoff rounds that spring. They still counted such luminaries on the roster as

Bob Gainey, Larry Robinson, Bobby Smith, Mats Naslund, Chris Chelios, and, of course, Patrick Roy in goal. Meanwhile, the one true elder statesman on the Flames, McDonald, hadn't even dressed since Game 2. Head coach Terry Crisp, the old Broad Street Bully who had succeeded Bob Johnson behind the Calgary bench, had been using hard-nosed winger Mark Hunter in McDonald's spot.

It was the cycle of a hockey player's life, as McDonald sees it now.

"As a rookie coming in, you're trying to do anything you can to find a spot, and stay in the lineup," he explains. "Then you become a mainstay, and you play all the time. Then, toward the end of your career, you're not a rookie, but you're finding whatever way you can to try to help the team, help the guys to be well prepared."

Now, in Game 6, Lanny was back in the lineup. Mike Vernon had let in a softie just 1:23 into the second period for a 1–1 tie, and seconds later McDonald found himself in position to restore the lead.

"Dana Murzyn had a shot on net, the rebound came out, and all I had to do was pull the puck straight sideways and I would have almost had an open net," he said. But over a week on the shelf, McDonald had grown cold. He had been watching games from the dressing room, which was not at all his style, and now the head and the hands weren't in sync like the old days.

He had scored only eleven times that year, and ten the season before. The old hands were, well, just that. Old hands. This wasn't 1978 anymore, when he'd swiftly beaten a diving defenceman named Dave Lewis to the puck, then snapped it calmly past Billy Smith to send the Leafs into Round 3 for the first time since 1967. It was eleven years later, and the miles had piled up along the gravel road that was McDonald's gritty career.

"I tried to do it too quickly," he remembers ruefully. "Patrick Roy makes the save, the puck goes in the corner, Bobby Smith picks it up, heading up the boards . . . And you want to get it back right away, and I take a stupid hooking penalty on Bobby Smith trying to get it back."

He had panicked on the chance and messed it up. Then, compounding the frustration, he'd made a poor decision to hook Smith. This is what happens when you're in the back nine of your career. Your hands can't do what your head asks of them anymore, and then your head, frustrated by a body that can't perform the way it used to, lets you down as well.

Now you're in the box, in a Game 6 in which you'd stood up and told your teammates how important every shift would be. Nice.

Meanwhile, on a stationary bike in the Flames dressing room, watching it all on television, was twenty-eight-year-old winger Jim Peplinski.

The first Flames practice jersey he'd pulled over his shoulder pads had the Flaming A of the Atlanta Flames on it, but already his career was closer to being over than he would imagine. While Lanny was out there, sitting in the box, Peplinski—and veteran tough guy Tim Hunter—had been made healthy scratches for a game that they had spent a career in anticipation of.

Peplinski wasn't saying much now. He was sour, and he'd spoken his piece when assistant coach Doug Risebrough had delivered the news prior to the game.

"Crispy says you're not goin' tonight, Pep," Risebrough had said.

"Tell Crispy to go &^%$ himself."

★

In 1989, free agency and the new NHL economy were only beginning to take hold. The Oilers had commenced their breakup, and the Flames would not be that far behind. Nobody had a clue how dry the province of Alberta would become after the last Cup was won by Edmonton in 1990. We'd had the Stanley Cup here for so long, it had simply become part of an Alberta summer, taken for granted like 10:30 p.m. sunsets.

Where parades had become a tradition in Edmonton, however, in Calgary they had only *played* in a Stanley Cup final in 1986. They hadn't actually *won* one. So while the rest of the country looked westward and thought, "Those Albertans are so lucky," you can imagine that Flames fans didn't quite see it that way. Not only wasn't their team winning the Cup, but the stupid Oilers were, most years. And when the Flames had finally cracked the code, climbing Bob Johnson's mountain in 1986, they had bungled the final ascent and lost to an underdog Montreal team.

"We knew we had blown it in Game 6 [of the Campbell Conference Final] in St. Louis in 1986," Lanny McDonald said. "We were up 5–2 and allowed them to score three goals in about the last twelve minutes. They tied it up and won the game in overtime, which meant we had to come back home, play a Game 7. We found a way to win 2–1, but that extra game took a tremendous amount out of us. We won Game 1 [of the Final], but after that it was over. We just didn't have the resources. This young guy by the name of Patrick Roy came in, besides, and he was playing pretty damned well."

They'd lost in Round 1 in 1987 and would be swept out by the Oilers in 1988. But in March 1988, two days before the NHL's trading deadline, the Flames made a move that only a Stanley Cup parade would be able to justify. General manager Cliff Fletcher traded Steve Bozek and a young prospect named Brett Hull to

St. Louis for backup goalie Rick Wamsley and a big, solid defenceman named Rob Ramage.

At that point, Hull had scored twenty-seven career goals, all for Calgary. He would go on to score 714 more times, and today there is a plaque for Bobby's son in the Hockey Hall of Fame.

"We knew we were trading a forty-goal scorer, but there were some shortcomings on the team," said assistant to the president Al Coates. (In fact, they were trading a five-time fifty-goal scorer who once had eighty-six goals for the Blues.) "I think I was on a pay phone on that decision for a minimum of three hours. Finally, the decision was made to go ahead, trade Hull for Wamsley and Ramage."

As it turned out, Gary Suter—father to Minnesota Wild defenceman Ryan and son to departed Miracle on Ice defenceman Bob— was knocked out of the playoffs with an injury in Round 1 that year and Ramage stepped into his spot. It had required a valuable piece to acquire Ramage, a former No. 1–overall draft pick who was right in his prime at age twenty-nine, and Hull was that piece. It was truly a brilliant, courageous move by Fletcher, who had tired of finishing second.

"Truth be known, if you're going to win you have to make some bold choices sometimes, to give yourself that chance to win. And it was not out of naivety. To a man, we all knew this guy was going to score forty goals. Knowing that, and everybody agreeing on that, the decision was still made to trade him," Coates said. "Suter goes out in the first round. Ramage moves to the left side, plays there for the whole playoffs. Ramage was a real integral part of that team, playing on his off side. Do you win the Cup in 1989 if you don't make that trade? Likely not."

Ramage, at that stage of his career, was a major upgrade on Hull. But it was just one upgrade from a 1986 team that did not have the depth required to survive four tough playoff rounds.

Where the 1986 Flames were led in scoring by the skilled but grit-less Dan Quinn, the 1989 Flames had Doug Gilmour at centre, and he was the full package. Joe Nieuwendyk, still at Cornell University in 1986, was coming off a fifty-one-goal season three years later. Brad "Sarge" McCrimmon had come on board to help man a blue line that had been revamped.

"In 1986 we'd gone to the finals with these seven defencemen," recalled Flames winger Jim Peplinski. "Terry Johnson, Jamie Macoun, Paul Baxter, Paul Reinhart, Gary Suter, Al MacInnis, and Neil Sheehy. It wasn't the best defence in the world.

"In 1989, Brad McCrimmon was a huge part. Rob Ramage had come in—two real competitors. [Czech winger] Jiri Hrdina—he could just skate right through people. Joey Mullen . . . they all just had the mental toughness to keep playing, no matter what. You just couldn't stop them. A guy like Colin Patterson was another. We had a core, that middle tier, that just played."

The problem for guys like Peplinski, Hunter, and McDonald was that that middle tier was younger, faster, and beginning to push the older guard aside. Lanny and Peplinski were rotating the captaincy all season long. Who knew that by the time they were playing for the Cup there would only be one lineup spot for the both of them?

"I remember going home after we'd won the first game against Montreal in 1986," said Peplinski. "I was listening to the radio, and they said that 85.4 percent of the teams that won the first game go on to win. I thought, 'We're going to win a Stanley Cup.' And I was wrong.

"In 1989, we had enough guys who knew the secret to winning the Stanley Cup. And that is, if you're lucky enough to get there, you've really got to slow it down. It goes so fast, even if you're playing every second night and you go to seven games, fourteen days passes by in a blink of an eye. And it's really hard to reset yourself if you mess up. In 1986, we won a game, then we lost four straight. We just hadn't figured out that you need to be absolutely on plan every minute.

"If you're good enough and lucky enough to get there, you have to take advantage of that. In 1989 we figured that out."

Ironically, one of the key changes for Calgary had not involved a Fletcher decision at all. It happened after the 1987 upset loss to Winnipeg in Round 1, after which Bob Johnson walked away to return to his roots at USA Hockey. As much respect as the Flames players had for Badger Bob, even they knew it was time for a change.

"Even though I believe we were coached better than any other team, I think the one thing that Bob Johnson wasn't willing to do was to press hard on guys," recollected Peplinski. "Human nature is such that very few individuals can run hills till they puke. It's hard to do. But if you've got somebody there whippin' you, you can. If you've got a buddy running beside you who is driving you, and you're driving him, you can. That was the one element that Bob required, to be not only a great coach but also an incredible, winning coach.

"I don't think there are a lot of people who will tell you that Terry Crisp was their best friend. But they will tell you, he knew when and how to push people."

The Flames won Game 1 again in 1989, this time at home in the Saddledome, but in identical fashion to 1986 Montreal bounced back to take Game 2. Lanny looked tired, and he was replaced in Game 3 by Mark Hunter. The Flames lost, and in Game 4 Peplinski joined McDonald, both captains watching the game from the dressing room as Calgary evened the series.

The series swung back to Calgary for Game 5. Tim Hunter came out, McDonald stayed out, but Peplinski returned to the lineup. He had three shots on goal and set Joel Otto up twenty-eight seconds into the game as Calgary won 3–2.

Now it was back to Montreal, and Stanley would be in the building. Crisp knew the decisions that lay ahead, and his guts were already churning as he boarded the flight at YYC. Hunter had taken how many punches, defended how many teammates since the day he joined the team in 1982? How could you not play him?

Peplinski was a Day 1er, playing in Calgary's original home opener at the Stampede Corral in 1980. He couldn't have much time left, but still, he was only twenty-eight at the time. Retirement did not appear imminent.

Then there was Lanny. He'd been cooling his heels since Game 2, and quietly, reporters covering the series wondered if this was how it would end for McDonald. Almost everyone wanted to see McDonald hoist the Cup, but after more than a thousand games, surely he would get the chance to play in the game that preceded the ceremony, wouldn't he?

We've all seen those Stanley Cup "win it for somebody" movements over the years, such as in 2001 in Colorado when it became all about winning one for Ray Bourque, who had gone Cup-less through twenty-two superb seasons. Or 2004 in Tampa Bay, when the Lightning were winning one for Dave Andreychuk, the veteran of more than sixteen hundred games who was almost certainly getting his last crack at a ring.

So, of course, there was a goodly portion of every Flames fan's heart that wanted to see McDonald, a Southern Alberta son who'd slugged it out through 1,111 regular-season games and scored exactly five hundred goals, raise the Cup. Same for Leafs fans, or most Canadians outside of Habs Nation, for that matter. But there was far more at play in Calgary in 1989 then there was in either Tampa in 2004 or Colorado in 2001.

Tampa was a one-off in 2004, much like the team they defeated in Game 7 that spring, the Calgary Flames. To compare Andreychuk and the Bolts with McDonald and the Flames, in that sense, was pure folly. Calgary had been much closer for much longer.

This was Calgary's second Cup appearance in four years, yet you didn't have tell a Flames fan that there were no guarantees another Cup final was around the corner. Now it was Game 6, the Flames led the series 3–2, and Big Stanley would be on hand that night at the hallowed Montreal Forum.

"What we tried to preach was, 'Look, we can't afford to take this back home,'" Lanny said. "It would be nice to win it at home, but Patrick Roy could win a Game 7 all by himself. I wanted no part of that."

There was a level of statesmanship attached to McDonald by this time. He'd made his name in Toronto and now had a far better team flanking him in Calgary. But it was a race to the finish line, with McDonald's waning abilities in one lane and in the other lane the thought that in a game like this one, you needed his veteran savvy in the lineup.

"They had some good players with high skill levels, like Reinhart, MacInnis, Loob, and Nieuwendyk," said Wayne Gretzky. "But what changed the whole complexion of the team was when Cliff went out and traded for Lanny McDonald. Lanny brought credibility to their group. That leader, the Jean Béliveau–type guy. He brought a certain calmness to their team."

★

It's game day in Montreal: May 25, 1989. A Thursday. "That day in Montreal," Crisp said, "it was the longest day I ever had."

By now it was pretty clear. The Flames had won two straight

and led the series 3–2. They were beginning to exert their dominance over Montreal, and anyone following the series could see it.

McDonald hadn't played since Game 2. Peplinski had sat out Game 4, and Hunter had sat out Game 5. All three were right-handed shots, and what was becoming obvious was, there was one spot on right wing for the three of them. The lineup was winning, and that trumped all loyalties. It was no time for an emotional decision, and nobody knew this better than Crisp, who had played in Philadelphia during their two Cup wins in 1974 and 1975.

"When I was with the Flyers in 1975 when we won the Cup in Buffalo, I'd played all the games up to that point. But in the final game, when we won the Cup, Fred [Shero] didn't dress me. I sat there all night wondering why," he said. "As a player it's hard to wrap your brain around it."

So Crisp knew exactly how crushing his decision was going to be to someone. Or, in this case, to two someones.

"I go back over it, and if it wasn't the longest day of my hockey career, it was the toughest," Crisp said. "We were in Montreal, going for the Stanley Cup. We had so much depth. We were so strong that you knew what you had to do. Every coach says the same thing: you sit down and decide on the lineup for that night, to win that game. I was looking over my lineup with [assistant coaches] Tom Watt and Doug Risebrough, going over and over and over it. I walked the streets of Montreal that day. It was a hard day.

"Tom and Riser, they came in and we had another meeting about the final lineup. The hardest part of all was this: Those two men, Tim Hunter and Jim Peplinski, were on the list of who sits out. Each of them had earned the right to be there in that game. But for that immediate game, the lineup that we as coaches decided on was the lineup we felt we needed to win this game. It was one of the hardest things I ever had to do, to sit those men out."

Crisp decided to play McDonald. Was it an emotional decision? Was it made out of loyalty? Out of deference? Maybe Crisp figured that, having not played for a full week, a fresh McDonald had one more big goal in him?

"It was a no-brainer," Crisp said. "Lanny was an icon, probably in his last season, and he'd never won a Cup. We were on the threshold of winning the Cup . . . How could you not [play him]?

"But Pep could have been in. Hunts could have been in, and we would have likely won the Cup that night anyhow. But a decision had to be made. You knew you weren't going to be popular," he said.

And Crisp, more than anyone, knew how much hurt he was about to dole out. "There's no antidote that's going to salve that wound. No antidote that's going to make you feel better—and there isn't an easy way to tell a player."

So, he sent Risebrough to tell them.

Peplinski, always good for an eloquent, thoughtful quote, did not dwell on the moment for long. He hasn't, publicly, in the twenty-five years since, really. It is as if he moved past it then, and it's not even clear if he's ever completely dealt with it, even today.

"When Riser came in and said, 'Crispy says you're not playing tonight,' I told Riser, 'Tell Crispy to go *&^% himself,'" he says. "That probably wasn't the right response."

The words flowed straight from Peplinski's heart, through the mouth of a hockey player. I've known hundreds of players, and no matter how much love they had for their coach, all of them would have thought what Peplinski said, and most would have verbalized it, as he did.

"I don't blame him," Crisp said, now twenty-five years later. "I understand where he's coming from. That's pride in an athlete, and everyone wants to play."

But something about the situation didn't sit right with Crisp, who was seventy-one when we spoke. He stewed on it for a while, then Crisp repeated: "Crispy?"

"I thought we were a coaching staff?" he mused. "I thought we had Tom Watt, Doug Risebrough, and myself making that decision. When you're making those decisions, do you think I'm going to do it without addressing Tom Watt and Doug Risebrough, who have been by my side all season long?"

Then he thought some more.

"I've often wondered, when we had functions, Tim Hunter and Jim Peplinski are always perfect gentlemen. What do they think about Terry Crisp? What do they think of Terry Crisp? We were a coaching staff. Three of us . . .

"Ah," he finally said, "I'd have probably told Terry Crisp to go *&^% himself too. Think about it. You've played all year, all of your career, and suddenly this hits you out of the blue? It upsets you."

"I was an assistant coach for a long time," added Hunter, who would go on to work for the Washington Capitals, San Jose Sharks, and Toronto Maple Leafs. "When things are going good, you're a real good guy. But when things go bad, you're a prick in a hurry, I'll tell ya."

So, while McDonald was out there messing up that scoring chance, and then taking that dumb penalty, Hunter and Peplinski were in the dressing room. "He was really sour," Hunter said of Peplinski.

Today the spare players get fully dressed in their gear and jerseys during the third period of a Cup-clinching game so that they look more like participating players in the post-game pictures with the Cup. But back then, there were few traditions. Only a year before, Gretzky had instigated the group picture around the Stanley Cup that has become de rigueur today, but it wasn't a thing back then. Peplinski and Hunter certainly weren't going to gear up. In fact, their gear was likely bagged and on a truck already anyhow.

"We rode the bike [during the game] because you had to stay ready in case there was a Game 7," Hunter said. "We watched [on TV] in the dressing room, popping our heads out once in a while. But he [Peplinski] didn't want to go on the ice and get the Cup with Lanny if we won.

"I said, 'Pep, tell you what. I'll go out, get the Cup with Lanny, and I'll bring it over to the concourse and you can run it around the concourse at the Forum. Okay?' He kinda laughed."

Even in his depression, it had begun to set in on Peplinski, the way it did on Crisp that 1975 night at the Aud in Buffalo—exactly fourteen years and two days prior—that if this was the way he was going to win his Stanley Cup, then he might as well enjoy it. There was only one of the three of them who was going to have the chance to make any special memories from this game—other than the outcome, of course—and that was Lanny McDonald.

And for the moment, McDonald was in the penalty box. "Praying like a good Catholic boy would that they don't score," he recalled.

The Canadiens did not convert on their power play, and McDonald's prayers were further answered when he stepped out of the box and his club had the puck. What ensued would be the last NHL goal he ever scored, and one that has been mis-labelled for years as the game-winner. It was, in fact, the second Flames goal in a 4–2 win, with Gilmour scoring twice more to seal the Cup victory.

But after all the angst, after fourteen playoff games without a goal, after a sixteen-year career that had reached its final night in hockey's most elegant showplace, what happened next for Lanny McDonald was nothing short of poetic.

"I jump out of the box," he began, the sequence burned into his memory. "Macoun moves the puck up to centre to Hakan Loob, and I jump into the play to make it a 3-on-2. When we get to their blue line, Hakan Loob throws the puck to the left side to Joe Nieuwendyk. And in one motion Nieuwendyk pulls it back and fires it in between Chelios's skate and stick to the right side [to McDonald]."

Watch the video. It was a masterful pass by Nieuwendyk, as much for the fact it hit McDonald on the tape as for the quickness with which he'd released it. Chelios was still edging the wrong direction toward Nieuwendyk, following the initial pass, when the puck was already on McDonald's stick, so fast were Nieuwendyk's instincts.

"We all knew," continued McDonald, "when Patrick Roy comes across his net he goes down in the butterfly and tries to cover as much net as he can. The only place to score is top shelf."

McDonald channelled his 1978 hands and buried the puck up under the crossbar. "When that baby went in? It was like, 'Yeah, baby!' I wanted the game to end right there, but we had a whole lot of game left to play."

Harry Neale, the former coach who had taken the chair next to Bob Cole working as a CBC colour analyst, quipped, "McDonald shows you a twenty-six-year-old's shot, from a thirty-six-year-old man, as he put it up and over Patrick Roy."

And, Neale added, "Crisp dressed Peplinski, and he got an assist at the thirty-eight-second mark of Game 5. Now he dresses McDonald, and McDonald puts him ahead in Game 6."

Of the 544 goals that McDonald scored in regular season and playoffs, it is clear which one is nearest and dearest to his heart. "When you're a little boy, you're trying to get to the NHL, but more importantly, you're playing the game to win a Stanley Cup. That was probably the most important goal I ever scored," he said.

Gilmour sandwiched a power-play goal and an empty-netter around a Montreal goal by Rick Green, and when it was done, with President John Ziegler waiting at centre ice to hand Captain McDonald the Cup, Lanny wouldn't go alone. Where most captains accept the Cup and then hand it off to their next in command, McDonald demanded that the two vets—dressed in red Flames workout strip—join him at centre ice.

They accepted the trophy as a trio, and the shot of Peplinski lovingly rubbing the top of McDonald's head is a snapshot you'll see in the bowels of the Saddledome even today.

"I wouldn't have gone on the ice if Hunts hadn't pulled me out there," Peplinski said. "It was a great moment to eternalize things. Lifting that Cup with Lanny, the three of us. One of my all-time favourite photos, regardless of whether I have sweats on or not. I played in 95 percent of the games to win a Stanley Cup. My name is on the Stanley Cup."

That everyone's name in this Flames organization reached that hallowed status that day in May 1989 is justice. It was, over a period of nearly a decade, one of the NHL's finest programs, just poorly situated behind the juggernaut in Edmonton that hogged five Stanley Cups and six finals appearances in eight seasons.

Today, there are conflicting mindsets from those Flames players who carted the Cup around the Forum ice in 1989. And the divide depends primarily on age—how long they'd fought to win that Cup, and how many more chances they had before hanging up their skates.

"The teams we had after 1989, we should have won at least one more Stanley Cup and we didn't. That's something I often think about," said Theo Fleury, who was a rookie in 1989. "After 1989 I never got another sniff until I went to Colorado [in 1999, a conference-finals loss to Dallas]. You don't realize how important, how significant those times were in your life. You're so young, you don't realize what's going on.

"I'm forty-six years old today, and I think about the year after. Us losing to L.A. in six games, and we were obviously a way better team than they were. We finished [twenty-four points] ahead of them in the standings and they beat us in six games. And there were a few other times after that," he said, the bitterness in his voice seeping through the phone line. "It just goes to show you how hard it is to win a Stanley Cup. You look at that dynasty the Oilers had. The Flames, we were trying to get there. We did one time, but we wanted to be there all the time. But because we played in the same division we had to play each other early in the playoffs, instead of meeting each other in a Stanley Cup final.

"Most times, if it was an Edmonton–Calgary playoff series, it *was* the Stanley Cup. Because the team that won it went on to win the Stanley Cup. Edmonton did that five times."

That spells out another dichotomy in the Battle, where members of the Oilers have five Stanley Cup rings while the Flames players have one. Having watched every minute of that rivalry, there isn't a chance that the Oilers were that much better than Calgary in the big picture. They were just a little bit better in every season but one, and most years, after getting past the Flames, the heaviest lifting was over for Edmonton.

Finally, the hockey gods had conspired to give the Flames their due, paving a path that did not include the Oilers that spring, after Edmonton had blown a 3–1 series lead to the Gretzky-led Kings. The Flames learned from 1986, the same way the Oilers had learned from their defeats at the hands of the Islanders, and given a chance to make it right, Calgary pretty much powered through those playoffs — after a Round 1 hiccup that required a Game 7 overtime goal against Vancouver.

"Hunts, Lanny, Peppy Joel Otto, Al MacInnis—those guys had been through it all. But it was as much for the city," Crisp said. "Our city was so desperate because up the road the Edmonton Oilers had won. It was the City of Champions, and all that. And Calgary finally broke through as a team and as a city to get one. Finally."

For Peplinski, who lives in Calgary to this day and has a very successful auto leasing business, it took him about thirty seconds to realize how much that Cup meant—and would mean— whether he'd been on the ice in that Game 6 or not. It's a spiritual thing for these guys, to finally get their hands on Big Stanley after a lifetime in the game. And as soon as he did, Peplinski's mind went back to all the times he'd played for that Cup in minor hockey rinks across Ontario as a kid.

"The thing that came together for me, at that moment, was the number of people who no one would know the names of, who were instrumental in my hockey and personal development," he said. "I was so friggin' lucky, over the course of my career, to have teachers, coaches parents . . . I remember at the moment, thinking about a lot of those different names, and calling a bunch of them afterwards to say, 'Thank you.'

"Then that moment passes, and I remember thinking on the plane home: 'I wonder, what now?' It's time to move on."

Peplinski took a couple of aborted, six-game runs at extending his NHL career over the next few years, but his heart was never really in it. It would almost have seemed like he was pushing his luck, after all the game had given him—and all the city of Calgary had given him—to try to squeeze more out of the game than he'd already enjoyed. Today, he is a product of what he calls "the notoriety that that Stanley Cup provided for each and every one of us for the past twenty-five years."

"I think back to guys who were with the team the year before and didn't stay with the team. Guys who could have just as easily been part of the success," he said. "I think back to getting lucky against Vancouver, arguably [in Round 1]. To different things that could have derailed that one championship, and all of the sudden your entire career isn't near the success that you want it to be just because you won the last series you played in.

"Thirty years later I am still amazed at how winning a Stanley Cup has defined our careers. I am still incredibly appreciative of just how lucky I got, and the fact that I ran into Al MacNeil, Pierre Page, and Bob Johnson, and then I got to room with Bob Murdoch, and then I met guys like Lanny McDonald, and Joey Mullen, Timmy Hunter and Hakan Loob and Doug Risebrough . . .

"I just have got very, very lucky in my career."

As for Lanny McDonald, he was never tempted to lace 'em up again in anger. Let's face it, he didn't have a whole lot left anyway. And after crafting an ending like he'd penned that night in Montreal, all a few more games might have done was mess up a good story.

"Well, [Gretzky] had mentioned Jean Béliveau before," he said when I asked him if he'd known that Game 6 would be his career finale. "And I was always disappointed I didn't have a chance to play against Jean Béliveau. He retired after they had won a Cup, and he could have probably played another two or four years. But he walked out the door on top, winning a Cup, and I always thought, 'Boy, that would be a pretty cool way to say goodbye.'

"When we won it, it was, 'Thank you very much. I am out of here.'"

13

STU GRIMSON VERSUS DAVE BROWN I AND II

The Night the Battle Went Too Far
"Don't be leaving for coffee."

Stu Grimson was the son of a Mountie, never a good recipe for putting down roots or forging lasting friendships. Staff Sergeant Stan Grimson spent thirty-one years in the Royal Canadian Mounted Police, and Stu, like so many kids of so many cops, quickly figured out that joining a hockey or football team was the surest way of meeting friends and fitting in quickly.

"We bounced around all over B.C., and Kamloops is as close to a hometown as I've got," Grimson said. "My earliest memories were skates on my feet pushing a chair around a pond somewhere. Learn how to skate, then chase a puck around."

Grimson was like every legitimate heavyweight you'll ever meet. Slow to grow into his frame. Gangly. A clumsy-looking gait as a teenager, like a baby moose on a frozen spring lake. But he was big, and that size bought him an extra second or two with the puck—and the ability to take it away from a smaller opponent that other players did not enjoy. When the coach needed what he brought to the table, Grimson would make the team. When they didn't, well, it was British Columbia, Canada. There was always a team that would have you. "There were years when I made the travel team, there were years I did not," Grimson said now, without any hard feelings.

It was the early 1980s, a time when even the best level of minor hockey player didn't play fifty games in a winter. It was the end of those healthy days before sport exclusivity, where kids played hockey in the winter, baseball in the summer, and, when you were Grimson's size, football in the fall. The spring hockey or three-on-three camps that ensure a young Canadian male can play hockey for twelve months a year? They did not yet exist. It was a wonderful time.

There was no bantam draft in the Western Hockey League then either, the way there has been since 1990. A team would just "list" a player on a scout's say-so, and so it was that a local bird dog named Glen Dirk was behind the wheel one evening when Grimson was out with a few of the boys from Sa-Hali Secondary School.

"Glen Dirk happened to be driving by the Kamloops movie theatre one night when I got into a scrape with some drill rig guy from out of town and kinda mopped up the street with him," Grimson recalled, chuckling. "Glen thought, 'This would be an interesting guy to have on our team . . .'"

Grimson, a well-built middle linebacker for the Sa-Hali Sabres, was walking in that familiar secondary-school pack of boys, all wearing their leather-sleeved football jackets, talking a big game on a midweek night. They epitomized strength in numbers, but as so often is the case, when push came to shove it was the biggest and bravest who were called upon to represent.

Of course, Grimson did not have to be asked twice. Some rough-necks started mouthing off at these younger boys, all dressed alike in their team jackets. They were younger, less experienced, and, the drillers figured, probably afraid of a bunch of rig pigs with five o'clock shadows and pockets full of oil money.

"Some guys were mouthing off," Grimson recalled, "so I sorted through the crowd, grabbed one of these guys, and cracked him in the face. I was always kind of aggressive by nature growing up."

☆

A couple of provinces to the east, Dave Brown was a similarly sized kid growing up in Saskatoon, the son of Phil Brown, a respected mechanic at the local Co-op Farm Implements dealer. His mom, Eleanor, was the secretary of maintenance and plan-ning at the University of Saskatchewan, organized and fastidious. Neither of them had any idea that young Dave, who inherited a work ethic as strong as both of his folks, would one day inhabit a dressing room stall next to the great Mark Messier. For now, he was just trying to stick on the Junior B Saskatoon Westleys.

"I wasn't a real good player," Brown said now, looking back through eyes that belong today to the head pro scout of the Philadelphia Flyers. He was sixteen years old, in a Junior B league that allowed six twenty-year-olds on every roster. It was the 1978–79 season, the year that Boris Fistric (father to NHL defenceman Mark) led the major-junior Western Hockey League with 460 penalty minutes—more than seven minutes per game played.

Some perspective: the penalty minutes leader in the NHL for the 2013–14 season was Vancouver's Tom Sestito—with a piddly 213 minutes. Only three players amassed more than 200 minutes in penalties that NHL season. In the 1978–79 Western Hockey League, the tenth-ranked PIMs leader was Dirk Graham, with

252. The NHL plays eighty-two games, while the WHL played seventy-two games that season.

Now, a team comparison: the Philadelphia Flyers led all NHL clubs with 1,180 PIMs in 2013–14. In the 1978–79 Western Hockey League, the Portland Winter Hawks were the most pacifistic of the twelve teams, amassing a conciliatory 1,728 PIMs. Portland averaged 24 PIMs per game, Philly 14, and while seven of thirty NHL teams eclipsed 1,000 minutes in 2013–14, there were seven teams with more than 2,000 PIMs in the Western League in 1978–79. Again, with ten fewer games played in junior.

So, these were violent times in hockey. The tail end, actually, of hockey's most violent period—the *Slap Shot* years—when bench-clearing brawls were a weekly occurrence somewhere in the hockey world. In the Western League, a couple of tough guys from the home team would sneak out early for the pre-game warmup, commandeer the other's team's net, and slide it to the corner in their own zone. When the visiting team skated out for warmup, they had two choices: either go through warmup like a bunch of pussies with no net or wade, en masse, into the home team's end, inviting a pre-game brawl.

Eventually, the men who governed junior hockey would outlaw such foolishness and mandate separate warmups in the WHL and elsewhere. But before Brown would reach the WHL, he would play senior hockey in Saskatchewan as a sixteen-year-old, facing off against men four years his senior. Tough men who liked to throw down, and Brown was big for his age. Looked more like eighteen than sixteen. As Johnny Cash sang in "A Boy Named Sue," Brown knew he'd have to get tough or die.

"We had fights every game. It was a tough league," said Brown, who found his calling as a hockey enforcer in that Saskatchewan Junior B league. "That's when I realized this is how you're going to have to play. You're going to have to play tough, if you're going to make it. It kind of made me grow up a little bit."

Like Grimson, Brown—a left-hander—also found that his ability to fight bought him extra time with the puck. He was destined to be a Flyer. He was big, aggressive, and played the game in a straight line. But first he would serve a couple of seasons in the Western League, a cup of coffee in Spokane, and then the entire 1981–82 season with the Saskatoon Blades. Grimson would not arrive in Regina until the following season, by which time Brown had moved on to minor pro.

"The Western Hockey League back then was probably the craziest it ever was. It was a wild time, man. A wild fuckin' time," Brown remembered. Led by Al Tuer's 486 minutes, the Regina Pats set the record for most PIMs as a team in 1981–82, a record long since broken. The intrepid Bill LaForge, whose teams always fought like caged wolverines, was the Pats' coach.

"We used to go in there and fight with them all the time," Brown said. "Must have brawled them five or six times that year 'cause we played them sixteen times a season. By the end, they didn't want to fight us anymore, but LaForge would send them out anyhow. Al Tuer? He had almost five hundred penalty minutes. He would have beat the record, but he got suspended."

Imagine that.

I've asked many a heavyweight this question over the years, and some—almost exclusively men who still had years left in the game—have lied when they answered. Brown, who was fifty-one when we spoke, his fighting days long past, easily answers the question: "Did you ever really enjoy fighting?"

"To a certain point you've got to enjoy it 'cause it's a tough thing to do if you don't," he reasoned. "You've got to enjoy wanting to win 'cause it can be tough if you're not winning fights, man. And at that point, I didn't have my sights set on the NHL. I didn't ever think I'd get there."

★

It was a silicone spray. The kind you'd find at any hardware store. There was also some everyday spray-on glue, perfect for keeping a hockey jersey locked on to a pair of shoulder pads. And a trainer's sewing kit, just to ensure there was nothing loose to grab on to.

The Oilers' head medical trainer, Ken Lowe (older brother to Kevin), had spent more than seven years working for the Edmonton Eskimos of the Canadian Football League. So when a young call-up nicknamed "The Grim Reaper" had successfully tied up Dave Brown's lethal left hand in a Sunday-night fight at Northlands Coliseum—on January 7, 1990—Oilers head equipment man Barrie Stafford wondered out loud if there was any way they could help Brown in the inevitable rematch.

"We should call Dwayne," advised Lowe. That was Dwayne Mandrusiak, the Eskimos' equipment man since 1971, and Lowe's buddy to this day. Football trainers have forever doctored equipment, with linemen on both sides of the ball requiring skintight jerseys so they can't be grabbed on to and manhandled in the trenches. There isn't a trick in the trade that Mandrusiak hasn't plied at one time or another, and so he arrived on a Monday morning to the back room behind the Oilers main dressing quarters, where Stafford doled out hockey gear and life lessons over a desk surrounded by skate sharpeners, a sewing machine, and riveting tools.

Stafford's favourite life lesson was known as The Six P Principle, and he passed it along often: "Proper Preparation Prevents Piss Poor Performance," he'd say with a smile, index finger raised. Well, the night before, the Oilers had lost 3–1 at home to Calgary. That never sits well, but what they liked even less was how they'd lost. Edmonton expected not only to win the games against Calgary but the fights too. And on this night a young buck who had been called up from the International League's Salt Lake City Golden Eagles had made his mark on the Battle.

His name was Stu (The Grim Reaper) Grimson, joined in the Flames lineup that night, according to then *Edmonton Journal* columnist Cam Cole, by Ken (The Grim Skater) Sabourin.

"I did not have a great sense of the broader picture," began Grimson, who still bears the scars of this particular chapter in the Battle. "I got it that [Tim] Hunter was there by himself. Lots of teams had a couple of guys my size, and he could use the support. I guess I kind of got that, but I was more focused on my own personal situation. It didn't have to be communicated to me: 'Stu, if you're going to stick here, of course we want you to play five-plus minutes a night, but we need the physical attributes. We need you to bang people for us, to go to the net for us, and we need you to shake your gloves off when appropriate and help establish a physical presence for the group as well.' I got that. I knew I had to provide that if I was going to stick as an NHLer."

Every NHL heavyweight will tell you about the ritualistic perusing of the week's schedule and the torturous mental process of linking buildings and/or opponents with upcoming bouts. In that particular season of 1989–90, a trip into the Met Center in Bloomington meant that big Basil McRae would be there, rolling out the welcome mat. The dark, dingy Cap Centre in Landover, Maryland? Alan May, a game journeyman whom I grew up with in Edmonton, who had taken the long road to his job with the Washington Capitals. Marty McSorley had been dealt alongside Wayne Gretzky to Los Angeles, working the old Fabulous Forum on Manchester Boulevard. Bob Probert, who would tally up 3,300 PIMs and several convictions in his long and storied career, policed Joe Louis Arena in the Motor City.

But this was the Battle of Alberta, and Grimson didn't have to buy a program that Sunday morning to know what time the movie started that night and who would be his co-star. "I knew, if was going to stick in the NHL, especially being a member of the Calgary Flames, all roads led through Dave Brown. I knew in the first game I suited up against the Oilers, Brownie and I were going to have to go."

Grimson was twenty-five, a veteran of just two NHL games. He'd broken his maiden the season before in Buffalo, on a line with Hunter and Joel Otto. He fought Kevin Maguire that night, then went back down to the minors for the rest of the year. He scarcely recalls that scrap. His next two, however, he would remember.

Now, after years of seemingly having one fewer heavy than the Oilers every night, Calgary had Grimson alongside Hunter, out there warming up in the most hallowed building of that NHL era. Four Stanley Cup banners hung overhead amid the laundry line of Presidents' Trophy, Smythe Division, and Campbell Conference pennants—with a fifth but a few months away.

All of that trivia, plus about six bucks, would have bought Grimson a Northlands beer that night. He probably could have used a belt or two, knowing what awaited him, dressed in the Oilers home whites.

"It was a pretty daunting proposition because in my estimation, that was the toughest, baddest, meanest man on the planet back then. The toughest man in the NHL back then, by most accounts. He was a big, tough guy," Grimson said. "I remember watching him looping over my side of the ice during the warmup, and I could hardly muster up the saliva to spit on the ice I was so nervous.

"We fought twice that night."

Now, of all the things that are fuzzy in the memory of a hockey player over the quarter-century between that scrap and today, the winner of a fight between a beloved teammate and a despised enemy perhaps tops the list. Teammates almost always give the decision to teammates.

Everyone remembers the outcome of the fight that would take place two nights later in Calgary, but the Grimson–Brown scrap that happened at the 11:24 mark of the first period on that Sunday evening in Edmonton? Well, Grimson won, we know that. How badly? That is up for debate.

"Grimson was this young guy," recalled Oilers defenceman Kevin Lowe, "and he wasn't causing a lot of shit." But he fought Brown, "and the papers the next day had it as a Grimson victory."

Flames trainer Bearcat Murray: "Grimson just kicked his ass, which we were very proud of. And in Edmonton!"

Dave Brown: "I'd been hit a couple of weeks before. Took a puck [above] the eye. It hit Gravey's [Adam Graves] skate and hit me in the face. I'd just got the stitches out, and it was tender. [Grimson] hit me there in the fight and cut me open. He might have got a little bit the better of me, but I think the fight was pretty close. He might have hit me a couple of extra times . . ."

Stu Grimson: "The first shift we were on the ice, I kind of elbowed him right off the draw, we dropped our gloves. I think he missed me with two or three left hands above my head. I finally got ahold of his left, and I clocked him twice and laid him out."

I finally got ahold of his left. . . Grimson would only wish he could say the same thing two nights later in Calgary. But Brown had something up his sleeve. And on his sleeve. And under his sleeve.

There was no doubt about it: this young stud from the farm in Salt Lake City had felled the mighty Dave Brown that night. They could argue over the scorecard, but not over who left Northlands Coliseum with the championship belt. In just the third game of his NHL career, the cop's kid from Kamloops had taken down the champ, but like the old Stampede Wrestling shows that played across Alberta, the same group of men would hit the same mat two nights later in Calgary. The only difference was, these results were not scripted the way they were in Stu Hart's Stampede Wrestling shows.

"It was the best of times, it was the worst of times," Grimson said now, a wry smile on his lips. "You knew you were going to have to answer for it eventually. We did fight again later that [first] night, but I'd clocked him twice pretty good [in the first bout], and I think he was a little wobbly. He came back for more, but he didn't have much. It wasn't much of a fight, though it was a different story Tuesday night in Calgary."

If what happened on Sunday and Tuesday night epitomized the Battle of Alberta for some people, for others it was the media circus that ensued in both cities at Monday's practices that made the Battle stand alone.

Had it been Gord Donnelly or Shawn Cronin of the Winnipeg Jets that had dusted Brown that night, the Oilers enforcer would have been just as miffed, but it would not have been the cause célèbre it was for the hockey writers in Alberta that Monday. L.A.'s Jay Miller and Vancouver's Garth Butcher were divisional foes, but Brown and the rest of the Oilers didn't see red when they looked at those players the way they did when Grimson rose from that fight with a triumphant swagger. It was a swagger he would come to regret.

"You and I both know, it doesn't matter who you are. Sooner or later you're going down," said Stafford, who had a front row seat for the first bout and would play a decisive role in Round 2. "[Grimson's post-fight behaviour] was less of a celebration than a release. He got up and shook his fist. Like, 'Yeah!' Well, Dave Brown was very, very upset."

You could imagine the tension release, the adrenalin rush, that coursed through Grimson's body when the fight was over and he had defeated the man he had thought of as "the toughest, baddest, meanest man on the planet." And he had hurt his hand in the fight, so shaking it came naturally—even if the Oilers had not seen it that way.

"It was a tough balance," Grimson recalled. "A snot-nosed rookie, feeling pretty good about himself, having shown well against one of the very best in the league. But at the same time, trying to keep yourself grounded, knowing that you're going to face the same guy a couple of nights later."

Alas, it wasn't the same guy. Dave Brown wasn't the same guy at all. Brown arrived at the rink for practice the next day without a word. He dressed in silence, practised the same way, a focused stoicism guiding him, his clock set to puck drop in Calgary the following night.

"Well, don't be leaving for coffee," Brown told the Edmonton media that day in a short, impatient interview. In Calgary, the press rushed to the Saddledome to introduce their new, young enforcer to Flames fans. "You only have so many chances to make an impression. I think we both knew what was going to happen," Grimson told the media that day. "He's a tough guy. One of the more legitimate heavyweights I've faced."

More legitimate. It probably didn't sound as cocky on Monday as it looked in print on Tuesday morning. Grimson was in a tough spot. There wasn't a thing he could say that would not pour fuel on the coals burning inside Brown's belly. But as a young newcomer, he wasn't really in a position to blow off the media either. He had to say *something.* The day off, he would later deduce, did not serve Grimson well. Both in what was said and what was brewing into the old bull up the highway, whose career as the king was suddenly in jeopardy.

"I had a couple of days to stew about it. I was pissed off," Brown recalled. "I wasn't pissed off because of the fight. I was mad because [the media] tried to make it like he'd really beat me up. I was really pissed off. It was just the thought that people may have thought I lost. Simple as that. He was just trying to come up and make a name for himself. There was no disrespect. It was just the fact I never ever wanted to lose. Then you've got to hear about it from other people? I didn't want to hear that. I was pissed off. *Pissed off.*"

Mandrusiak arrived during practice that morning, entering through the back hallway into Stafford's open office. When Brown was off the practice ice, his gear hanging to dry in his dressing room stall, Stafford retrieved Brown's shoulder pads, the skimpy non-protective shoulder pads of a fighter. Built more for falling off than stopping pucks. There was an old trick that Mandrusiak had picked up from a colleague in the National Football League, where they would apply a spray-on glue to a player's shoulder pads, then slip the jersey overtop. Once the glue set, it was impossible to grab the jersey.

"The player just sneaks into the shoulder pads from the inside," Stafford said. "Then Dwayne said, 'You know what we also do? We silicone-spray the outside of the sweater.' So, not only did we spray his shoulder pads so that they were skintight to the jersey—he could hardly get his sweater on it was so tight—but we siliconed the shit out of the whole front of his sweater and his left arm.

"It was a very competitive world. We're trying to help our players, whether they're scoring goals or winning scraps. And I'm sure Grimson had help on his side."

"I watched the game on TV, and I was laughing," said Mandrusiak. "It was neat that I was able to help. We're all friends, Spark, Barrie, Kenny, and I. It was a nice collaboration."

Brown, meanwhile, was in a catatonic state.

"I don't think he slept for two days, according to his wife, who has since passed away," said Kevin Lowe. "We flew down the day of the game, and me, Mess, and a bunch of guys at the back of the plane, it was like, 'Holy Christ . . .' He wasn't looking at anybody, he wasn't talking to anybody. He was just sitting in his seat, kind of rocking. It was like an assassin, or a guy walking into a shootout at the O.K. Corral. He knows that either he's inflicting damage or there is going to be damage inflicted on him."

"I don't remember any of that stuff, no," Brown said now. "I didn't hardly talk for two days. I knew what was going to happen. I was pissed off. I was pissed off, man. I was ready. Ready for whatever was going to happen."

Rod Phillips, the radio voice of the Oilers, travelled every inch of the way with the team. From the team flight, to the bus, to the hotel, and back on the bus to the rink. While other media walk into the Saddledome, say, sixty to ninety minutes before game time and head straight to the press meal, Phillips rode with the team from the hotel, and his stature and position as the hometown radio voice allowed him to hang around the dressing room for some time after arrival.

"I go down into the equipment room in Calgary," recalled Phillips. "Barrie Stafford is there, Brownie has his uniform on already, and they're in the back. Barrie is sewing the left sleeve of Brownie's jersey, sewing it really, really tight. Nothing to grab. Then they smeared over it with Vaseline, after that.

"I remember I said, 'Wow, you're really going after him.' And big Brownie looked at me, and he said, 'Rod, I'm gonna hurt him.'"

"It was like he had a polio arm," said Stafford's right-hand man in the Oilers equipment room, Lyle (Sparky) Kulchisky. "He had one regular arm, and the other one was just so tight. I don't know how they didn't see it in warmup."

All hockey players have their rituals, but go to ice level some time for a pre-game warmup and you'll see that the fighters' rituals naturally must involve the opponent. So where Gretzky could go through his pre-game routine without incorporating the opponent in any way, it only figures that the only way to be an intimidator is to find an intimida*tee*.

"It was shaping up much like it did two nights prior," Grimson said. "Warmup, Brownie does his traditional looping across my side of the red line. It became clear, even before regulation started, that he and I were going to go at it again."

Brown's stare would bring a normal person to their knees. He is big, imposing, and if he wants them to be that way, his eyes can be dead. Like a shark. Meet him today, and they are friendly, welcoming eyes, as he extends his hand for a shake. Beat him in a scrap, and you get the Dave Brown that's all business. And his business, that night, involved dealing with this young kid who'd come up from the minors.

Many accounts of the fight have Grimson somehow not ready for what ensued, though that seems hard to believe. Even his trainer, Bearcat Murray, had weighed in that day. "I talked to Stu in the morning," Murray said. "I said, 'You've got to be alert. You embarrassed the hell out of him up there. Please be alert.' I begged him. But he didn't seem to pay attention to me. I said, 'Stu, I'm serious.'"

This wasn't anything that every one of these hockey people hadn't seen before. Hell, this was the Battle of Alberta, its very existence built on the back of copious fisticuffs. Hunter–Semenko, Jackson–Peplinski, McClelland–Sheehy. Grimson versus Brown was just another in a long line of anticipated rhubarbs, and the truth was, on so many nights of the Battle when an excess of violent behaviour seemed inevitable, sometimes even imperative, those were usually the nights when nothing much happened.

On this night, Grimson was right. It was unavoidable, and his memories of the warmup douse any theories that he wasn't ready for the scrap. The officials were expecting the worst, as referee Kerry Fraser recalls.

"As I came in to Calgary for the game the night before, I checked the papers the next morning, and all the hype was around this rematch," Fraser said. "I remember talking about it in the dressing room before the game. It was like, 'Listen, guys, we've got some bad blood here tonight, and this is going to be a rematch. Let's be ready for it. They're two big guys, and they've got a job to do. Let's not rush in there.'

"For me, I don't condone fighting, certainly now. But back then I felt like, if the inevitable was avoided—if it was somehow put on hold—the game tended to get chippier. It was, 'Let these guys go, and if they're standing up throwing punches, let 'em go right to the end. Don't rush in there unless some guy is really getting throttled.' Two big guys. They're gonna go. And when they do, let's let it happen. And it should be over for the rest of the night."

Really, it didn't matter much what those zebras said to each other in that officials room, deep in the bowels of the Saddledome. "There was nobody who was going to get in Dave Brown's way to get to Stu Grimson on that first shift," Fraser admits. "The intensity that he brought on to that ice, in his demeanour, in his focus. Wherever the puck went, it didn't matter."

Don't be leaving for coffee.

"I knew it was going to happen," Brown said. "I was going after it. I felt a little embarrassed . . . I was going to set it straight. That's what I did. I just threw my gloves off and went after him. Went straight to him. It's more of a blur now. I don't remember a lot about the fight, from punch to punch. I was focused on what I needed to do, and I don't know. Maybe it was over and I [intentionally] forgot. I just did what I needed to do."

"I remember it quite vividly," began Grimson. Of course he

did, the way one recalls the unfolding of a horrible car wreck or a high-speed ski crash that landed them in the hospital. The way that memory of the deer slows down as the front end of your truck buckles its ribs at 110 km/h.

Grimson had plenty of time to recount the evening, as it would be his last NHL shift that winter. Even the coaches, John Muckler and Calgary's Terry Crisp, would follow protocol and allow the fight to be attended to early, so that the game might play out afterwards.

"Less than five minutes into the game. Faceoff in our zone. Muckler sent Brownie out, and Crispy sends me and my line out. The puck was dropped, and it was a matter of seconds before Brownie and I got into it."

Linesman Randy Mitton: "They dropped their gloves, and we were kicking the gloves and the sticks out of the way, when we really could have got in the way and broken it up. But everyone wanted to see this, and it would have [happened eventually] anyway. We ended up getting in trouble because of kicking the gloves out of the way. Grimson ends up getting badly hurt, and we were in trouble from the league. We were 'promoting the fight.'"

Bearcat: "Brown just annihilated him. Destroyed him. He was a mess. Everyone was just down. Quiet. Amazed. It was such a vicious fight. I was just tore to pieces because of it, because I knew it was going to happen."

It happened with clinical precision. Like a professional pickpocket, but with more pain. Brown went straight to Grimson along the right-wing boards as the puck drifted into the left-wing corner, herding Grimson to his fists like a cutting horse directs a calf.

"I remember I was kind of late getting my gloves off. I groped for his left hand, and I just wasn't able to find it on this night," Grimson said. Brown landed a few hard shots, and Grimson again slowed the piston enough to take a second run at grabbing that left arm. But it was impossible to get a grip. There was just nothing to grab on to, and Brown began raining lefts down on Grimson.

"I know now, Brownie and his trainers spent a lot of time siliconing the sleeves of his jersey and tightened it up so it was impossible to get ahold of it. Missing the left hand, groping for the left hand, and he tagged with about three or four left hands. He clipped me pretty good.

"Put me down, not out. But I remember as I was down on the ice, taking my right hand and wiping under my right eye, because I thought surely there has got to be a cut under there. Then I felt this really distinct impression under my right eye. I thought, 'I've never felt anything like that before. That's kind of peculiar.' Then I skated over to the penalty box, we served our majors."

What follows is a testament to how tough these guys are, and how much pain they can withstand. Sometimes, when hockey arrives in one of commissioner Gary Bettman's new Southern markets, the locals just assume that the fights aren't real. That bare-knuckle chuckin' would be too painful to actually occur in earnest. Well, on this night Grimson served his major penalty with several broken bones in his face, sitting, aching until the gate opened and his ambulance was accessible.

"When I first sat down [in the penalty box], I thought, 'This guy embarrassed me in my own building. I've got to set it straight; I've got to go out there and fight him again.' But the longer I sat there, the heavier my head got. And this really, dull, throbbing sense of pain started to become pretty significant.

"By the end of my major I skated over to the other side and I said, 'Bearcat, I'd better see a doctor because I think there is something fairly seriously wrong with my right eye. I had broken my cheekbone and fractured my orbital in three different

"The Montreal–Toronto (rivalry) was unbelievable. Philadelphia–Toronto was pretty heated. But nothing compared to Calgary–Edmonton." —Lanny McDonald

Kevin Lowe played in all five playoff installments of The Battle.

Look at the hook on that Sherwood PMP! Al MacInnis had the biggest blast in The Battle.

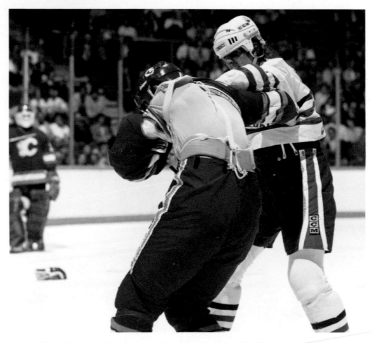

Paul Baxter finds out that Kevin McClelland is a lefty.

Marty McSorley was a tough, valuable defenceman/policeman who Gretzky demanded be included in his trade to L.A.

The only team in NHL history to score 400-plus goals in a season was Edmonton. They did it five times from 1981–82 to 1985–86.

The 1985 All-Star Game was played in Calgary, and the Oilers dominated the Campbell Conference roster.

Joel Otto and Mark Messier went Cooper to Winwell over many a draw. "He's unpredictable," Otto said. "I approached him like I was going into the cage with a lion. You had to be careful."

A little Stampede wrestling.

A young Glen Sather mastering "The Smirk."

Scrumming it up at the Saddledome.

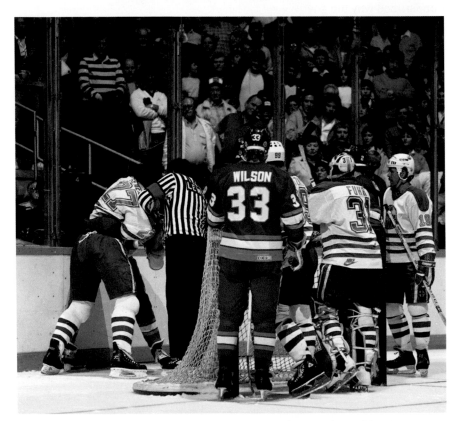

Semenko, seen here tussling with Hunter, on fighting: "I didn't like the thought of it. But once it was going, I was fine with it."

Neil Sheehy: "I was there to be a pest. To be an annoying SOB, OK? Listen, I understood why the guy [Wayne Gretzky] would despise and hate me. Because I was an annoying prick, you know? OK?"

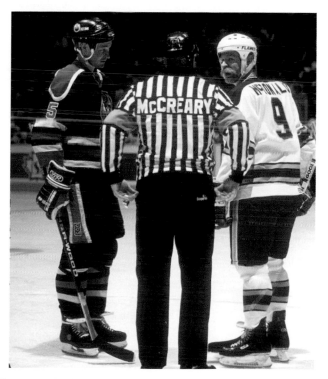

"I think of mean, I think of tough . . . I think of a game that would border on mayhem." —McCreary, on The Battle

Mike Vernon and the Flames are the only visiting team to hoist the
Stanley Cup in Montreal.

Gretzky in his office.

places. I had to have reconstructive surgery to square it all away.

"Straight to the hospital, had surgery that night. I was recuperating by the next day."

Typically, Brown's account of his victory was short. Like almost every heavyweight I've ever known, he'll talk about the ones he lost far longer than the ones that went his way. When they lose, the other guy was super tough. When they win, it was mostly luck, really.

"I never gloated about what happened," Brown said. "That could have been me. He was coming up, a young guy, lookin' to make a name for himself. He was doing what I was doing for my team, standing up for your team and being a tough guy. At that time, I didn't know him. That could easily have been me on the losing end."

In the papers the next day, Grimson became labelled The Grim Receiver. That's how fleeting it can be, when your reputation rides on bare-knuckle fighting on skates.

How many scraps had the Battle witnessed, from the big boys like Semenko and Hunter to the middleweights like McClelland and Sheehy? Nobody ever got seriously injured in these fights. Until this one.

"In all of those battles, no one really got hurt," said Calgary winger Colin Patterson. "You might have got hurt, but not to that degree, although Jamie Macoun broke his jaw when Messier hit him from behind. The number of times I saw Tim Hunter and Dave Semenko fight, it wasn't like when Stu and Dave Brown fought. Kudos to Stu. He came back, and that could have crushed a guy's career."

Even the Oilers felt a certain sympathy for the new kid from Calgary that day. The blood feud had always spilled a little bit of the red stuff, but ironically, Grimson didn't bleed at all that night. The bones under the skin on the right side of his face, however, were cratered. The Battle would not endure much further into the 1990s, and that night a decade of tough hockey had climaxed with a fight that truly scared everyone in attendance. It was, perhaps, a time to take a step back.

For players like Lowe, at that point thirty years old and eight hundred games into his NHL career, or Patterson, also a thirty-year-old veteran of the wars, watching that fight was somewhat of a seminal moment. It was a three-day process that played out in front of an entire province of hockey fans, readers, and viewers. Everyone had an opportunity to save Grimson the kind of beating that most thought would end his career that day, but the thought of doing so had occurred to no one.

"Stu had hurt his hand in the [Sunday] fight,' Patterson said. "Looking back, we probably shouldn't have played him. Unfortunately, the next fight didn't go as well. It is what it is. It was like Stu wasn't expecting the fight to happen right then. I don't know why he wasn't thinking that. Dave Brown was thinking that way."

"That was as wild a moment . . . Top five for me, for sure, in hockey," said Lowe, who would go on to enjoy a career spanning nineteen seasons and 1,468 games, including playoffs. "It was just a beatdown. But the whole building, it went from excitement to dead still, to quiet, to almost a sickening feeling to the people in the building. Including us.

"Your body, your mind—you go through the whole range of emotions. It went from, 'Get him, Brownie! Get him!' Then, 'I hope he's doing well . . .' Then, 'Holy shit, stop, Brownie!' Then it was, 'Oh my God . . . He just killed that guy.' It was almost like premeditated murder."

Nobody played more meaningful games in the Battle than Lowe, on either side. He joined the Oilers in 1979–80, the year before the Atlanta Flames relocated to Calgary, and played for

Edmonton through all five Stanley Cups before leaving for the New York Rangers after the 1991–92 season. By then, the Battle was cooling, on its way to what it is today.

The retribution. The machismo. The utter hatred of that opposing sweater and the disregard for the health of those inside of it. Did it all go too far that night at the Saddledome?

"When guys get hurt like that? For sure," said Lowe. "Everybody's view of a beatdown is that a guy gets knocked to the ice. He gets up right away, and it's, 'His feelings are hurt, but he's not hurt.' When it gets to that extent, that's too much."

Grimson awoke the next day in a Calgary hospital bed in rough, rough shape. As is the custom in hockey, a young Flames teammate named Marc Bureau arrived at his bedside. They had been called up from Salt Lake together, and the two were roommates at the Calgary Westin. The morning after Grimson's surgery, Bureau was among the first visitors to the Calgary hospital room where Grimson lay resting.

"He brought my shaving kit, and some of my personal effects from the hotel," said Grimson, laughing at the memory. "He walks into the room and saw me after I had reconstructive surgery on my face. He took one look at me, and he started crying. I must have been really in rough shape because he's sitting in a chair beside my bed, and I'm holding his hand and patting it. I'm saying, 'Frenchy, it's going to be all right. I'm going to be okay.' This hockey player, he's weeping. Honestly, I looked like a truck had backed up over my face."

For Grimson, as you might guess, January 9, 1990, was a life-changing moment—but in a positive way. He recovered from his injuries, rejoined Salt Lake City later that season, and would forge a tidy career of his own, playing another 725 games over thirteen seasons for Chicago, Anaheim, Detroit, Hartford/Carolina, Anaheim again, then closing it out in Los Angeles and Nashville. He logged another 2,091 minutes in penalties in his career, and fought all the big boys along the way. Even fought Brown again.

About the only thing that Stu Grimson did not do after that fateful meeting with Brown was play another game for the Calgary Flames. His chapter in the Battle had closed, and Grimson moved on. He went to camp the next fall in Calgary and was put on waivers by the Flames. The Chicago Blackhawks picked him up.

The insecure heavyweight has always been one of hockey's great ironies, and in the end, Brown was just another in a long line of them. We look at men like him, Grimson, Semenko, Hunter, Probert, John Kordic, Brian McGrattan, and we see physically imposing, take-matters-into-their-own-hands men who have quite literally carved a lucrative career out of kicking ass. They should be at ease, right? Confident and comfortable in their own skin.

Today, with the gradual extinction of the heavyweight position in hockey, one can understand if some job insecurity is creeping into the picture for those whose sole job is to protect their more skilled teammates. But even back before the instigator penalty, the more heavyweights I met, the more I could see it is a generally insecure breed—worried about what their teammates thought of them more than any other position on the team.

Think about it: if the top centreman goes through a couple of scoreless weeks, he might get demoted to the second line, or perhaps be furnished with different wingers to perk up his game. It is traditionally couched in terms like "mixing things up" or "putting the lines in the blender." The process involves a support network comprised of coaches and teammates working together to help the struggling player out of his slump. He's never completely alone in his troubles.

When a heavyweight starts to slip, there's nowhere to fall—except for off the roster completely. Losing fights at this level—as

Grimson will testify—isn't a whole lot of fun. There is no good luck or hard work that can to help you out of a fighting slump the way a player can have a point shot bounce in off the seat of his pants or get teamed up with a red-hot player on a real good run, where there are easy points to be had.

When you consider how seldom these guys really fight, the role of the enforcer becomes more of an emotional or cerebral thing. He must retain his teammates' belief in his abilities to protect the tribe. It is an unspoken yet well-known element within the team.

"All Brownie wanted to do was contribute to the team, be considered a consistent, reliable player—especially in the defensive zone," Stafford said. "That's the kind of player those guys are. Semenk, McClelland—they want to be considered hockey players first, and that they can be relied upon by their coaches and their teammates. Davey Brown was no different.

"He was an old-school player. No coach ever had to tap him on the shoulder. He knew his job very well. His number-one priority was . . . looking after his teammates."

Brown had been sat down for a few games and could see his value to the team waning. Then he got back into the lineup and lost to this Grimson kid. It explains his singular focus for that forty-eight-hour period between the two scraps. He was a twenty-seven-year-old heavyweight who had just lost a fight to a virtual nobody. Brown's career, in his mind, was literally on the line.

"For me, the most important thing of all was what the rest of your teammates think of you in the room. I always wanted everyone to think I was doing my job for the team, and that's probably what motivated me the most to go out and do what I did there," he said.

"I didn't want to be the guy sittin' in the room with everybody thinking I didn't do my job. I wanted everyone to think that I was doing my part. If I wasn't, that made me sick to my stomach. That's what drives you the most. Everything outside the dressing room, it doesn't mean much. Are you doing your job for the team? That's what mattered. The team."

The guys. The room. The camaraderie. It's what they all talk about when their careers are over and you ask them what they miss the most.

Said Brown, "To play hockey in the NHL was fun, man. You'd play forever if you could."

Brown played another six seasons, returning to the team that drafted him and employs him today, the Flyers. He is as well respected a hockey man as there is in the game, soft-spoken and humble. He has never gloated about a fight won, or an opponent he bested, and in fact took considerable cajoling to recount this particular chapter in the Battle of Alberta. Talking about a one-sided win is simply out of character for big Dave Brown.

As for Grimson, well, from great depths begin heroic rises, and Grimson couldn't have been any lower at that point in his career. He was a twenty-five-year-old heavyweight who had just failed the Big Test in a young heavyweight's career. That damned silicone had meant he couldn't even tie Brown up and play for the draw, and it wouldn't surprise anyone if Grimson had just faded away into obscurity. Maybe follow in his father's footsteps, enroll in the academy.

It's almost fortunate that such an injurious event had been inflicted on a man bright enough to process it all. Before earning a law degree in his post-hockey life, Grimson weighed the evidence of that January 9, 1990, altercation, and somehow found a way to turn it into a positive experience.

"It's kind of peculiar, but it *was* a turning point for me, personally and professionally," Grimson said. "That was a bad beat— make no mistake about it. That's as bad a beat as a guy doing what I did could take. But I kind of came to a place in my mind: 'If that's the worst I can suffer, and if I can bounce back from that, then I've got nothing to fear.' It turned into a liberating thing for me."

Liberating. From where most people sat, the only liberating element of Brown versus Grimson II was when Dave Brown liberated Stu Grimson of his senses. Grimson is a religious man, however, and a scholar. Two key recipes to turning this life experience lemon into lemonade.

"I came to that realization that, if I can bounce back from something like this, then I have nothing left to fear. This isn't going to cause me to pack it up and play a different game. Or terminate my attempt to find a niche in this league. It's only going to reaffirm that this is what I'm going to do. I chose the tougher path, I guess," he said. "When you face trials like that, but you're able to grab yourself by the boot straps, move through them, and come out the other side, it steels you as a person. It galvanizes your character. There's no question: Being able to move past something like that made me stronger as a human being. Without question. I think it was Shakespeare who said, 'Whatever doesn't kill us makes us stronger.' That certainly was true in my situation.

"There is nothing more exhilarating than being able to confront your fears. And fear number one for me was the heavyweight champion of the NHL, Dave Brown. Regardless of the outcome."

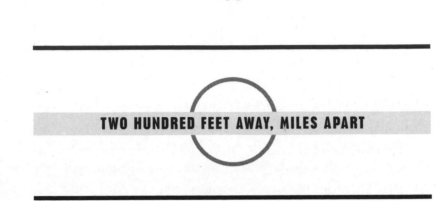

14

TWO HUNDRED FEET AWAY, MILES APART

Flame Réjean Lemelin versus Oiler Grant Fuhr
"We made kick saves, we made glove saves.
We were not on our knees trying to stop everything
with our chest. It wouldn't have worked anyway."

It was autumn of 1974 in Philadelphia.

The Flyers' Dave (The Hammer) Schultz would embark upon the NHL's single-season record for penalty minutes (472) that still stands today. The Broad Street Bullies would pound their way to a second of back-to-back Stanley Cups in the spring of 1975, the last ever Cup-winning roster comprised solely of Canadian-born players. And after two years of the Flyers' reign, the sport of hockey would reach its nadir, marred by the bench-clearing brawls and violent punchups that would manifest itself on the Hollywood screen in the Paul Newman classic *Slap Shot.*

In downtown Philly, a little Denis Lemieux lookalike named

Réjean (Reggie) Lemelin was settling into his first pro hockey job as a goalie for the Philadelphia Firebirds of the North American Hockey League (NAHL). This was the league from which the *Slap Shot* movie was derived, and Lemelin was playing in a town where hockey had morphed into hooliganism, in the process producing two Stanley Cup championships.

It was tough, goofy hockey played in the old Philadelphia Convention Hall and Civic Center, a 1930-built, art deco landmark where Martin Luther King, Pope John Paul II, and Nelson Mandela had delivered speeches and The Beatles, The Rolling Stones, and The Jackson 5 had performed.

"There was a lot of fighting [in the NAHL]. The bus rides, the fan clubs . . . There were plenty of similarities to the movie," said Lemelin, who would go on to backbone the Calgary Flames in the early 1980s. "I barely spoke English when I got there. And when you don't speak that well, and you're trying to figure out what's going on in that place . . . Well, it was a bit crazy."

If you watch the movie, you'll see a scene where Newman's Charlestown Chiefs are playing against the Firebirds. The little goalie in Philly's net is wearing a mask and pads that are identical to Lemelin's. "They used all of our replicas. We had to sign releases and everything," he said. You couldn't blame him if, at the time, Lemelin might have thought that he was watching his five minutes of fame play out on that movie screen in Philadelphia, where he and his teammates gathered on an off day to watch the movie about their lives.

"It was Philadelphia's second minor-league team, basically," Lemelin began. "It was more of a veteran league. Guys in their later twenties, just trying to hang on to the game. We had Dave Schultz's brother [Ray], Rick MacLeish's brother [Dale] . . . It was a bunch of misfits, basically. I'm just a nineteen-year-old kid, and I show up there and get paired up with an older, washed-out goalie named Danny Sullivan. A real good guy. I didn't know anything. I was kind of lost."

But there was an ember of hope for our little Denis Lemieux lookalike. "I ended up winning the Rookie of the Year in the league."

Lemelin's Firebirds came with their own personal Reggie Dunlop behind the bench, a former minor-league lifer-turned-coach named Gregg Pilling. In thirteen years of playing and coaching—all but one spent below the American Hockey League level in the nether regions of professional hockey in the 1960s and 1970s—Pilling's only championship would come during Lemelin's second pro season in Philly.

To say Pilling is a barrel of laughs is to say that Wayne Gretzky was merely a decent player. If someone wrote a book on characters in the game, "Pill" would get at least a chapter. If only he was more handsome, he'd get the cover.

When Pilling runs across one of his old goalies today, he greets them all with the same salutation. "Hey, ya leaky bastard! How the hell are ya?" he'll say. "You know what? They all answer when you say that."

Pilling was coaching a team of second-tier Flyers prospects, with a handful of guys who couldn't make their WHA clubs tossed on the heap. He'd brought along Sullivan—a five-foot-nine goalie from Kimberley, B.C., whose career apex would consist of two WHA starts—from their time together in the soon-to-be-defunct Southern League, pairing him up in the Firebirds crease with Lemelin.

"You never knew what you were going to get from the parent team. Sometimes you'd get saddled with their financial mistakes," Pilling said. Other times, as he was finding out in Philly, you'd get the older brothers of the team's NHL stars, as a favour to Rick MacLeish and Dave Schultz. "I had a goaltender I knew could play in the Southern League [Sullivan], and I had Reggie. Didn't know too much about Reggie."

That made for an even start to their relationship, considering Lemelin did not have a hot clue what to think about this Pilling guy either. He was a wildcat of a hockey man who realized that there wasn't going to be a lot of money down this minor-league hockey trail, so he might as well have as many laughs as possible.

Lemelin recalls Pilling walking across the ice to the bench for the third period wearing a ref's striped jersey, shades, and holding a hockey stick taped white, like a cane. Another time, Pilling flipped the guy inside the mascot suit a few bucks to borrow his costume, and thrilled the folks in Lewiston, Maine, when he pulled the Bear's head off during a ceremony to reveal who was inside. Another time, Pilling sent the entire team to the penalty box to serve a bench minor he had been assessed—just to further rile the referee. "You're gonna call penalties on all my guys all night? Then here. Have 'em all. I'll save you some time!"

Still another time, Pilling decided he would switch his goalies every shift. "He said to me, 'You're going to start the game, but on the first faceoff I'm going to pull you and I'm going to put Danny in,'" Lemelin remembered. "So he pulls me, then I go back in. He pulls me, I go back in. Then there's another faceoff, and he pulls me again! That's three times now. So, the next shift I'm on my way out to the goal, I say to Danny, 'He wants to play this game? I'm comin' out on the fly. So get [bleep]in' ready.'

"So we break out of our own end, there's a long pass up to centre ice, and I'm comin'. Danny jumps the boards and he goes flyin' into the net, and now I'm on the bench. Pill comes storming down the bench, like he's gonna beat me up or something. He says, 'That was fucking great!'

"I don't think there were ever goalies who changed on the fly in professional hockey, but we did it," said Lemelin. "Pill? He was nuts, but guys played for him so hard because he was such a great guy. He was a players' coach. But that's also why his career never went anywhere, because he did too many goofy things like that. No one wanted to hire him."

Lemelin was, as it turns out, the Accidental Goaler. He grew up in a little town north of Quebec City, Orsainville, which has since been swallowed up by the Quebec capital. About twelve thousand people lived there, but to Lemelin's good fortune, one of them was a kid named Réal Cloutier, who would become one of the greatest goal scorers of his generation. Cloutier would score ninety-three goals in his final junior season and pot seventy-five one year for his hometown team, the Quebec Nordiques of the WHA.

"We were awesome because he scored four, five goals every game, and I could stop the puck. We had a small population, but we did some good things," Lemelin said of his childhood teams. Lemelin would give up on being a goalie after his pee wee season. "In Quebec, once you got to bantam you had to go back outside to play your games. I didn't want to play goal outside, so I went back to forward for a couple of years."

Eventually talked back into goal by a junior scout, by the time Lemelin was draft eligible in 1974 he would become the first goalie drafted out of the Quebec Major Junior Hockey League that season. "I was kind of proud of that," he admitted. It would be the beginning of one hell of a journey for the man who would spawn "The Reggie Lemelin Pool" along the scribes in the press boxes of the Battle nearly a decade later.

Lemelin was drafted in Round 7 of that 1974 draft by the Flyers, in a time when the entry draft was a simple conference call conducted from the league offices in Montreal. No TV, no glitzy two-day event, and no eighteen-year-old draftees, surrounded by their families and their agents, pulling on a jersey on a big stage under the bright lights. In fact, the 1974 draft was even more clandestine, having been quietly moved up on the calendar because of the emergence of the World Hockey Association in 1972 and the reality that the WHA was beginning to poach a lot of talent from the NHL.

Undeterred, the Chicago Cougars would select Lemelin in the thirteenth round of the subsequent WHA draft. In an interesting twist, the same draft would see the Minnesota Fighting Saints select a left-shooting defenceman named Dave Hanson. He would quickly be assigned to the Johnstown Jets and go on to star as Jack Hanson, one of the famed brothers in *Slap Shot*. Lemelin, meanwhile, had no intentions of attending the camp of the Cougars, a second-rate team in a second-rate league. But he also knew the path would be a long one with the Flyers.

Only days before selecting Lemelin, Philadelphia had won its first Stanley Cup. The Broad Street Bullies were set in goal, with Bernie Parent in the midst of winning the Conn Smythe Trophy as the top playoff performer in both Cup runs. Now they'd chosen a Parent prototype—a kid out of a Quebec City suburb who barely spoke English —whom they would assign to the Firebirds.

Lemelin logged four hard seasons with the Firebirds, where he met his wife, Rona. Eventually, Lemelin's time with the Flyers came to a close and he signed on with the Atlanta Flames—who promptly sent him back to the Firebirds. He couldn't escape the movie, and like that little goalie, Lemelin was beginning to feel like he was in some goalie penalty box, "feeling shame."

Even when Lemelin made the Flames though, it didn't feel to Lemelin like he was in the big leagues. The crowds at the Omni Coliseum in Atlanta were small, and the newspapers barely acknowledged the Flames amid all the NBA, NFL, and NCAA interest in Georgia. It wasn't hockey country then, just as it was not in 1999 when the Atlanta Thrashers were reinvented ı inglorious seasons before shuffling off to Winnipeg. Lemelin was still going up and down from the minors as Atlanta relocated to Calgary for the 1980–81 season and had now been passed by in the Flames system by a newcomer out of the WHA named Pat Riggin. Lemelin was sour about that, and on November 19, 1980—Lemelin's twenty-sixth birthday—he got the fateful phone call while playing in Birmingham.

"The Flames were going on a six-game road trip and they wanted me to join the team," Lemelin said. "The whole trip I sat as the third goalie. Practised every day. We got back to Calgary, and the first game we were going to play the Islanders— the Stanley Cup champs. I'll never forget this. I already knew I was leaving the next day and going back to Birmingham. Dan Bouchard was going to start, and Pat Riggin was the backup. But Riggin came down with the flu. They were going to dress him as the backup anyhow, but during the warmup, I'm in the stands eating popcorn, and somebody came and tapped me on the shoulder.

"I said, 'Okay, I'll come in and dress up," he laughed. "Well, at the twelve-minute mark of the first period, Dan Bouchard goes down with a pulled groin. I have to go in, out of the blue, and we tie the Stanley Cup champion. I was the first star in the game."

Bouchard was on the shelf for quite some time, so Lemelin's plane ticket to Birmingham was cancelled. Then he got the next start, two nights later. "I win the game, and I go on to win eleven straight games. And the rest is history."

The Flames would trade Bouchard and Riggin not long after, and little Réjean Lemelin of the Philadelphia Firebirds was finally an NHL No. 1. There was only one problem: "Our team was not as good as the Oilers when Reggie was playing," said Calgary assistant coach Bob Murdoch. "We just weren't as good as them, and I don't think anyone believed, subconsciously, that we were as good as them. There was a psychological factor, and there is also that intimidation factor."

You know what they say when a team gets poor goaltending? That if affects the psyche of the entire team? That they play differently, and nothing can work the way it is supposed to when a team plays in fear that a long wrist shot from the side boards is going to end up in their net? Well, the opposite can be true as well.

When a goalie knows that his team knows it isn't going to win, it isn't very often that he is able to win a game for them. For the Calgary Flames of the early 1980s, it was only a matter of time before the Oilers started scoring goals by the bunches, most nights.

So it was not Lemelin's fault that he became the subject of the "Reggie Lemelin Pool" in the press boxes of the Olympic Saddledome and the Northlands Coliseum. But for a few seasons at least, the Edmonton and Calgary scribes would put a $5 bill in the pot prior to puck drop, picking a number between one and ten out of a coffee cup. If the number you had drawn coincided with the number of shots Edmonton had when their first goal got behind Reggie, you won the pot.

It became a running joke: if, by the time you were drawing, the numbers one through five were gone, you would moan about making a charitable donation and having no chance to win. It was half-joke, half-truth. Edmonton was just that strong offensively in the early years of the Battle, and Calgary had not acquired the roster or devised the defensive system to hold the floodgates for long.

"They could have done that against every team," Lemelin said when I told him about the pool. "I don't give a shit. I was doing my thing. I'm very proud of my career.

"You just played the games, and you knew that you were going to try to keep it under four, and then maybe you'd have a chance,"

Lemelin continued. "If you got into a power-play game, then you had no chance because their power play was scary. You didn't want to be embarrassed, was the whole thing. And sometimes, you know, they did [embarrass you]."

Almost two hundred feet away stood a much younger goalie, whose path to the NHL had been paved in rose petals compared with Lemelin's.

Grant Fuhr grew up in a suburb of Edmonton called Spruce Grove, played his junior in lovely Victoria for the old Cougars of the Western Hockey League, and was chosen at No. 8, the Oilers' first-rounder in 1981. As a nineteen-year-old rookie, he would play more than half the games for Edmonton, and spent only ten games in the minors on his way to becoming an NHL star.

Oh, and Fuhr had a team in front of him that would score five goals a game. Edmonton was indeed a soft landing spot, compared with Lemelin's career path.

"Reggie and Donnie Edwards," Fuhr recalled of the Flames tandem of the day. "You knew that if they stood on their head it might be a close game. But we knew we would get thirty-five or forty shots against them, and probably twenty, twenty-five of them were going to be good ones. So, they were in a tough spot. We always assumed we were going to win."

Lemelin saw it from pretty much the same angle, frankly. But when Fuhr was breaking in as a teenager in his own hometown, comfortably destined to be the number-one goalie on the most powerful offensive team in the history of the game, Lemelin was already a grizzled veteran in his eighth pro season. By Fuhr's rookie season, Lemelin had already donned six different uniforms in four different pro leagues.

The only adversity that Fuhr would face, it turns out, was self-induced. Off the ice, he fell into some financial issues, going a round or two with the fashionable cocaine lifestyle of the 1980s.

Then there was the time that he called Oilers fans a bunch of "[bleep]in' jerks."

"Yes I did say that," Fuhr admitted today. "Nineteen years old, and a size 9 right in the mouth." It earned him his ten games with the Moncton Alpines of the American League.

"I was struggling, and hadn't really struggled before that," he said. "I decided to make things easier on myself and stuck my foot in my mouth. It's not hard enough. You might as well make it a little harder."

That was perhaps the last time anyone ever saw any visible signs of stress on Fuhr's face. It is the trademark of a great goalie — never let the last goal affect you, lest it turn into the next goal — and Fuhr was Teflon. Nothing stuck to him. He was the antithesis of the high-strung, high-maintenance goalie you always hear about.

"Equipment would come from the factory, he'd put them on for a few practices, then he'd wear them [in a game]," said Oilers equipment man Lyle [Sparky] Kulchisky. "A new mask would come. He'd put it on. Grant was a low-maintenance guy. He rolled with it. 'Oh yeah? Oh, well, okay.'

"Grant, your pants didn't come in. 'Hmm? Okay.'"

And that made Fuhr the perfect man for the job in Edmonton, where supporting the goalie was priority number ten in those early years. The Oilers gave up more prime scoring chances in an important playoff game in 1982 than the Los Angeles Kings or New York Rangers of today would give up in half a series. If your feelings were going to be hurt by a few three-on-ones, then surely you weren't the man to tend the twine in Edmonton.

In the best-of-three final of the 1987 Canada Cup—a meeting between Canada and Russia in the time before the Iron Curtain had fallen, believed by many to the highest pedigree of hockey ever played—Fuhr allowed sixteen goals. Each of the three games ended in an identical 6–5 score, yet no one ever said, as they would today, "You can't win letting in five goals a night."

"That's the fun of playing offensive hockey. You can make some mistakes," Fuhr said. "It was a new style to the league at that time. We just played run 'n' gun. We knew we were going to get our four or five every night, and we [as in, he] just had to keep the other guys to one less. It wasn't about numbers. It was about winning and losing.

"I think people get hung up on that now. They're so worried about what a goalie's numbers look like. But at the end of the day, if you have a great average and your win–loss record is 10–20, people aren't going to be happy. If you're 20–10, all of a sudden people are happy."

Every great goalie becomes known for some trait. Like Patrick Roy's cockiness, or the way Ron Hextall could play a drumroll on his posts with the blade and knob of his goalstick. Maybe it's a piece of equipment, like Gerry Cheevers's mask. Or Dominik Hasek's weird but effective style that somehow kept even the most impossible puck out of his net.

Fuhr's contemporaries—and that included Lemelin—were the last of the "small equipment" goalies who played before men like Roy and Garth Snow made a mockery of the position by introducing chest protectors the size of bus benches and pants that could have been worn by a circus clown. Fuhr caught with a serpent-like right hand, which made him unique. And because those early-1980s goalies didn't have the help of equipment manufacturers to make them bigger, it was a common sight to see goals like that Guy Lafleur classic, a blast off the boards from above the faceoff dot. Or Gretzky, coming down the wing and blasting high over Mike Vernon's shoulder.

As such, goalies would leave their crease to cut off the angle, which left them far out of position on rebounds. Then they'd have to scramble back through traffic to try to make the next save.

It was a far more athletic position in the early 1980s, played by smaller, more acrobatic men compared with the giants of today.

"To maintain a [goals-against] average under 3.50 in my day was pretty good. A .900 saves percentage meant you were an All-Star goalie," said Lemelin. "Look at the equipment, and the size of the goalie. We were not big. Andy Moog was just a little guy but a really good goaltender. Today, they go down and they block everything with their chest. If the puck beats them, it's in the net, but there is almost no net open to shoot at.

"We made kick saves, we made glove saves. We were not on our knees trying to stop everything with our chest. It wouldn't have worked anyway."

The undisputable calling card that would belong to Fuhr, the way Martin Brodeur will always be known as the best puck-handling goalie there ever was, was less about stopping pucks and more about which ones he stopped. Like Lemelin, Fuhr never had a saves percentage in the .900s (until late in his career with St. Louis). It was never about the fact that Fuhr would let a few pucks past every night. It was about when he would slam the gate shut—for good.

He had the uncanny ability to recognize when his team could no longer afford "the next one." Whether that meant pitching a shutout in a 1–0 victory in Game 1 of the 1984 Stanley Cup final or holding the Calgary Flames to four in the final installment of the Battle, a 5–4 Oilers win in overtime of Game 7 in 1991.

"It still comes down to, can you make the right save at the right time. Growing up, watching goalies, nothing has changed: you still have to make the right save at the right time," Fuhr said.

There is less room in today's game for the mistakes Fuhr speaks of because goals are more precious. A goalie's team does not score four or five goals a night in front of him anymore: the highest-scoring team in the NHL in the 2013–14 season, the

Anaheim Ducks, averaged just 3.21 goals per game. Anaheim, along with Boston and Chicago, were the only three teams whose goals-per-game average began with the number three.

Contrast that with the early-1980s Oilers: in each season from 1981–82 to 1985–86, Edmonton scored in excess of four hundred goals per season. For that span of five dazzling seasons, the Edmonton Oilers averaged exactly 5.29 goals per game. But they allowed, on average, 3.83 goals per game.

How many coaches have you heard today say, "Well, it's a 3–2 league?" Back in the day it was a 5–4 league—at least in Edmonton—with a lot more fights. Which brand of hockey seems more entertaining to you?

"The numbers don't matter," said Fuhr of his personal stats. "I just had a sense of, when the momentum of the game changes, you know you have to make that next save. Hockey is a game of momentum. If you're up 3–2 and it's early in the third period, you have to make that save to keep that momentum. [No matter how you've played in the game,] if that third goal doesn't go in, you probably win that hockey game. You have to make that save, just to keep that momentum. At the end of the day, you need the W out of it.

"I talk to people now, and they say, 'Your numbers aren't great.' Well, the numbers may not be great. But four hundred-and-some wins? No one can complain about that. People get hung up on numbers and they forget what the essence of the game is. You still have to win."

Fuhr retired with 403 wins, ninth on the all-time list at the time of this writing. Were most of those wins due to the quality of the team in front of him? Perhaps. But what of the fact that Fuhr practised every day against the most prolific scoring machine in National Hockey League history?

Facing Wayne Gretzky every day in practice? Fuhr admits

there was something to be learned every day—even if that lesson often boiled down to being glad you weren't Lemelin or Vernon.

"Even today, Gretz would easily be the best passer in the game, so first and foremost, you had to respect that. Which made his shot that much better," Fuhr said. "He never really shot the puck hard, but he was very accurate. If you gave him a foot, he could hit that spot. But because he was such a great passer, you always had to be aware of him not taking that shot.

"It was a vicious cycle of covering the net the way a goalie would for any opposing player within shooting range, but diverting your attention—and perhaps compromising your positioning—to account for where Kurri or Coffey was. You were never really in balance," Fuhr said. "I saw it every day in practice. For Reggie only seeing it eight or nine times a year would be a big adjustment. That's something that helped me in Canada Cups because that's the way the Russians played. It wasn't a huge change for me."

Ask Lemelin who had the best shot on the Edmonton Oilers and his answer comes quickly, and with little thought. "They all did, it seemed to me." It was the variety in players the Oilers had that gave Lemelin fits, coming from every angle, including the defensive corps.

"Coffey was all about speed, and cutting left to right. Gretzky, he was just waiting, waiting. He just floated down and made passes absolutely perfectly on everyone's stick," Lemelin said. "Messier was the bully. He ran through everybody. The great complimentary guys, Anderson, Simpson for a while, Hughes for a while . . . And Fuhr was a pretty good goalie. But it's nice to start the game knowing your team is going to score four or five goals. I'm not taking anything away from him. He did his job. But that's a nice start for a goalie."

It became the balance every NHL coach tried to walk. If he played run and gun, he had to believe his shooters could outscore Edmonton's. Well, there weren't any coaches who thought that. So the other side of that coin was to limit chances. But playing a defensive game to limit Edmonton's chances meant cutting down on the numbers of shots and scoring chances your team generated as well.

Now the question became "Is my goaltending likely to be better than theirs?" With Fuhr in net, most nights the answer to that question was also a resounding no. And so, you have an idea what it was like to be an NHL coach in the 1980s.

"The Oilers had so much confidence in their goaltending," Murdoch said. "If you break down the scoring chances from so many of those games, we might have a 17–9 lead in scoring chances. But we'd lose the game 8–2 because whenever the Oilers had a scoring chance, they were so bloody skilled they'd score. They were willing to trade chances, and if you did, they'd eventually beat you."

Then a kid named Mike Vernon graduated from the Calgary Wranglers junior team. It was as if the Flames had been waiting for his arrival—the local kid in goal, to match Edmonton's local kid in goal—because almost the moment Vernon became a regular, for the 1986 playoffs, the Flames began to beat the Oilers with regularity. Edmonton had not lost a regular-season series to Calgary in the five years before the 1986 playoff upset. The Flames would win that series, go 6–1–1 versus Edmonton the next season, and would not surrender a season series to Edmonton again until 1996–97, long after the Battle had been tamed.

"Vernon was the young phenomenon coming through, a local guy, and he took them to the Cup. Which was great," said Lemelin. "I played in the building years, but you go through what you go through. I'm proud of what I accomplished, to set the path.

Unfortunately I wasn't there when it all happened (in 1989), but I went to Boston and we went to the Cup twice, in (1988 and 1990). Of course, it was against Edmonton again. I still live here [near Boston], my family was raised there . . . You can't be upset because the Flames won after you left. It's no big deal."

Was Vernon a better goalie than Lemelin? Well, he played four more seasons (19), nearly 275 more games (781), had nearly 150 more wins (385), and won two Stanley Cups to Lemelin's none. But when it came to the Battle, Vernon surely had a stronger team in front of him. As Murdoch pointed out, his was a team that truly believed it could beat Edmonton, where Lemelin's was not.

15

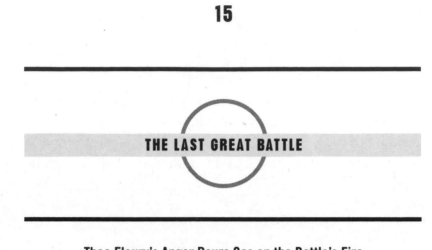

THE LAST GREAT BATTLE

Theo Fleury's Anger Pours Gas on the Battle's Fire
"[MacInnis] looks up at me and he says,
'What the fuck are you doing here?'"

By 1991, the Battle had been waged for more than a decade since
Calgary had become the second Alberta city to get an NHL franchise in 1980. The two clubs had met in the playoffs four times —
in 1983, 1984, 1986, and 1988 — with one more vicious, memorable
series about to begin. It would turn out to be the last playoff
meeting between the teams, and in 2014 the prospects of both
clubs making the playoffs at the same time and meeting in a
series seemed almost like science fiction.

By 1991, Lanny McDonald and Jim Peplinski were gone from
Calgary's lineup, as were Wayne Gretzky, Jari Kurri, and Paul
Coffey from Edmonton's. Doug Risebrough was now coaching
the Flames while John Muckler had succeeded Glen Sather
behind the Oilers bench. This would mark the final Battle of

Alberta for Edmonton's great tandem of Mark Messier and Glenn Anderson, as the dismantling of a dynasty was in full gear in Edmonton.

Alas, 1991 would also become the first year since 1983 that neither Calgary nor Edmonton would represent the Campbell Conference in the Stanley Cup final. Gretzky and his Los Angeles Kings had walked away with the Smythe Division that regular season for the first time in team history, the first time in eleven seasons that somebody other than the Oilers or Flames had stood atop the Smythe standings heading into the post-season. So, in the spring of 1991, it was No. 2 Calgary hosting No. 3 Edmonton in that Round 1 series, another first in the Battle of Alberta, and a sign that the glory years of these two franchises were drawing to a close.

Calgary had finished twenty points ahead of Edmonton in 1990–91 and were the prohibitive favourites.

"Look at it on paper," said defenceman Jeff Beukeboom, who was wading into his first Battle as an everyday, top-six defence-man for Edmonton in April 1991. "Their top-three centremen were [Joe] Nieuwendyk, [Doug] Gilmour, and [Joel] Otto. They had [Gary] Roberts, [Theoren] Fleury . . . [Al] MacInnis and [Gary] Suter on the points. [Mike] Vernon in goal. They were stacked and we were the underdogs. We knew it, but we didn't care. We were battle-tested from before, and the guys who weren't—such as myself—we were ready for the challenge, and knew what it took.

"This was eight, nine years in the making."

And it did not disappoint.

"Best series I have ever covered—anywhere, any time, between any two teams," said veteran Calgary hockey writer George Johnson. "What I remember the most was how visceral it was. Beukeboom was Nieuwendyk's cousin. Well, he must have broken ten sticks over his cousin's back. This wasn't the new, 'we're-looking-after-your-health' NHL. This was out-and-out tong warfare.

"There were guys who'd been on those earlier Calgary teams, when the Oilers had just kicked the hell out of them. They remembered. That's what made the Battle so great. It built to this point."

Even though the Oilers were the defending Stanley Cup champions from 1990, with Gretzky in L.A. and Mario Lemieux and his Pittsburgh Penguins about to win their first of back-to-back Stanley Cups, it would have taken the most rednecked Albertan to argue that the Battle still contained the two best teams in the game. Sure, the Oilers and Flames had won six of the past seven Stanley Cups. But the page was turning, and turning fast.

There was one big difference, however. Edmonton still had its two true heart-and-soul leaders through all the years: Mark Messier up front and Kevin Lowe on the blue line. Calgary, well, ever since that Oilers sweep in 1988 there had been some question as to who—if anyone—really made this team tick. They'd won their Cup in 1989, sure. But the Flames had been a better regular-season club than Edmonton for some time now, and the book on the Flames was that they'd never have the intangibles to fulfill their promise on a grander scale.

They had boatloads of skill, but in hockey parlance, the Calgary Flames needed more guts. Enter Theoren Fleury, an angry, petulant, five-foot-eight winger raised in Russell, Manitoba, who, we would learn later, had every right to be pissed off at the world. He'd been a victim of sexual abuse by former junior coach Graham James, carrying that secret with him through an alcohol- and drug-fuelled NHL career.

We didn't know about any of that in 1991, however. All

Beukeboom knew about Fleury was this: "He was a rat." It was, in fact, a kinder description than Fleury uses today to describe his on-ice persona then.

"It had started with him long before," began the big Oilers defenceman, who at six-foot-five and two hundred and thirty pounds had nine inches and fifty pounds on Fleury. "I think it was a pre-season game that year. I was going up ice and got two-handed on the back of the legs by him. Whack! Then, later on, there was a pileup in the corner, after Simmer [Craig Simpson] had taken out their goalie, and Fleury was running his mouth. 'You guys suck. You can't skate, you big —s.' He's on top of me, but when we come out of it together, I've got him. Now he's saying, 'It's okay. I've got you. No problem.' Like, now he's being a nice guy."

So, what did Beukeboom do? Exactly what Fleury would have done.

"I suckered him. Cut him open for stitches," he said. "It was one of the few times Muckler paid me a compliment."

With the series set to open, *Edmonton Journal* columnist Cam Cole described Fleury as "a healthy heartbeat on a screen full of flat-liners." He referenced Fleury's long-standing feud with Beukeboom, and Fleury told Cole, "It's been going on ever since that pre-season game when he suckered me. Then he was mouthing off in the paper, how it was such a great feeling and all this stuff."

This from the man who, as a junior, was part of the famous "Punch Up in Piestany." When Czech officials turned the lights off on that 1987 World Junior brawl between Canada and Russia, what did Fleury do? "I went out there and tried to punch as many Commies as I could," he once said.

Ah, a true patriot indeed. In fact, Fleury was exactly what the Battle needed. He was a fresh new antagonist. A match to ignite the fumes of history. A straw to stir the drink or to deliver the cheap shot that would take everyone's emotions over the top.

Fleury had arrived in the NHL, fittingly, with much agitation. An eighth-round draft pick out of the Moose Jaw Warriors, there were folks at the Flames' own draft table who didn't want any part of him.

"Al MacNeil went nuts," Flames former general manager Cliff Fletcher said of his assistant general manager. "He says, 'How can we draft a little guy like this?' But we had one of the real great amateur scouts, one of the legends in the scouting business, Ian McKenzie. And Ian said, 'You've got to draft this guy. He'll play in the NHL. He'll play for us.'"

Fletcher, as many general managers will do, gave that late-round pick to his top junior scout as a sign of allegiance. If McKenzie felt that strongly about Fleury, then Fletcher would reward his bird dog for all of that bad arena coffee, all of those ice-cold drives between prairie junior rinks, by donating an eighth-round pick.

"In my own mind, I took the middle road," Fletcher admitted today. "I thought, 'Even if he doesn't play in the NHL, he's going to really sell tickets in the American League.' So we drafted Theo in the eighth round."

When a player is still available that late in a draft—the way Detroit snapped up Pavel Datsyuk at No. 171 or Henrik Zetterberg at No. 210—not even the team that picked him can say they truly knew he'd turn into even a decent player. Any one of twenty-one teams could have had Fleury, who ranks eighth in NHL games played from that draft, despite being chosen at No. 166. Only one took a flyer on him.

"I didn't think he could play. Thought he was too small," said Oilers chief scout Barry Fraser. "He was a good skater, not an exceptional skater. But one thing about him I've got to give him credit for, he has a big heart. He worked his ass off all the time. As miserable an asshole as he was back then—and he was a real prick—nobody liked him. His own teammates didn't like him."

Now, his teammates didn't mind Fleury in 1990–91 when he became the smallest man in NHL history to score fifty goals. But being liked was never high on Fleury's priority list.

"He came in with a lot of fanfare, playing extremely well in the minors," recalled Lanny McDonald of Fleury's entrance three years earlier. "He comes in and promptly told us our troubles were over. He was here. He was a cocky, brash little pepperpot."

Fleury had joined the Flames midway through a 1988–89 season in which Calgary was stocked and ready to win its first Stanley Cup. His act didn't go over particularly well—especially with an old hand like Lanny, who hadn't won a Cup yet in seventeen NHL seasons and knew his days were numbered.

"We very quickly, as a leadership group, tried to make him understand: 'You can be cocky, you can be arrogant. But you still have to find a way to fit into the team concept, and the team philosophy,'" McDonald said. "This was not all about him. This was about finding a way to win."

What the old moustachioed ex-Maple Leaf didn't know was that his relationship with Fleury went back farther than McDonald knew. When Fleury was a kid, his team won tickets to a Winnipeg Jets game, where McDonald's Colorado Rockies happened to be on the visiting team that same night.

"My parents couldn't rub two nickels together—we were always poor," Fleury began, "but I managed to get enough money together to buy a program in Winnipeg. So I got this program and I went down to where the Colorado bench was during warmup, and sure enough Lanny is coming off the ice, so I got his autograph.

"Fast-forward to my first NHL training camp. The rookies usually dress in the bowels of the rinks, right? But, for some reason, I was in the main room for camp. I get into the main room and I'm looking for my stall, and sure enough I'm sitting next to Lanny McDonald. I remember saying, 'Hey, been skating a lot this summer?' He's like, 'No. First time I've put my skates on.' I'm thinking, 'Shit, I like this guy!'

"Eighteen months later, him, I, and the rest of the team are carrying the Stanley Cup around the Montreal Forum."

Fleury's reputation preceded him. He was called up on New Year's Eve of 1988 from the Flames farm team in Salt Lake City, where he'd racked up seventy-four points in forty games. "The Flames were in a mini-slump. They'd lost, like, one game in a row," laughed Fleury. "But they call me up. So the next day I walk into Flames dressing room for practice, and I'm walking by Al MacInnis.

"He looks up at me and he says, 'What the fuck are *you* doing here?' I said, 'Well, I don't really know at this point . . .' Nice way to greeted by one of the veterans, eh?"

It didn't take long to discern what Fleury had been called up to do. He played thirty-six games in that first season and had thirty-four points. The next year he scored thirty-one goals. The next, fifty-one. Fleury also had a firm grip on what the Battle meant inside that Flames room. Even a guy like MacInnis had to respect him for that.

"I knew how big this Edmonton–Calgary rivalry was, and I knew that if I played real well against the Oilers it would go a long ways to me making the Flames as a regular," Fleury said. "I scored my first two NHL goals on *Hockey Night in Canada* against Grant Fuhr, against the Edmonton Oilers.

"From that moment on, I played some of my best hockey against the Oilers."

Fleury was very good. Extremely quick and creative, and wholly unafraid for a man his size. He had been told since he was a pee wee player that he was too small and shouldn't bother trying to play in the NHL. He'd never make it, they said, and with each evaluation the chip on Fleury's shoulder grew bigger and bigger.

That chip became as valuable as his scoring touch, prompting his coach, Doug Risebrough, to say this leading into the 1991 series against Edmonton: "I would say that the day Theoren is comfortable, that all the questions have been answered, will not be a positive thing in his career. The challenge at one time was to play pro, then to play in the NHL, then be a regular in the NHL. Now, he's in another dimension."

Fleury, we know now, was a troubled young man. He had the inner drive to prove everyone wrong, which meant he refused ever to back down. But he also harboured an anger that Graham James was responsible for. A confusion, no doubt, about how to deal with what had happened. The burden of not revealing what James had done was clearly a heavy one, a statement borne out when you see his transformation from a dark, troubled, drug-abusing NHLer to the fabulous role model and positive influence Fleury has become since admitting that he was victimized.

"I hadn't started using those street drugs back then. I was still partying and drinking, like everyone else was," he said. He was angry, but he'd been angry all the way up through juniors. He had to be.

"I realized it somewhere along the way, maybe it was when Dave Manson hit me when I was in Prince Albert, one of my first games in the Western League," he said. "I thought my collar bone was on the other side of my body when he hit me that night, and I realized right then and there that, if I was going to make it, I was going to have to set myself apart from every other small guy that's ever played the game. I just never backed down from anything or anybody."

Manson's nickname was "Charlie." Today he is a mild-mannered father of the Anaheim Ducks defenceman Josh Manson, but back in the day the moniker suited Dave. He was not only one of the toughest, meanest players of his day, but in his early days he was also known as what hockey people call "a snapper." He had become a more gentle, polite person whom I got to know and quite liked when he played for the Edmonton Oilers back in the early 1990s. But in his prime, when Charlie snapped, nobody wanted any part of him. That much was a fact.

"He was fuckin' scary in junior, let me tell ya. And his defence partner was Ken Baumgartner!" Fleury recalled, laughing. "So I went up to P.A. with Moose Jaw. I was five-foot-three, a hundred and twenty-five pounds, playing in the Western League my first year."

That Manson hit framed Fleury's career. It left him in deep pain, and deep in thought as to how he was going to survive in a bigger man's game. "You'd better figure out how you're going to protect yourself," Fleury challenged himself. "How you're going to get room out on the ice here because this can't be happening much more. Otherwise, I'm not going to make it."

Not unlike Stu Grimson and Dave Brown, Fleury was well served to have apprenticed in the pre-politically correct WHL. It toughened him up, and when you were Fleury's size, it honed your survival skills. "[Craig] Berube, Manson, Baumgartner, Wendel Clark . . . There were tough guys everywhere in the league. So in order to get room out there, I had to become this fuckin' hatchet man," Fleury said. "And I had no problem fuckin' cutting your eye out. Wouldn't have bothered me a bit.

"Hey, you're trying to fuckin' kill me? This was survival. It was that unpredictability that allowed me to have the room that I had."

The 1991 Battle of Alberta began with a 3–1 Oilers win in Calgary. With that, home-ice advantage had been eliminated by Edmonton. The Flames won by the same score two nights later, then two nights after that, at the Northlands Coliseum, a tight 4–3 Oilers win on a goal by Joe Murphy with fourteen ticks left on the clock. Edmonton also won Game 4, and in the first game that had not been a one-goal affair until late in the third period, the usual fisticuffs ensued.

It was in this game that Oiler Dave Brown administered a beating on Jim Kyte—exactly fifteen months and one day after his fight with Stu Grimson—in which Kyte ended up lying on the ice face up with Brown straddling his chest. Kyte made the poor choice of throwing a punch or two from his back, prompting Brown to fire up the left hand again from his perch atop Kyte. The sequence prompted sportscaster Darren Dutchyshen to proclaim, "There goes Brownie! He's startin' the lawnmower on Jim Kyte!"

The series shifted back to Calgary for Game 5, the Flames' lives on the line. It was then that Tim Hunter did his best Billy Graham impression, which lacked only a "Hallelujah!!" or a "Praise the Lord!" to have been fit for a Sunday-morning service.

"We're going to win this series," Hunter promised the Calgary press on the off day. "We have twenty believers in this room, and if we have any disbelievers, they're not going to go out on the ice."

Three hundred kilometres to the north, they were asking Brown about his fight with Kyte. "It was self-explanatory," he said.

Calgary would win Game 5 with their best effort. Off the ice, the series was heating up, to the point where Flames' goalie coach, the Hall of Famer Glenn Hall, attacked a reporter who he claimed had misquoted him. "You writers are out to get us. I'll teach you a lesson!" the fifty-nine-year-old Hall shouted before gripping *Herald* reporter Gyle Konotopetz's melon in a python-like headlock. "Fight, you yellow —! Fight!"

On the ice, the series had also become brutal. It was still the one-referee system, and if they were to make a video about why the NHL switched to two referees, they could have begun with footage of the lumber being swung in the 1991 Battle of Alberta.

"It was absolute war. War. War. War," said Fleury. "If we played that series today, all of us would be suspended for one hundred games each. There were full baseball swings, slashing each other. There was no little tap, tap. If you were using your stick, it was to either maim someone or hurt them."

The Oilers defence, without Coffey or depth defenceman Randy Gregg, had transformed itself somewhat, and the Edmonton pairing that leading scorer Fleury would see all night every night was known as the "Twin Towers." Six-foot-five Jeff Beukeboom and six-foot-three Steve Smith were assigned not only to defend Fleury but also to inflict as much pain upon the little dynamo as possible.

Staying within the rules was merely a suggestion by head coach John Muckler. And, of course, Beukeboom and Fleury had their special friendship that went back to the pre-season.

"Beuk would absolutely punish Theo Fleury every chance he got," marvelled Craig MacTavish. "Fleury was tough, he kept coming back. But Beuk would just punish him. He was a tough, tough, tough guy. Theo, back in those days, was also a tough, hard-nosed competitor."

Recalled Fleury: "My left side and my right side were two different colours, and not the colour they are supposed to be. It was brutal. But it was one of the best series I've ever been involved with. And one of the best series I've ever played."

"He was dirty. Everyone knew it," Beukeboom said of Fleury.

"You had a lot of respect for him, but at the same time, a lot of hate toward each other. I gave it to him every time I could because I didn't want him to be the determining factor that he tried to be. It was all fine."

Fleury had just a lone assist in the first four games of that 1991 series, and his Flames trailed 3–1 at that point. He added an assist in Game 5, and then, in a 2–1 Flames win at Northlands in Game 6, Fleury had an assist in regulation and the all-important overtime winner just four minutes and forty seconds into overtime.

Messier, on the ice in overtime with Esa Tikkanen and Petr Klima, was stood up near the blue line by Jamie Macoun and stubbornly refused to shoot the puck in. Instead, he tried a risky cross-ice pass to Steve Smith, flawlessly anticipated by Fleury.

"I just read the play perfect, and it was a foot race between me and Jeff Beukeboom. So, who's going to win that one?" asked Fleury, a full twenty-three years later, still seizing the chance to get a shot in at Beukeboom. The goal was on Messier, not Beukeboom, but it was the defenceman who was left to chase the speedy Fleury as he bore down on Grant Fuhr.

Asked if he'd planned to go five-hole on Fuhr, as Fleury did that night to extend the series to a seventh game, Fleury referenced author Malcolm Gladwell and his book *The Outliers.* There, Gladwell writes of "The 10,000 Hour Rule." His premise is, in order to be an expert at anything, you must put in at least 10,000 hours of repetition. In Fleury, and most NHLers, that manifests itself in a clutch moment like Game 6.

"When you're going in on a breakaway, it's not about knowing where you're going to shoot or knowing the goalie's tendencies," Fleury said. "It's a split-second decision. All those hours that I spent in Russell on the ice by myself shooting pucks, doing all that [practice], that takes over in a situation like that.

"I just went in, shot the puck, and fortunately it went in. We lived to play another day."

You've likely seen Fleury's celebration after that goal, and if you have not, do yourself a favour and Google it. On the evening of April 14, 1991, Fleury enacted a celebration that stretched 175 feet, from the corner to the right of the beaten Fuhr, across the blue line and the Northlands emblem at centre ice, and on to the half-wall in the Flames zone. There, Fleury lay on his back like a puppy waiting for a tummy rub when Joe Nieuwendyk finally caught up to him for a bear hug.

"It is the biggest goal I ever scored," said Fleury, who scored 489 NHL goals, regular season and playoffs. "Everybody has a goal that sort of defines their career. That one was it for me. Being an emotional guy—I wear my heart on my sleeve, I tell it like it is—that's just all part of that."

"Theo was a clutch player," said Glenn Anderson. "Certain things he said back then, you'd kind of wonder why he'd say them. He had a lot of frustration and anger built up inside of him. But that was great 'cause it showed on the ice. He wanted control of the game. Like a Cliff Ronning or Martin St. Louis, who always heard that they were too small and not going to be any good in the NHL, he proved all those critics wrong."

Fleury couldn't be more matter-of-fact as he recollects things that happened more than twenty years ago, puffing on a smoke while the questions are asked, exhaling during the first few words of each answer. Perhaps the cards that Fleury has been dealt in his life—and having made so much of himself—leaves him this way. He truly does not care what others may think of him, so comfortable is Theo Fleury in his own skin these days.

One of the things you learn, however, when you leave the world of hockey fans and talk with those players we all watched from those arena seats, our couches at home, or seats in the press box is that those of us who never played at the pro level stress over the minutiae of games gone by so much more than the actual players ever do.

How many times over the course of interviewing for this book did a player recollect the wrong play, in the wrong game, in the wrong town? "Who did we play the series before?" they'll ask. "Vancouver?"

"No, it was Los Angeles."

"Oh yeah, that was a great series. How many games . . . ?"

"Game 7 was 3–0 or 3–1, I can't remember," Fleury begins. "The other team is trying to win just a badly as we are, right? And back then, the game was a lot more wide open. What did it go, to double overtime? And a shitty goal goes off of Frank Musil's shin pad and in the top corner. It could have gone our way."

The irony of this final Battle of Alberta lay in the fact that it took the Flames five games to realize they could not be drawn into the physical battle with Edmonton. Just as Bob Johnson had bogged down the game in the early 1980s in order to slow down the offensively superior Oilers, in 1991 the Flames had to eschew the natural affinity to get even on players like Beukeboom, Smith, and Craig Muni and open up the ice for players like Doug Gilmour, Nieuwendyk, Robert Reichel, and Paul Ranheim. Oh, how the skate was on the other foot from the days when Neil Sheehy would attempt to drag Gretzky down to his level of play—but that's where we'd come to. Full circle. Calgary was the better team now; it was the Flames who had led the league in goals scored in 1990–91, scoring nearly a goal per game more than Edmonton.

But it had taken Calgary too long to solve the puzzle, and now we were heading into a Game 7. It was Johnson who had laid out, as the last entry in his Seven Point Plan, "Force them to a Game 7." Then anything can happen.

Anderson, along with Messier and Fuhr, would dress for this final game in the Battle of Alberta that night, on April 16, 1991, at the Saddledome. After all they had been through in that visiting team's dressing room over the past decade; after all the blood shed, the Cup runs, and ultimately the success that the blue team had enjoyed over the red one, Anderson felt it in his bones that day that his team would do what it almost always had done to Calgary when the chips were down.

They would win.

"To knock off the Stanley Cup champions is a very, very difficult thing to do," he said, referring not only to the previous spring but also the four Cups that preceded 1990. "We've got the will, and we had the nucleus. We had guys who had been there for five Cups—Kevin Lowe. Mark Messier, myself, Fuhrsie . . . You had a nucleus of guys who had been around the block a million times. If you're going to try to knock us off, you'd better be bringing your A game, plus. 'Cause we're not going down without a fight."

The Oilers had enough Game 7 experience, having beaten Calgary in seven games in 1984, lost to them in seven in 1986, won Game 7 in the final against Philly in 1987, lost Game 7 to L.A. in 1989, and defeated Winnipeg in 1990. If one learns as much from losing as they do from winning, a 3–2 Game 7 record was a pretty good education. Especially considering that, over the same time, Calgary had a 3–1 mark in Game 7s themselves.

"In a Game 7, it's never over," Anderson said. "You've always got an opportunity, and you never say die. Once you've won it once, you've got it in your heart, in your mind, in your soul, that you're never going to surrender.

"And that's the hardest things to beat: The heart, the mind, and the soul."

Calgary jumped to a 3–0 lead in Game 7, the kind of advantage that would seal the deal in today's game. But, as Reggie Lemelin and Grant Fuhr have said in these pages, goalies were more fallible back in those days, unaided by the giant equipment of today. And sure enough, late in the first period, Esa Tikkanen unloaded one from just inside the Calgary blue line that would leak through Vernon's pads, planting that seed of doubt in a Flames team that, sadly, was experienced at allowing that seed to germinate.

Before long it was 3–3, then 4–3 for Edmonton before Ronnie Stern jammed home a puck at 17:50 of the third period to force overtime.

"Any time any game goes to Game 7, anything can happen," said Fleury. "And if you're the favourite? There's even more pressure on you. 'Cause you should never let a team get you to that point in a series."

After Fleury had brought the series back home with his Game 6 heroics in Edmonton, conventional wisdom had dictated that the Flames had exorcised their demons. They had looked adversity in the eye, down 3–1, and put themselves back in the driver's seat of the series. Then they led the game 3–0 on home ice. With what everyone considered to be a better hockey team . . .

"'That Game 7," Flames play-by-play man Peter Maher recalled, "that's when I started not to believe so strongly in momentum. In Game 6, when Fleury scored that OT goal and slides across the ice and everything . . . And on top of that, the Flames jumped ahead 3–0 in the first period? So I'm thinking, What more can you ask for?

"Then Tikkanen got his first goal, right at the end of the first period. It was a long shot, and that turned the game. Next thing you know, you lose in overtime and you're done."

Overtime was not yet seven minutes old when Tikkanen, who had an assist and two goals already that night, picked up a loose puck at centre with his back to the Flames net. He circled to his left, was picked up at the blue line by a helmetless Flames defenceman Frank Musil, and taken wide on his off-wing down the right-wing boards. MacInnis cruised in as support, and neither Flames defenceman, at the end of a long shift, played a red-hot Tikkanen aggressively enough, allowing a lethal shooter to have a shot off the wrong wing through traffic.

The puck glanced off of Musil's leg and rifled past Vernon, a harmless chance transformed into a stake in Calgary's heart, just like that. The goal was unassisted, and truly, a goal of that import should have required more work than Tikkanen did to score that series-winner.

After a decade of violent, emotional hockey that had brought two Alberta cities to the forefront of perhaps the most entertaining eras of hockey history, Tikkanen had simply waltzed down the right side and zipped home a wrist shot. No one laid a stick on him. Nobody put a glove in his face.

"This is one of the finest wins. One of the greatest series we've played," Sather said post-game.

And that was it. With that goal, the Battle of Alberta was over. Or, at least, it entered a long period of hibernation.

"The highlight of my career, having an opportunity to play in one the greatest rivalries ever, in the history of the game," Fleury says today. "Calgary didn't give a shit about the other twenty-something teams. They only cared about beating Edmonton.

"We hated everybody on their team. We hated Edmonton, they hated us."

Yet, everybody loved the Battle, and the hockey that it spawned.

"I thought the Edmonton–Calgary rivalry would run forever," said Grant Fuhr. "I am a little surprised — and I think everybody is — that it's still not back [to that high level]. Both teams are rebuilding, but you'd think it would still be a hard-fought rivalry."

CONCLUSION

You never want to become that dinosaur. The one who can't listen to a song, go to a movie, or watch a game without squawking on about how much better things were back in the day.

The Battle of Alberta wasn't "better" than the hockey we watch today per se. It was, in fact, played with far less structure than the coaches of this era demand. Reggie Lemelin and Grant Fuhr whiffed on shots from outside the hashmarks far more often than goalies do now, while teams allowed more end-to-end rushes in one game by the two Pauls—Coffey and Reinhart—than you'd see in a month of current hockey.

They fought far more often in the Battle than what we now consider to be an acceptable amount of violence. Not only to defend a teammate or to change the tone in the game that was being played but often to set a tone for the next meeting. The "just in case" fight that hockey has pretty much done away with.

Truly, there was always an accepted justification to drop the gloves in the Battle, and at the time we loved that. Today, with concussion awareness, we know better.

The lineups in the 1980s were not nearly as deep with fast-skating, physically fit players as they are now. Those players didn't shoot the puck as hard with their wooden Sher-Wood PMP 5030s—or Gretzky's classic white-and-red Titan—as the guys do with those composite rocket launchers they use today. And from a fan's standpoint, there were probably thirty games or more a season that weren't even on TV—anywhere—with no Centre Ice package or streaming video to pull in games from afar.

No, yesterday's game lacks a lot of the elements of today's hockey. Above all, predictability.

Every game is on TV now. Every player is in shape and executes the system he is told to play (or at least he tries). Goalies stop a little more than nine out of ten shots, and a goal from long range is now most often deemed a mistake by the netminder. Defencemen pass the puck three or four times before it reaches centre ice for a dump-in because modern defensive systems have deemed skating the puck up the middle to be too risky.

Maybe that's where the game they played during the height of the Battle grabbed me. That same lack of complexity, of systematic preparedness, also gave us an absence of predictability.

Mix in nine or ten Hall of Fame players, some of the funniest characters in hockey, and several of the toughest fighters in the game, and you had the kind of hockey that Albertans fell in love with in the 1980s.

I never heard Glen Sather lament, as coaches do today, "It's a 3–2 league," as if his troops would not even attempt to score eight or nine goals that night. Sometimes, Edmonton or Calgary scored five times in the opening period during the 1980s. Gretzky would have four points in the first fifteen minutes, and the building buzzed in anticipation of the possibility of a record-breaking night.

The average score of an Edmonton game in the mid-1980s was 5–4 for the Oilers. That meant the old Oilers were splitting up nine goals a night, or nearly twice as many as they do today in the same sixty-minute game. Yet the size of the netminders' equipment still left plenty of room for spectacular goaltending.

You just didn't know what would greet you when you went to

the rink in those days, and for me, unpredictability is the necessary ingredient of any good sporting event.

You might see Doug Gilmour score four goals for Calgary, or on a night when Gretzky was absent from the Oilers lineup, I once saw Pat Hughes score five. You might have been present when Doug Risebrough ripped Marty McSorley's jersey to shreds with his skates while sitting in the penalty box after a five-on-five brawl. Or perhaps you were there when Flames trainer Jim (Bearcat) Murray ran out on the ice to tend to an injured player while his team scored a goal. And the goal counted.

We all knew Gretzky would score fifty goals in fewer than fifty games in the 1981–82 season, as he had forty-one goals in his first thirty-seven games. But did anyone even consider the possibility he would score nine times in Games 38 and 39? That he'd set an unreachable bar of fifty-in-thirty-nine with a five-goal performance that night against Philly, providing the highlight of a diving Bill Barber—festooned in the long pant Cooperalls of the day—that is etched on my brain?

It was the anticipation each night that maybe, just maybe, you'd see history when Edmonton and Calgary met. Or you'd see a brawl. Or likely both.

At the time of this writing, the Alberta hockey landscape is once again emerging. Calgary had not hosted a playoff game in six years or won a playoff series in more than a decade, but went two rounds in the spring of 2015. After a string of nine straight playoff misses the Oilers cleaned house, adding a new general manger (Peter Chiarelli) and head coach (Todd McLellan), drafting Connor McDavid, and upgrading almost roughly one-third of its lineup through trades and free agency.

As Sather lamented after his Rangers had dispatched the Oilers by a 2–0 score one night in December, "Nobody wants to hit anybody and that's the way the rules are today. Move the puck, skate, dump it in, dump it out, and wait for a break. It's all it is."

The two lineups in Calgary and Edmonton are filed with youth, speed, and the promise of a Battle of Alberta that may never be as violent, but could be as exciting as it once had been.

With McDavid, Taylor Hall, et al, Edmonton looks like a team that could once again lead the NHL in scoring one day soon. It may never be like 1985 again, but a 2015 version of the 400-goal Oilers would be just fine with hockey fans.

"That's the fun of playing offensive hockey. You can make some mistakes," Grant Fuhr said. "It was a new style to the league at that time. We just played run 'n' gun. We knew we were going to get our four or five every night, and we [as in, he] just had to keep the other guys to one less. It wasn't about numbers. It was about winning and losing."

Goals, saves, end-to-end rushes. Hits and fights.

If you grew up watching the Battle, you expected more than one prize in the box of Cracker Jack because that is what the games delivered nightly. They never played 2–0 hockey; there weren't any no-hitters.

The players let their emotions get away from them, and they did dumb things.

It didn't always make for an instructional video. But, boy, were there highlights.

ACKNOWLEDGEMENTS

Jack Cookson's photographs provided the inspiration for *The Battle of Alberta*, and they are available at proamsports.ca. Colin Patterson and Tonya Young didn't know me from Adam when I first contacted them, but they generously opened up their contact lists and pointed me in the right direction. Wayne Gretzky, Reggie Lemelin, Mark Messier, Theo Fleury, Glenn Anderson, Neil Sheehy, and so many other survivors of the Battle found time to answer my calls and texts, long after they'd given me a lengthy interview, for follow-ups. Thank you.

Among my colleagues, Al Maki, Eric Duhatschek, Jim Matheson, and George Johnson were generous with their memories, old books, and newspaper clippings that I could not possibly have unearthed myself. HockeyDB.com was essential, and is unmatched in the industry. And Dean Bennett, an old and dear friend who once kept me in the business when I was literally walking away, lent his keen eye to this manuscript. Thanks, Dean. Without you, I might have had to get a real job.

Thank you all.

INDEX

Ali, Muhammad, 106
Ambrose, Ricky, 34, 35
Anderson, Glenn, 46, 167–68,
    264
    and 1986 playoffs, 124, 132, 133
    and Mark Messier, 91–93
    on Theoren Fleury, 262
Ashley, John, 169
Atlanta Flames, 9, 239

Baxter, Paul, 115, 164, 171
Béliveau, Jean, 209
Berezan, Perry, 18, 134, 147
Berthiaume, Daniel, 185
Beukeboom, Jeff, 10–11, 251, 253,
    260–61
"blackout game," 171
Boston Bruins, 52, 171
Boston Garden, 171
Bouchard, Pat, 240
Bourgeois, Aurele, 32–34
Bourgeois, Charlie, 32–35
Bowman, Jamie, 71
Bozek, Steve, 195
Brookside Training School, 142
Brophy, John, 145

Brown, Dave, 259
    fight with Stu Grimson,
        103–4, 153, 215, 217–28
    in junior hockey, 212–14
Bullard, Mike, 3, 12, 170, 173,
    185–86, 188
Bureau, Marc, 229

Calgary Flames
    and 1986 playoffs, 18–19, 72,
        124–40, 146–47
    and 1988 playoffs, 185–90
    and 1989 championship,
        191–209
    and 1991 playoffs, 251, 259–66
    collegiate players, 21–31, 62
    management, 24
    mascot, 17
    ownership, 15
    power play, 116–17
    record vs. Edmonton, 63–64,
        122, 131, 248
    style of play, 7–8, 25, 127, 263
Canada Cup, 73, 186, 243–44
Canadian Broadcasting Corp.
    (CBC), 124–27, 135–36

Chelios, Chris, 205
Chiarelli, Peter, 269
Chicago Blackhawks, 17–18
Chicago Cougars, 239
Chubey, Dick, 181
Cincinnati Stingers, 81
Cloutier, Réal, 238
Coates, Al, 23, 27, 56, 59–63, 196
Coffey, Paul, 38, 46–47, 130, 140,
    247
Cole, Cam, 99, 253
Crisp, Terry, 12, 13, 225
    and 1989 playoffs, 193,
        198–203, 205, 208

Dirk, Glen, 211
Drake, Clare, 61–62
Dryden, Dave, 43
Dryden, Ken, 43
Duhatschek, Eric, 70, 110, 112
Dutchyshen, Darren, 259

Eaves, Mike, 90
Edmonton Eskimos, 5, 215
Edmonton Flyers, 83
Edmonton Oilers
    and 1986 playoffs, 124–40,
        145–55
    and 1988 playoffs, 185–90
    and 1991 playoffs, 98, 251,
        259–66
    acquisition of Gretzky, 41–42
    "blackout game," 171
    and Clare Drake, 61–62
    depth of roster, 87
    early playoff defeats, 84–87
    influence of Winnipeg Jets, 103

and media, 150–51
    offensive dominance, 150
    ownership, 15, 24–25
    playoff success, 182–85
    record vs. Calgary, 63–64, 122,
        131, 248
    record vs. Winnipeg, 184–85
    roster depth, 54–56, 78–79
    style of play, 6–9, 243, 246,
        248, 270
    team personality, 6, 10
Edwards, Don, 242
equipment managers
    cooperation between, 16
    doctoring of equipment, 215,
        221, 222
ESPN, 127
Evans, Daryl, 85

Ferreira, Jack, 22, 62
fighting, 1–3, 10, 11, 14, 103–4,
        112–14, 123, 164, 177–78,
        212–33, 267
Fisher, Red, 96
Fletcher, Cliff, 7, 195–96, 254
    and 1986 playoffs, 133, 137, 138
    availability to media, 104–5
    on Bob Johnson, 62
    on collegiate players, 26–27
Flett, Bill, 7
Fleury, Theoren, 164, 165, 206–7,
        252–65
Ford, Betty, 106
Ford, Gerald, 106
Fotiu, Nick, 167–68
Fraser, Barry, 22, 37–38, 45–47,
        144, 254–55

Fraser, Kerry, 156–57, 161–63, 167–68, 170, 224
Freeman, (Bullet) Bob, 48
Fuhr, Grant
  and 1984 playoffs, 90
  and 1986 playoffs, 129, 130, 132, 134, 147
  on end of rivalry, 266
  on his statistics, 246–47
  off-ice problems, 49, 242–43
  on Oilers' style of play, 270
  personality, 243–44
  scouting and drafting of, 37–38, 47

general managers
  availability to media, 104–5
  and drafting, 37, 254
Gilmour, Doug, 197, 204, 206
Gilmour, Lloyd, 170
Gladwell, Malcolm, 261–62
goaltending, 8, 235–49, 264, 267, 268
Goldthorpe, Bill (Goldie), 144–45
Graves, Adam, 218
Green, Rick, 206
Gregg, Randy, 31–32, 151
Gretzky, Phyllis, 132–33
Gretzky, Wayne, 172–90, 247
  and 1986 playoffs, 130, 132–33, 136
  and 1988 playoffs, 186–89
  acquisition by Edmonton, 41–42
  attempts to defend against, 179–81

  on Bob Johnson, 71
  on Calgary Flames, 189–90
  competitiveness, 174–76
  favourite goal, 172–73, 187–89
  on Glen Sather, 39
  on Kevin McClelland, 1–3
  and media, 97, 107
  and Neil Sheehy, 27, 109–10, 115–19
  offensive dominance, 173–74
  and referees, 165–66
  and tickets to Toronto games, 126–27
Grimson, Stan, 210
Grimson, Stu, 103–4, 153, 210–21, 223–33
Guidolin, Armand (Bep), 42
Gustafsson, Bengt, 41

Hall, Glenn, 259–60
Harvey the Hound, 17
Hayter, Ron, 5
Hislop, Jamie, 88
Hrdina, Jiri, 197
Hryniuk, Al, 71
Huddy, Charlie, 100, 133
Hughes, Pat, 55–56
Hull, Brett, 195–96
Hunter, Bill, 15
Hunter, Dave, 106
Hunter, Mark, 193, 198
Hunter, Tim, 216
  and 1989 playoffs, 194, 197, 201–4, 206
  and 1991 playoffs, 259
  ability to intimidate, 8, 11, 171

and Kevin McClelland fight,
1–3
Hutchison, James, 33, 34, 35

Iafrate, Al, 96
Indianapolis Racers, 41–42, 81

Jackson, Don, 11, 128
James, Graham, 257
Johnson, (Badger) Bob, 7, 58–74,
90–91, 127, 133, 186
coaching style, 61, 62, 64–67,
105
contrasted with Sather, 14–15,
25
death of, 73–74
departure from Calgary, 72–73
hiring of, 26, 84
personality, 58–60, 68
and referees, 162–63
Seven Point Plan, 18, 69–71
superstitions, 66–67
as tactician, 68–72, 117, 131,
168, 181
Johnson, George, 54, 68, 97, 138,
251–52

Keenan, Mike, 162
Klein, Ralph, 5
Knox, Swede, 159, 163–64
Konotopetz, Gyle, 260
Krushelnyski, Mike, 132, 134
Kulchisky, Lyle (Sparky), 11, 15,
16–17, 151, 222
Kurri, Jari, 47, 92, 130, 133, 188
Kyte, Jim, 259

LaForge, Bill, 214
LaForge, Patrick, 20
Lemaire, Jacques, 168
Lemelin, Réjean (Reggie), 128,
235–42
Lewis, Bryan, 158–59, 160
London Knights, 143–44
Loob, Hakan, 133, 178, 205
Los Angeles Kings, 84–85
Lowe, Ken, 16, 215
Lowe, Kevin, 16, 171
and 1986 playoffs, 131, 133, 134,
140, 147, 149
on Brown–Grimson fight,
228–29
on Dave Brown, 221–22
drafting of, 45–46
on fighting, 14
on Stu Grimson, 218
on toughness of Calgary
games, 10, 11, 178
Luff, Glenn, 125
Lumley, Dave, 124, 128

MacInnis, Al, 90, 256
MacNeil, Al, 254
Macoun, Jamie, 261
and 1986 playoffs, 138
and 1989 playoffs, 205
on Bob Johnson, 64–65
and Mark Messier, 52, 89
on Neil Sheehy, 109
signing with Calgary, 21–24
MacTavish, Craig, 105, 182, 260
and 1986 playoffs, 132
and 1991 playoffs, 98
and Flames mascot, 17

on Glen Sather, 50, 51
and linesmen, 164
on Mark Messier, 91
on toughness of Calgary
    games, 9–10, 19–20, 178
on Wayne Gretzky, 174–75
Maguire, Kevin, 217–28
Maher, Peter, 66–68, 122–24, 134,
    139, 265
Maki, Al, 13, 58–59, 98–99, 107,
    110, 118–19
Mandrusiak, Dwayne, 215, 221
Manson, Dave, 257–58
Matheson, Jack, 48
Matheson, Jim, 48, 100, 101, 106
Mayerthrope massacre, 32–35
McCammon, Bob, 105
McCauley, John, 158
McClelland, Kevin, 1–3, 113–14,
    117
McCreary, Bill, 158, 168–70
McCrimmon, Brad, 180, 197
McDonald, Lanny
    and 1986 playoffs, 18–19, 128,
        135
    and 1989 playoffs, 191–202,
        204–6, 209
    on Bob Johnson, 59
    on Theoren Fleury, 255–56
McIntosh, Paul, 143
McKenzie, Ian, 254
McSorley, Marty, 3, 12, 13, 128, 170
media, 94–107
    access to management, 103,
        104–5
    access to players, 94–98,
        101–2, 150–51

and Bob Johnson, 68
and Glenn Hall, 259–60
and Glen Sather, 39–40
predominance of newspapers,
    100–101
and Steve Smith, 154
television coverage, 30–31, 41,
    104, 124–27, 135–36
travel with teams, 105–6
Meredith, Greg, 112
Messier, Doug, 28, 75–76, 80–81,
    261
Messier, Mark, 75–93
    and 1986 playoffs, 130, 132, 133
    and 1988 playoffs, 187
    on Bob Johnson, 84
    childhood, 75–76, 80–81
    drafting of, 37
    on influence of Calgary
        Flames, 4
    and Joel Otto, 28–29
    as leader, 37, 75–77, 91
    maturing of, 49
    on Oilers style, 6–7
    physical style of play, 52,
        88–91, 178, 247
    on Wayne Gretzky, 175–77
Messier, Paul, 76
Minnesota North Stars, 73
Miracle on Manchester, 85
Mitton, Randy, 159–60, 163–66,
    225
Moncton Alpines, 144–45
Montreal Canadiens, 96
    and 1986 playoffs, 72, 139
    and 1989 playoffs, 192–94, 198
Moog, Andy, 47

Morel, Denis, 159, 162, 167, 171
Morrison, Scotty, 170
Muckler, John, 50–51, 225, 260
Mullen, Joe, 132, 187, 197
Munro, Scotty, 15
Murdoch, Bob
   and 1986 playoffs, 127, 139, 150
   on Bob Johnson, 63, 67–70
   on goaltending, 240–41, 248
   on Wayne Gretzky, 179–81
Murphy, Joe, 259
Murray, Jim (Bearcat), 13, 16,
   218, 223, 225
Murzyn, Dana, 193
Musil, Frank, 101, 263, 266

National Hockey League (NHL)
   amateur draft, 238–39
   defensive emphasis, 245–46,
     268
   entertainment value, 52–54,
     267–70
   merger with WHA, 41, 44–45,
     102
Neale, Harry, 205
Neilson, Roger, 69
New York Islanders, 85–87
New York Rangers, 77–78
Nieuwendyk, Joe, 197, 205,
   251–52, 262
Nilsson, Kent, 8
North American Hockey League
   (NAHL), 235
Northlands Coliseum, 9–10

O'Leary, Michael, 33–34
Orr, Frank, 95

Otto, Joel, 29–30, 109
   and 1986 playoffs, 129, 130, 136
   and 1989 playoffs, 199
   and Mark Messier, 28–29
   on Oilers' personality, 6, 15–16
The Outliers (Gladwell), 261–62

Pagé, Pierre, 109
Parent, Bernie, 239
Patterson, Colin, 122, 123, 128,
   197
   on Bob Johnson, 65, 70
   on fighting, 227, 228
   on Flames' collegiate players,
     25–26
   on Oilers roster, 55
   on television coverage, 30–31,
     125
   on Wayne Gretzky, 180–81
Pavelich, Matt, 169
Peplinski, Jim, 29, 178
   and 1986 playoffs, 129, 133
   and 1989 playoffs, 194, 197–99,
     201–4, 206, 208–9
   on Bob Johnson, 7–8
   on Oilers' personality, 9, 10
   on toughness of Edmonton
     games, 19
Philadelphia Firebirds, 235–39
Philadelphia Flyers, 238–39
Phillips, Rod, 31, 103–4, 106, 134,
   222
physical play, 11–14
Pilling, Gregg, 80, 236
Pittsburgh Penguins, 73
Pocklington, Peter, 15, 24–25,
   41–42, 103, 106, 138, 151

Quinn, Dan, 197

Ramage, Rob, 196–97
Ranford, Bill, 155
referees, 156–71
  "non-calls," 168–69
  playoff assignments, 159–60
"Reggie Lemelin Pool," 241
Regina Pats, 214
Reichel, Robert, 101
Reinhart, Paul, 90
Riggin, Pat, 240
Risebrough, Doug, 3, 13, 194,
  201–2, 203, 257
Roberts, Gary, 12
Roy, Patrick, 72, 194, 205

St. Albert Saints, 81
St. Louis Blues, 72, 125, 139
Sather, Glen (Slats), 6, 13, 30,
  36–57, 138
  and 1991 playoffs, 266
  on Bob Johnson, 71–72
  as coach, 42–44, 51–52
  contrasted with Johnson,
    14–15, 25
  and fans, 17
  management style, 36–38
  on Mark Messier, 81–82
  and media, 39–40, 49–50,
    104–5
  as mentor, 38–39, 47–49, 82–83
  on modern NHL hockey, 270
  as motivator, 9, 181–82
  and referees, 157, 161–63
  roster management, 54–56,
    78–79

scouting, 21–22, 37–38, 44–47
Semenko, Dave, 11, 45, 57, 106,
  117, 123, 166–67
Shannon, John, 31, 70, 125, 127,
  135
Sheehy, Neil, 27, 74, 97, 108–20
Sheehy, Tim, 110
Sinden, Harry, 171
Six P Principle, 215
Skalbania, Nelson, 9, 41–42
Slap Shot, 144–45, 235
Smith, Bobby, 194
Smith, Rae, 142
Smith, Steve, 1, 141–55
  and 1986 playoffs, 100, 128, 133
  and 1988 playoffs, 186
  and 1991 playoffs, 260, 261
  childhood, 142
  on fighting, 11
  in junior hockey, 142–43
  and media, 154
  own goal in 1986 playoffs, 18,
    134, 137, 141, 147–50
Spruce Grove Mets, 76
Stafford, Barrie, 16, 136, 137, 174,
  215, 219, 221, 222, 231
Stampede Corral, 9
Stein, Raymond, 33
Stern, Ronnie, 265
Stewart, Bobby, 16
Strachan, Al, 96, 98, 101, 105
Sullivan, Danny, 236–37
Summanen, Raimo, 128
Suter, Gary, 123, 128, 188, 196

team meetings, 19, 39, 69, 91,
  105, 182–83

television coverage, 30–31, 41,
104, 124–27, 135–36
Tikkanen, Esa, 128, 132, 265–66
Tonelli, John, 132
Toronto Maple Leafs, 125
trainers, 16–17
Tuele, Bill, 126–27, 137, 151, 152
Tuer, Al, 214
Turchansky, Ray, 152

Udvari, Frank, 169
USA Hockey, 72–73

Vernon, Mike, 14, 128, 132, 187,
193, 248–49

Wamsley, Rick, 196
Watt, Tom, 201, 203
Western Hockey League (WHL),
213–14, 258
Whitney, Floyd, 48
Wilson, Carey, 100, 133
Winnipeg Jets, 26, 72, 103, 184–85
Wittman, Don, 148
World Hockey Association (WHA),
41–45, 61–62, 81, 239
merger with NHL, 41, 44–45,
102

Ziegler, John, 206